EXAM CRAM™

PRAXIS

Diana Huggins

PRAXIS Exam Cram

International Standard Book Number: 0-7897-3262-9

Library of Congress Catalog Card Number: 2004108923

Printed in the United States of America

First Printing: April 2005

08   07   4   3

Trademarks

Warning and Disclaimer

Bulk Sales

Que Publishing offers excellent discounts on this book when ordered in quantity for bulk purchases or special sales. For more information, please contact

    U.S. Corporate and Government Sales

    1-800-382-3419

    corpsales@pearsontechgroup.com

For sales outside the U.S., please contact

    International Sales

    international@pearsoned.com

Publisher
Paul Boger

Executive Editor
Jeff Riley

Acquisitions Editor
Carol Ackerman

Development Editor
Steve Rowe

Managing Editor
Charlotte Clapp

Project Editor
Tonya Simpson

Copy Editor
Margaret Berson

Indexer
Mandie Frank

Proofreader
Tonya Fenimore

Technical Editors
Amelia Askren
Karl W. Riebs

Publishing Coordinator
Pamalee Nelson

Multimedia Developer
Dan Scherf

Page Layout
Cheryl Lynch
Michelle Mitchell

To my oh-so-handsome and perfect son, Brandon.

&

About the Author

Diana Huggins has spent several years working in the field of education. After completing her Bachelor of Education degree, she began her career as an elementary school teacher and then moved into adult education. As an adult educator, she was responsible for overseeing adult learning programs, spent some time on courseware development for the Department of Education, and she also continued to spend time teaching in the classroom.

Diana is currently an independent contractor providing both writing and consulting services. Prior to this, she worked as a senior systems consultant. Some of the projects she worked on included a security review of Microsoft's official curriculum and content development for private companies, as well as network infrastructure design and implementation projects.

Although she switched to the Information Technology industry, Diana has never given up her love of educating. She has been able to combine the two passions, and over the past few years has been writing certification study guides. To complement her efforts, she also spends a portion of her time consulting for small- to medium-sized companies in a variety of areas. She continues to work as an independent technical trainer and a substitute teacher.

Along with a Bachelor of Education degree, Diana holds several Information Technology certifications. She currently has her Microsoft Certified Systems Engineer (MCSE) and Microsoft Certified Trainer (MCT), along with several other certifications from different vendors. Diana also runs her own company, DKB Consulting Services. The main focus of the company is on developing certification training courseware and online practice exams, as well as content delivery.

About the Contributing Authors

Karl W. Riebs finds teaching and helping young people one of his greatest pleasures and plans to be a full-time teacher someday. He is a graduate of the U.S. Naval Academy and majoring in math and science. He currently works for a large retail chain.

Debbie Forkner is a math teacher and girls basketball coach at Fishers Junior High School in Indiana.

About the Technical Editor

Amelia Askren is a 5th-grade teacher at Gallberry Farm Elementary in Hope Mills, North Carolina. She graduated in July 2003 with a bachelor's degree in elementary education from Ball State University in Muncie, Indiana. Amelia's educational training included teaching as an instructional assistant at Fishers Junior High in Fishers, Indiana, as a daycare teacher for school-aged children at Children's World Learning Center in Fishers, Indiana during the summer of 2003, and as a student teacher in a 5th-grade classroom at Hamilton Heights Elementary School in Arcadia, Indiana during the spring semester of 2003. Amelia also successfully completed several PRAXIS exams between 2000 and 2003 as a prerequisite to receiving her teaching license.

Acknowledgments

I'd like to begin by saying thanks to "everyone"—that is, everyone in my life who continues to offer me encouragement and support every day.

Thanks to my seven-year-old son, Brandon. You're always so patient and understanding when I have deadlines looming. However, no deadlines are as important as your soccer, baseball, and hockey games! Also, thanks to "papa" for always being there.

Thanks to Jeff Riley and Que Publishing for giving me the opportunity to work on this title and for seeing the value in the *Exam Cram* series. Thanks to Carol Ackerman for keeping the project on track. As always, it has been a pleasure working with you all.

There are so many other people I need to thank, and I always seem to remember one more after everything is said and done. So here it goes, "Oscar" style. Thanks to my mom for being such a great source of inspiration. Thanks to Wayne for being my punching bag when the pressure is on. Thanks to all my friends who manage to drag me away from work on Friday evenings. Finally, thanks to Felicia, my best friend; we are the girls in the bright white U-Haul!

Contents at a Glance

Table of Contents

Part II PLT

Chapter 5
PRAXIS II Principles of Learning and Teaching 145

Chapter 6
PRAXIS III Classroom Performance Assessment 177

Part III Appendixes

We Want to Hear from You!

As the reader of this book, *you* are our most important critic and commentator. We value your opinion and want to know what we're doing right, what we could do better, what areas you'd like to see us publish in, and any other words of wisdom you're willing to pass our way.

As an executive editor for Que Publishing, I welcome your comments. You can email or write me directly to let me know what you did or didn't like about this book—as well as what we can do to make our books better.

Please note that I cannot help you with technical problems related to the topic of this book. We do have a User Services group, however, where I will forward specific technical questions related to the book.

When you write, please be sure to include this book's title and author as well as your name, email address, and phone number. I will carefully review your comments and share them with the author and editors who worked on the book.

Email: feedback@quepublishing.com

Mail: Jeff Riley
            Executive Editor
            Que Publishing
            800 East 96th Street
            Indianapolis, IN 46240 USA

For more information about this book or another Que Certification title, visit our Web site at www.examcram2.com. Type the ISBN (0789732629) or the title of a book in the Search field to find the page you're looking for.

Introduction

This introduction provides you with some general information about the layout of this book and what you can expect to find in an *Exam Cram*. This is followed by a brief overview of the chapter content and basic test information such as question format, number of questions, and passing score, as well as recommendations for preparing for and taking the exam.

About This Book

The chapters in this book have been structured around the exam objectives developed by Educational Testing Services (ETS). This ensures you are familiar with the content that you'll encounter on the PRAXIS Pre-Professional Skills Test (PPST) and Principles of Learning and Teaching (PLT) exams.

I recommend that you work through the book from start to finish for your initial reading. After you've read the book, you can brush up on a certain area by using the Index or the Table of Contents to go straight to the topics and questions you want to re-examine. I've tried to use the headings and sub-headings to provide outline information about each given topic. After you've completed the PRAXIS I exam, I think you'll also find this book useful as a study resource for the PRAXIS II exam.

Who This Book Is For

This book has been written as a study resource for the PRAXIS I and PRAXIS II exams. It is intended for those individuals who are currently completing or have already completed their college training and are now preparing to take the PRAXIS I and/or PRAXIS II exams. The book assumes that the reader has some background knowledge in high-school level math, reading, and writing.

Chapter Formats

Each chapter of *Exam Cram* follows a regular structure, along with graphical cues about especially important or useful material. The structure of a typical chapter is as follows:

➤ *Opening hotlists*—Each chapter begins with lists of the terms you'll need to understand and the concepts you'll need to master before you can be fully conversant with the chapter's subject matter. I follow the hotlists with a few introductory paragraphs, setting the stage for the rest of the chapter.

➤ *Topical coverage*—After the opening hotlists, each chapter covers the topics related to the chapter's subject.

➤ *Exam Alerts*—Throughout the topical coverage section, I highlight material most likely to appear on the exam by using a special Exam Alert element that looks like this:

 An Exam Alert stresses concepts, terms, or any other bit of information that will most likely appear in one or more exam questions. For that reason, I think any information that's offset in Exam Alert format is worthy of unusual attentiveness on your part.

Even if material isn't flagged as an Exam Alert, *all* the content in this book is associated in some way with test-related material. What appears in the chapter content is critical knowledge.

➤ *Notes*—This book is an overall examination of the different content areas on the exam. As such, I'll dip into many different aspects of reading, writing, and mathematics. Where a body of knowledge is deeper than the scope of the book, I use notes to indicate areas of concern or specialty training.

 Cramming for an exam will get you through a test, but it won't make you a competent professional. Although you can memorize just the facts you need in order to pass an exam, your daily work in the field will rapidly put you in water over your head if you don't know the underlying principles in a specific content area.

➤ *Tips*—I provide tips that will help you to build a better foundation of knowledge or to focus your attention on an important concept that will reappear later in the book. Tips are helpful ways to remind you of the context surrounding a particular area of a topic under discussion.

You should also read the section in the beginning of the book titled "Self-Assessment." The information contained in this section will help you to determine your readiness to challenge the PRAXIS I exam.

➤ *Exam Prep Questions*—This section presents a short list of test questions related to the specific chapter topic. Each question is followed by an explanation of both correct and incorrect answers. The practice questions highlight the areas I found to be most important on the exam.

➤ *"Need to Know More?" Section*—Each chapter ends with a listing of additional resources offering more details about the chapter topics.

The bulk of the book follows this chapter structure, but there are a few other elements that should be pointed out:

➤ *Practice Exams*—The practice exams, which appear in Chapters 8, 10, and 12 (with answer keys in Chapters 9, 11, and 13), are very close approximations of the types of questions you are likely to see on the PRAXIS I exam.

➤ *Answer Keys*—These provide the answers to the practice exams, complete with explanations of both the correct responses and the incorrect responses.

➤ *Glossary*—This is an extensive glossary of important terms used in this book.

➤ *The Cram Sheet*—This appears as a tear-away sheet inside the front cover of this *Exam Cram* book. It is a valuable tool that represents a collection of the most difficult-to-remember facts and numbers I think you should memorize before taking the test. Remember, you can dump this information out of your head onto a piece of paper as soon as you enter the testing room. These are usually facts that I've found require brute-force memorization.

You might want to look at the Cram Sheet in your car or just before you walk in to take your exam. The Cram Sheet is divided into sections, so you can review the appropriate parts just before each test.

Test Information

The PRAXIS I Pre-Professional Skills Test (PPST) is designed to measure your knowledge and understanding in three different content areas: *reading*, *writing*, and *mathematics*. You must pass the PRAXIS I exam to demonstrate basic competency in these three content areas. The exam is also broken into different sections based on these content areas. The three content areas are outlined in the following list:

➤ *Reading*—This portion of the PRAXIS I exam will test your ability to understand and evaluate written passages. The questions will vary in difficulty with some including passages with 200 words and others with only a few sentences.

➤ *Writing*—The questions covering this content area are designed to test your basic knowledge of grammar and sentence structure. The writing portion of the exam is broken down into two sections: multiple-choice questions and an essay question.

➤ *Math*—The mathematics section of the PRAXIS I will measure your knowledge of basic math skills and concepts. Along with focusing on basic math skills, the questions will also test your ability to reason and problem-solve.

PRAXIS Written Test Versus PRAXIS Computer Test

The PRAXIS I exam is available in two different formats: a *paper-based exam* or a *computer-based exam*. Both exam formats cover the same content areas and include the same types of questions. The main difference between the two exam formats is the number of questions and the time allocated to answer the given number of questions. Table I.1 outlines the number of questions that will appear on the two different exams.

Table I.1 Written and Computer Exam Questions		
Section	**PRAXIS Written**	**PRAXIS Computer**
Reading	40 questions/60 minutes	46 questions/75 minutes
Writing	45 questions/60 minutes	51 questions/45 minutes
Essay	1 essay/30 minutes	1 essay/30 minutes
Math	40 questions/60 minutes	46 questions/75 minutes

Registering for the Exam

As you already know, there are two different versions of the PRAXIS I exam. When you determine which exam format you prefer, you can register for the exam.

Registering for the PRAXIS Written Exam

The PRAXIS I exam can be taken at specific times throughout the year. You can view the current dates when the exam is being offered at the following URL: http://www.ets.org/praxis/prxdates.html.

After you've decided on a date to take the exam, your next step will be to register for the exam or one of its components. Remember that you do not need to take all the components of the PRAXIS I exam at the same time. You can register for just a specific component if that's what you prefer. You can register for the exam in three different ways. You can do so by phone at the following numbers:

➤ Within the U.S., U.S. Territories, and Canada call 1-800-772-9476.

➤ For all other locations, call 1-609-771-7395.

You can register for the exam online at the following URL: http://www.ets.org/register.html. If you choose, you can also register for the exam by mail. You must obtain a printed copy of the Registration Bulletin and return it to the address on the preaddressed envelope that is included with the registration information.

Registering for the PRAXIS Computer-Based Test

The process for registering for the PRAXIS I computer-based test is slightly different. You can register for the computerized version by calling a testing center near you or by calling Candidate Services at Prometric at 1-800-853-6773.

How to Prepare for the Exam

Preparing for most exams requires that you obtain and study materials designed to provide comprehensive information about the specific exam for which you are preparing. The following list of materials can help you study and prepare:

➤ *The Educational Learning Services Web site (www.ets.org)*—This site provides comprehensive information about the PRAXIS I exam, including what you should know for each exam and specific exam details such as the number of questions and time alotted.

➤ *www.examcram2.com*—You can find exam-preparation advice, practice tests, questions of the day, and discussion groups on the *Exam Cram* e-learning and certification destination Web site, at www.examcram2.com.

➤ *Preparation programs*—Many organizations offer preparation programs. These would entail more formal instructor-led training.

➤ *Other publications*—There's no shortage of materials available covering the content on the PRAXIS I exam. The "Need to Know More?" resource sections at the end of each chapter in this book give you an idea of where I think you should look for further discussion.

This set of required and recommended materials represents an unparalleled collection of sources and resources for the PRAXIS I exam. I hope you'll find that this book belongs in this company.

What This Book Will Not Do

This book will *not* teach you everything you need to know about mathematics or the English language, or even about a given topic. This book will review what you need to know before you take the test, with the fundamental purpose dedicated to reviewing the information covered on the PRAXIS I and PRAXIS II exams.

This book uses a variety of teaching and memorization techniques that will help you analyze exam-related topics and provide you with ways to input, index, and retrieve everything you'll need to know to pass the test.

What This Book Is Designed to Do

This book will discuss the areas of knowledge upon which you will be tested. In other words, you may want to read the book one time just to get an insight into how comprehensive your knowledge of the various topics is. Then, as you find weak areas in your content knowledge, you will need to seek out more information on those topics from college textbooks, friends, teachers, or any other source that you deem trustworthy. The book is also designed to be read shortly before you go for the actual test and to give you a distillation of the important information as a last-minute "brush-up." I think you can use this book to get a sense of the underlying context of any topic in the chapters or to skim-read for Exam Alerts, bulleted points, summaries, and topic headings as part of this brush-up.

Study Tips

It's every candidate's goal to succeed on any exam the first time around. Of course, being well prepared and ensuring you're familiar with all the objectives for each of the domains increases your chances of success. However, don't be discouraged if you don't succeed the first time. Sometimes, just being in an exam situation is enough to throw off your train of thought. If you don't pass the first time, think positively, as you'll know exactly what to expect the second time around.

Good study habits get you one step closer to achieving success on any exam. I suggest that as you begin studying for the PRAXIS I and PRAXIS II exams, you take a close look at the objectives for each of the content areas. These objectives provide an excellent starting point for determining what topics you need to study. You can obtain the objectives for each content area from the Educational Testing Services website at www.ets.org.

A number of resources are available that you can use to prepare for the PRAXIS exams. As already mentioned, preparation programs provide one method. Although it can cost several hundred dollars, instructor-led training is a valuable exam preparation tool. Alternatives to classroom instructor-led training are computer-based training and web-based training. The nice things about computer-based and web-based training are the affordability and flexibility they offer.

Several publishers offer PRAXIS I and PRAXIS II study guides. Some of the guides are geared toward a higher level of knowledge, teaching you everything you need to know. Others provide you with the information you absolutely need to know to pass the exam. I recommend that if you're studying for the exam on your own, you begin with a complete study guide and work through it from start to finish, and then finish with a book that points out the "need-to-know" information for the exam. Que's *Exam Cram 2* does an excellent job of distilling all the information that you must know for exam success.

Practice exams are a wonderful way to test your knowledge after you've studied all the required material. A lot of study guides include practice exams designed to mimic the questions you're likely to encounter on the actual exams. There are also an abundance of Web sites that offer PRAXIS I and PRAXIS II practice exams, some of which are free and others that must be purchased. The one tip I have when using sites that offer free practice questions is to be wary of the answers. I have often encountered questions where the stated correct answer is actually incorrect.

In any case, when you are taking the practice exams, pay close attention to the answers as well. For any questions you answer incorrectly, use the explanations to understand where you went wrong and why the correct answer is indeed correct. Be sure to review study materials pertaining to the questions you answered incorrectly before taking the real exams.

Test-Taking Tips

Obviously, the most important tip is to make sure you are fully prepared for the exam by using some of the study tips outlined in the preceding section. Aside from that, there are a few other tips and tricks you can use to increase your chances of performing well on the exams.

Before you begin the exam, make sure you know how much time you have to complete all the questions. You can then average how much time you can spend on each question. Of course, you may need to spend more time on some questions than others. It's generally a good idea to do a quick clock check every few questions to ensure you aren't running behind. A general rule of thumb is to plan to spend approximately one minute on each question.

The majority of test questions are multiple choice in format, so you will be presented with a minimum of four answers from which to choose. You can usually eliminate one or more of the answers immediately as being incorrect. From there, you can use your knowledge about the topic to begin eliminating the remaining answers. If you are unsure of the correct answer, try reading the question over.

Don't be surprised if you encounter an exam question for which you cannot determine the correct answer. It often happens to those of us who have fully prepared for an exam and have thoroughly studied all the necessary topics. In such cases, do not leave the question unanswered. Why? An unanswered question becomes a wrong answer. Therefore, when all else fails, a guess at least gives you a chance of answering it correctly.

In some cases, you might be able to narrow the correct answer down to two choices. Then, carefully reread the question. Sometimes one word can throw you off.

Some of the best advice ever given in such situations is to always go with your first instinct. When in doubt, always go with the answer that first jumped out at you as being correct.

Self-Assessment

A self-assessment has been included in this Exam Cram to help you evaluate your readiness to tackle the PRAXIS I exam. It should also help you understand what you need to master the topics of this book—namely, the PRAXIS I exam, which includes PRAXIS Reading, PRAXIS Writing, and PRAXIS Math. Before you take a look at the self-assessment, however, I'll talk about the concerns you might face when pursuing a teaching career and what an ideal candidate might look like.

Teachers in the Real World

In the next section, I describe an ideal teaching candidate, knowing full well that only a few actual candidates meet this ideal. In fact, my description of that ideal candidate might seem downright scary. But take heart; although the requirements to obtain a teaching degree may seem formidable, they are by no means impossible to meet. However, you should be keenly aware that it does take time, it requires some expense, and it calls for a substantial effort.

You can get all the real-world motivation you need from knowing that many others have gone before you, and you can follow in their footsteps. If you're willing to tackle the process seriously and do what it takes to gain the necessary experience and knowledge, you can take—and pass—the PRAXIS tests. In fact, the *Exam Crams* are designed to make it as easy as possible for you to prepare for these exams, but prepare you must!

The Ideal Teaching Candidate

Just to give you some idea of what an ideal teaching candidate is like, here are some relevant statistics about the background and experience such an individual might have. Don't worry if you don't meet these qualifications (or, indeed, if you don't even come close) because this world is far from ideal, and where you fall short is simply where you'll have more work to do. The ideal candidate will have the following qualifications:

➤ Academic training in basic high-school–level English and mathematics

➤ College-level training in basic English and mathematics

Many candidates who apply to an education program do not meet these requirements. In fact, most probably meet less than half of them (at least when they begin the certification process). However, all those who have their certifications have already survived this ordeal, and you can survive it, too—especially if you heed what this self-assessment can tell you about what you already know and what you need to learn.

Put Yourself to the Test

The following series of questions and observations is designed to help you figure out how much work you'll face in passing the PRAXIS I exams and what kinds of resources you can consult on your quest. Be absolutely honest in your answers, or you'll end up wasting money on exams you're not ready to take. There are no right or wrong answers, simply steps along the path to certification. Only you can decide where you really belong in the broad spectrum of aspiring candidates.

Two things should be clear from the outset, however:

➤ Even a modest background in English and mathematics will help.

➤ Essay-writing experience is an essential ingredient for achieving exam success.

Educational Background

1. Have you ever taken any college-level English and mathematics classes? (Yes or No)

   If yes, proceed to question 2; if no, proceed to question 4.

2. Have you taken any classes on English grammar and language? Have you taken any classes on basic mathematical functions? (Yes or No)

   If yes, you will probably be able to handle the types of questions you will encounter on the PRAXIS I exams. If you're rusty, brush up on the basic English and math concepts. If the answer is no, consider some basic reading in these areas. I strongly recommend good college-level textbooks.

3. Have you taken any classes requiring you to write essays? (Yes or No)

If yes, you will probably be able to handle the essay-writing and short-answer questions. If you're rusty, brush up on basic essay-writing concepts and terminology. If your answer is no, you might want to check out some books that will teach you how to develop and write a good essay.

4. Have you done any additional reading above high-school–level English and mathematics? (Yes or No)

If yes, review the requirements from questions 2 and 3. If you meet them, move to the next section, "Testing Your Exam Readiness." If you answered no, consult some additional readings. This kind of strong background will be of great help in preparing for the PRAXIS I exams.

Testing Your Exam Readiness

Whether you attend a formal class on a specific topic to get ready for an exam or use written materials to study on your own, some preparation for the PRAXIS I exams is essential. At $30 a try for each paper-based test and $85 for the computer-based test, pass or fail, you want to do everything you can to pass on your first try. That's where studying comes in.

In this book, I have included several practice exam questions for each chapter and three sample tests, so if you don't score well on the chapter questions, you can study more and then tackle the sample tests at the end of each part. If you don't score well on a chapter test, you'll want to investigate the other practice test resources available via the Web. (You can locate them by using your favorite search engine.)

For any given subject, consider taking a class specifically designed to help you pass the PRAXIS I exam if you've tackled self-study materials, taken the test, and failed anyway. If you can afford the privilege, the opportunity to interact with an instructor and fellow students can make all the difference in the world.

If you can't afford to take a class, visit the Educational Testing Services web page at www.ets.org because it includes test preparation information. Even if you can't afford to spend much at all, you should still invest in some low-cost practice exams from commercial vendors because they can help you assess your readiness to pass a test better than any other tool.

5. Have you taken a practice exam on your chosen test subject? (Yes or No)

If yes—and you scored well—you're probably ready to tackle the real thing. If your score isn't above that crucial threshold (you can find out more about the passing scores for each exam through your college or ETS), keep at it until you break that barrier. If you answered no, obtain all the free and low-budget practice tests you can find (or afford) and get to work. Keep trying until you can comfortably break the passing threshold.

 There is no better way to assess your test readiness than to take a good-quality practice exam. When I'm preparing, I shoot for 80% or higher, just to leave room for the "weirdness factor" that sometimes shows up on exams.

Onward, Through the Fog!

After you've assessed your readiness, undertaken the right background studies, obtained the knowledge and skills that will help you understand the concepts at hand, and reviewed the many sources of information to help you prepare for a test, you'll be ready to take a round of practice tests. When your scores come back positive enough to get you through the exams, you're ready to tackle the real thing. If you follow my assessment regimen, you'll not only know what you need to study, but also know when you're ready to make a test date. Good luck!

PART I
PPST

PRAXIS I Math

Terms you'll need to understand:

- ✓ Fraction
- ✓ Numerator
- ✓ Denominator
- ✓ Area
- ✓ Ratio
- ✓ Factor
- ✓ Volume
- ✓ Exponents
- ✓ Mean

- ✓ Mode
- ✓ Median
- ✓ Angles
- ✓ Lines
- ✓ Triangles
- ✓ Circles
- ✓ Volume
- ✓ Surface Area
- ✓ Variable

Techniques you'll need to master:

- ✓ Understand numbers and number properties
- ✓ Understand how to work with fractions
- ✓ Understand how to manipulate decimals
- ✓ Understand how to add and subtract fractions
- ✓ Understand how to multiply fractions and whole numbers
- ✓ Understand how to divide fractions
- ✓ Work with ratios and proportions

- ✓ Manipulate percentages
- ✓ Convert percentages to decimals
- ✓ Know the place values of numbers
- ✓ Understand basic arithmetic
- ✓ Understand the English and metric systems of measurement
- ✓ Understand scientific notation
- ✓ Understand probability
- ✓ Understand common graphical techniques and data tables

This chapter focuses on the math skills required to pass the PRAXIS I math exam.

Arithmetic

Arithmetic covers the basic math skills: addition, subtraction, multiplication, and division.

Addition and Subtraction

When you *add* two or more numbers together, you find how many you have in all, or the *sum*. *Subtraction* involves removing some objects from a group. The result of a subtraction problem is called the *difference*.

```
 320      320
+ 40     − 40
-----    -----
 360      280
```

Multiplication and Division

The result of multiplication is referred to as the *product*. Multiplication results can be obtained by repeated addition, but because this method is time-consuming and impractical for multiplying large numbers, multiplication problems are solved by breaking the operation down into smaller steps. Here is an example of how to find the product of larger numbers:

```
  450
×  21
------
  450
 900
------
 9450
```

Division is the opposite of multiplication. Division can be as simple as dividing a two-digit number by a one-digit number, such as $42 \div 7$, or it can be long division with larger numbers, such as $4,320 \div 150$. The following is an example of division:

```
      20
25 ) 500
    − 50
    ----
      00
```

Some division problems produce a *remainder* (the amount left over when one number does not divide an exact number of times into another), as shown in this example. If you divide 564 by 25, the result will be 22 with a remainder of 14. The solution to this problem may be written as 22 R 14 or, more commonly, with the remainder shown as a fraction. This produces a mixed number: $22 \frac{14}{25}$.

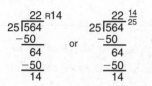

Positive and Negative Numbers

Positive numbers are any numbers greater than zero, such as 1, 2.9, 3.14159, 40,000, and 0.0005. For each positive number, there is a negative number that is its opposite. We write the opposite of a positive number with a negative or minus sign in front of the number and call it a *negative number*. The opposites of the numbers in the list earlier in this paragraph would be –1, –2.9, –3.14159, –40,000, and –0.0005. Negative numbers are any numbers less than zero. Similarly, the opposite of any negative number is a positive number. For example, the opposite of –12.3 is 12.3. We do not consider zero to be a positive or negative number.

The sum of any number and its opposite is 0.

The *sign* of a number refers to whether the number is positive or negative; for example, the sign of –3.2 is negative and the sign of 442 is positive.

Absolute Value of Positive and Negative Numbers

The absolute value of a number is that number's distance from zero (0). You specify the absolute value of a number n by writing n in between two vertical bars: $|n|$.

For example, $|6| = 6$, $|-0.004| = 0.004$, and $|0| = 0$.

Adding Positive and Negative Numbers

When adding numbers with the same sign, we add their absolute values and give the result the same sign.

Consider the following examples:

$2 + 5.7 = 7.7$

$-100 + -0.05 = -|100 + 0.05| = -100.05$

When adding numbers with opposite signs, we take their absolute values, subtract the smaller absolute value from the larger one, and give the result the sign of the number with the larger absolute value.

The following examples demonstrate this technique:

$7 + (-3.4) = ?$

The absolute values of 7 and -3.4 are 7 and 3.4. Subtracting the smaller from the larger gives $7 - 3.4 = 3.6$, and because the larger absolute value was 7, we give the result the same sign as 7, so $7 + (-3.4) = 3.6$.

Here's another example:

$-2.2 + 1.1 = ?$

The absolute values of -2.2 and 1.1 are 2.2 and 1.1. Subtracting the smaller from the larger gives $2.2 - 1.1 = 1.1$, and because the larger absolute value was 2.2, we give the result the same sign as -2.2, so $-2.2 + 1.1 = -1.1$.

Subtracting Positive and Negative Numbers

Subtracting a number is the same as adding the opposite of the number. Review the following examples to view how to convert the subtracted number to its opposite sign (+) and add the two numbers:

$7 - 4.4 = 7 + (-4.4) = 2.6$

$-8.9 - 1.7 = -8.9 + (-1.7) = -10.6$

Multiplying and Dividing Positive and Negative Numbers

When you multiply or divide a pair of numbers and both numbers have the same sign, their product is the product of their absolute values (their product is positive). If the numbers have opposite signs, their product is the opposite of the product of their absolute values (their product is negative). If one or both of the numbers is 0, the product is 0.

In the following examples, both numbers are positive, so we just take their product or quotient.

$0.5 \times 3 = 1.5$

$7 \div 2 = 3.5$

In the next two examples, both numbers are negative, so we take the product or quotient of their absolute values.

$(-1.1) \times (-5) = |-1.1| \times |-5| = 1.1 \times 5 = 5.5$

$(-2.4) \div (-3) = |-2.4| \div |-3| = 2.4 \div 3 = 0.8$

When you multiply or divide a negative number by a positive number or a positive number by a negative number, the answer will be a negative number. See the following examples:

$(-3) \times 0.7 = -2.1$

$(-1) \div 2.5 = -0.4$

To multiply several numbers, there are three steps to consider. First, count the negative factors. Second, take the product of their absolute values. Finally, if the number of negative numbers counted in step 1 is even, the product is just the product from step 2. If the number of negative numbers is odd, the product is the opposite of the product in step 2. (In other words, give the product in step 2 a negative sign.) If any of the factors is 0, the product is 0.

Table 1.1 gives you some quick reminders about what sign to give to the solution of a multiplication or division problem that may have the same signs in the numbers or different signs in the numbers.

Table 1.1 Multiplying and Dividing Positive and Negative Numbers	
$+ \times + =$	$+$
$+ \div + =$	
$- \times + =$	$-$
$- \div + =$	
$+ \times - =$	$-$
$+ \div - =$	
$- \times - =$	$+$
$- \div - =$	

Arithmetic Concepts

The PRAXIS math exam will also test your knowledge of a variety of arithmetic concepts. The following sections discuss the important concepts you need to be familiar with.

Rounding

Rounding helps make large, unwieldy numbers easier to work with. Use rounding to get an answer that is close but does not have to be exact. The following list gives you the general rounding rules:

➤ Round numbers that end in 1 through 4 to the next lower number that ends in 0. For example, 74 rounded to the nearest ten would be 70.

➤ Numbers that end in a digit of 5 or more should be rounded up to the next even ten. For example, the number 88 rounded to the nearest ten would be 90.

You can also round decimal numbers. For example, if you need to round the number 84.76 to the nearest tenth, the second decimal place (that is, the hundredths place) number will determine whether you round up or round down. Because the second decimal place value is 6, the number is rounded up to 84.8.

Averages

To average any set of data, you add up all of the data and then divide by the number of elements in the series.

For example, to average the following four numbers, you would begin by adding 11.935 + 11.936 + 11.937 + 11.938 to get 47.746. You would then divide by 4 because we added four numbers. The average of these numbers is 11.9365.

Mean, Median, and Mode

You are likely to come across an exam question that will ask you to determine the mean, median, or mode for data. The *mean* is the average of a list of numbers. Note the following example:

23, 25, 25, 27, 29, 33 = 162 ÷ 6 = 27

The *median* is the middle value in a list. If the list has an odd number of terms, the median is the middle term in the list (after you have sorted the list into increasing order). For example, the median for the following list would be 26.

23 24 25 **26** 27 28 29

However, if the list has an even number of terms, the median is equal to the average of the two middle numbers (after they are sorted into increasing order) divided by 2. For example, the median for the following list of numbers would be 25.5:

23 24 **25 26** 27 28   { (25 + 26) ÷ 2 = 25.5}

The *mode* for a list of numbers is the number that occurs most often. Keep in mind that a list can have more than one mode. For example, in the following list, the mode is 26 because this number occurs twice and all other numbers occur only once. It is also possible for a data set to not have a mode if one number doesn't appear more than once.

23 24 25 26 26 27 28 29

Place Value

Each digit in a number has a different place value. Figure 1.1 shows the different place values for the six-digit number 495,784.

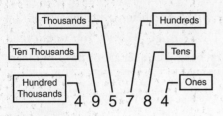

Figure 1.1   Place value.

For the PRAXIS math exam, you should also be familiar with the place value for decimal numbers (tenths, hundredths, thousandths, and so on) as shown in Figure 1.2.

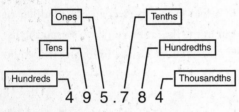

Figure 1.2   Decimal place value.

Estimation

Estimation can be used to quickly determine an approximate answer. For example, a quick way to estimate the sum or difference of two numbers is to round each number and then add the rounded numbers. Although estimating won't produce the exact answer, it may yield a result that is close enough for some purposes.

Ratios

Ratios are used to make comparisons between two things. The most common way to write a ratio is as a fraction, such as $\frac{5}{8}$. You could also write it by using the word *to*, as in 5 *to* 8. Finally, you could write this ratio using a colon between the two numbers, as in 5:8.

Multiplying or dividing each term by the same nonzero number will give an equivalent ratio. For example, the ratio 2:4 is equivalent to the ratio 1:2 because you can multiply each number in 1:2 by 2 to get 2:4, or you can divide each number in 2:4 by 2 to get 1:2.

Some other equivalent ratios are shown in the following example. Remember that you can multiply or divide by the same number (other than zero) to work between equal ratios:

$3:6 = 12:24 = 6:12 = 15:30$

Some ratios are not equivalent. For example, 3:12 and 36:72 are not equivalent because to go from 3 to 36 you must multiply by 12. To be equivalent, you must multiply 12 by 12 as well. However, 12×12 gives you 144, not 72.

Fractions

A *fraction* is a number that expresses part of a group. Fractions are written in the form $\frac{a}{b}$, where a and b are whole numbers and b is not 0. When describing a and b, a is referred to as the *numerator* and b is referred to as the *denominator*.

The following numbers are all fractions:

$\frac{1}{2}, \frac{3}{4}, \frac{6}{7}$, and $\frac{9}{16}$

Equivalent Fractions

Equivalent fractions are different fractions that have the same value. For example, $\frac{1}{2}, \frac{2}{4}, \frac{6}{12}$, and $\frac{300}{600}$ are all equivalent fractions. Each of these fractions is equal to one-half, or 50%. To test whether two fractions are equivalent, *cross-multiply* the numerators and denominators. The result of cross-multiplication is also called the *cross-product*. For example, to test whether $\frac{3}{7}$ and $\frac{18}{42}$ are equivalent, you begin by cross-multiplying, as seen in the following example:

$\frac{3}{7} \times \frac{18}{42} = 3 \times 42 = 126$ and $7 \times 18 = 126$

As you can see, the result of each cross-product is 126, which makes the fractions equivalent.

Another example would be to test whether $\frac{2}{4}$ and $\frac{13}{20}$ are equivalent fractions. In the following example, when you cross-multiply, you find that the cross-products are different. Thus, the fractions are *not equivalent*.

$$\frac{2 \times 13}{4 \times 20} = 2 \times 20 = 40 \text{ and } 13 \times 4 = 52$$

Converting and Reducing Fractions

For any fraction, multiplying the numerator and denominator by the same number (if that number is not zero) gives an equivalent fraction. We can convert one fraction to an equivalent fraction by using this method.

Consider the following:

$$\frac{1}{2} = \frac{(1 \times 2)}{(2 \times 2)} = \frac{2}{4}$$

$$\frac{4}{5} = \frac{(4 \times 3)}{(5 \times 3)} = \frac{12}{15}$$

You can also convert one fraction to an equivalent fraction by dividing the numerator and denominator by the greatest common factor of the numerator and denominator. Let's look at an example:

$$\frac{14}{20} = \frac{(14 \div 2)}{(20 \div 2)} = \frac{7}{10}$$

When you divide the numerator and denominator of a fraction by their *greatest common factor*, the resulting fraction is an equivalent fraction in lowest terms. Take the following as an example of division where the greatest common factor is 12:

$$\frac{12}{36} = \frac{(12 \div 12)}{(36 \div 12)} = \frac{1}{3}$$

A fraction is in *lowest terms* when the greatest common factor of its numerator and denominator is 1. There are two methods of reducing a fraction to lowest terms.

Method 1:

Divide the numerator and denominator by their greatest common factor.

$$\frac{12}{30} = \frac{(12 \div 6)}{(30 \div 6)} = \frac{2}{5}$$

Method 2:

Divide the numerator and denominator by any common factor. Keep dividing until there are no more common factors.

$$\frac{12}{30} = \frac{(12 \div 2)}{(30 \div 2)} = \frac{6}{15} = \frac{(6 \div 3)}{(15 \div 3)} = \frac{2}{5}$$

Proper Fractions, Improper Fractions, and Mixed Numbers

A *common fraction* is simply a number written with a numerator and a denominator. A proper fraction is less than 1. This means that the numerator is always smaller than the denominator.

Improper fractions have numerators that are greater than or equal to their denominators. For example, $\frac{11}{4}, \frac{5}{5}$, and $\frac{13}{2}$ are improper fractions.

Mixed numbers have a whole number part and a fraction part. For example, $1\frac{1}{2}, 6\frac{3}{4}$, or $15\frac{3}{7}$.

To change a mixed number into an improper fraction, multiply the whole number by the denominator and add the product to the numerator of the fractional part. The following example demonstrates this:

$$2\frac{3}{5} = \frac{((2 \times 5) + 3)}{5} = \frac{13}{5}$$

To change an improper fraction into a mixed number, divide the numerator by the denominator. The remainder (R) becomes the numerator of the fractional part. See the following example:

$$\frac{9}{4} = 9 \div 4 = 2 \text{ R } 1 = 2\frac{1}{4}$$

Adding and Subtracting Fractions and Mixed Numbers

If the fractions have the same denominator, the sum of the fractions is the sum of the numerators, and that sum is placed over the denominator. For example:

$$\frac{3}{8} + \frac{2}{8} = \frac{(3 + 2)}{8} = \frac{5}{8}$$

If the fractions have the same denominator, their difference is the difference of the numerators over the denominator. Do not add or subtract the denominators.

$$\frac{7}{9} - \frac{3}{9} = \frac{(7 - 3)}{9} = \frac{4}{9}$$

Reduce (put in simplest form), if necessary. A fraction is in its simplest form if there are no common factors between the numerator and denominator. To simplify a fraction, you divide both its numerator and its denominator by their greatest common factor.

$$\frac{1}{6} + \frac{2}{6} = \frac{(1+2)}{6} = \frac{3}{6}$$

However, $\frac{3}{6}$ can be simplified by dividing both the numerator and denominator by their greatest common factor: 3.

$$\frac{3}{6} = \frac{\left(\frac{3}{3}\right)}{\left(\frac{3}{6}\right)} = \frac{1}{2}$$

If the fractions have different denominators, follow these instructions for adding or subtracting the fractions:

1. Find the least common denominator (also referred to as the least common multiple).

2. Write the equivalent fractions using this denominator.

3. Add or subtract the fractions.

4. Reduce (simplify) if necessary.

Let's take a look at some examples of how to do this.

Add the following fractions:

$$\frac{3}{4} + \frac{1}{6}$$

Begin by finding the least common denominator, which is 12.

$$\frac{3}{4} + \frac{1}{6} = \frac{9}{12} + \frac{2}{12} = \frac{11}{12}$$

$$\boxed{\frac{3 \times 3}{4 \times 3} = \frac{9}{12}} \quad \boxed{\frac{1 \times 2}{6 \times 2} = \frac{2}{12}}$$

Note from our example how you received $\frac{11}{12}$ for an answer. You found that 12 was the least common denominator, and then used this to find the equivalent fractions of $\frac{9}{12}$ and $\frac{2}{12}$.

Let's put the principles you just discovered in the preceding example to work in a subtraction problem. Subtract the following fractions:

$$\frac{9}{10} - \frac{1}{2}.$$

The least common denominator is 10, so you would proceed like this:

$$\frac{9}{10} - \frac{1}{2} = \frac{9}{10} - \frac{5}{10} = \frac{4}{10} = \frac{2}{5}$$

Notice again how you derived the equivalent fractions and then did a simple subtraction problem to arrive at $\frac{4}{10}$, which was then reduced to $\frac{2}{5}$.

On the PRAXIS exam, you will need to know how to add, subtract, multiply, and divide mixed numbers. To add or subtract mixed numbers, simply convert the mixed numbers into improper fractions, and then add or subtract them as fractions.

For example, add the following mixed numbers:

$$9\frac{1}{2} + 5\frac{3}{4}.$$

Begin by converting each mixed number to an improper fraction:

$$9\frac{1}{2} = \frac{19}{2} \text{ and } 5\frac{3}{4} = \frac{23}{4}$$

Then calculate

$$\frac{19}{2} + \frac{23}{4}$$

The least common multiple of 2 and 4 is 4. Thus, you need to make an equivalent fraction for $\frac{19}{2}$ that has a denominator of 4. Recalling how to make equivalent fractions, you will get an equivalent fraction of $\frac{38}{4}$, as in the following example.

$$\frac{19}{2} + \frac{23}{4} = \frac{38}{4} + \frac{23}{4} = \frac{(38 + 23)}{4} = \frac{61}{4}$$

The last step is to convert the answer back to a mixed number:

$$\frac{61}{4} = 15\frac{1}{4}.$$

An additional example uses a whole number within the equation:

$$13 - 1\frac{1}{3}.$$

$$13 - 1\frac{1}{3} = \frac{39}{3} - \frac{4}{3} = \frac{(39-4)}{3} = \frac{35}{3}, \text{ and } \frac{35}{3} = 11\frac{2}{3}$$

Multiplying Fractions and Mixed Numbers

To multiply two fractions, place the product of their numerators over the product of their denominators. Then, simplify the resulting fraction (if needed). The following is an example:

$$\frac{2}{3} \times \frac{3}{4} = \frac{(2 \times 3)}{(3 \times 4)} = \frac{6}{12} = \frac{1}{2}$$

To multiply a fraction and a whole number, write the whole number as an improper fraction with a denominator of 1, and then multiply the fractions.

For example, multiply $8 \times \frac{5}{20}$:

$$8 \times \frac{5}{20} = \frac{8}{1} \times \frac{5}{20} = \frac{(8 \times 5)}{(1 \times 20)} = \frac{40}{20} = 2$$

Dividing Fractions and Mixed Numbers

To understand how to divide fractions, you must first have an understanding of *reciprocals*. Two fractions are reciprocals if their product equals 1. Note the following example:

$$\frac{1}{2} \times \frac{2}{1} = \frac{2}{2} = 1$$

To find the reciprocal of a mixed number, first convert the mixed number to an improper fraction:

$$12\frac{1}{2} = \frac{25}{2}$$

Next, switch the numerator and denominator to find the reciprocal:

$$\frac{2}{25}$$

You use reciprocals when you divide two fractions. To do this, change the division into a multiplication problem using the second fraction's reciprocal. Note the following examples:

$$\frac{1}{5} \div \frac{2}{7} = \frac{1}{5} \times \frac{7}{2} = \frac{7}{10}$$

or

$$2\frac{1}{9} \div \frac{3}{7} = \frac{19}{9} \div \frac{3}{7} = \frac{19}{9} \times \frac{7}{3} = \frac{133}{27} = 4\frac{25}{27}$$

To divide a whole number by a fraction, multiply the whole number by the reciprocal of the fraction.

For example, calculate $7 \div \frac{1}{5}$.

$$7 \div \frac{1}{5} = 7 \times \frac{5}{1} = 7 \times 5 = 35$$

Also consider the following example, $\frac{1}{5} \div 16$:

$$\frac{1}{5} \div \frac{16}{1} = \frac{1}{5} \times \frac{1}{16} = \frac{(1 \times 1)}{(5 \times 16)} = \frac{1}{80}$$

 To divide mixed numbers, you should always convert them to improper fractions, and then multiply the first fraction by the reciprocal of the second.

Decimals

For the PRAXIS exam, it is important for you to be familiar with adding, subtracting, multiplying, and dividing decimal numbers. These topics will be summarized in the following sections.

Adding and Subtracting Decimals

Whether you are adding whole numbers or decimals, the procedure is the same. However, you must ensure that you have lined up the numbers correctly. The important thing to remember is that the decimal places must be lined up. You can add zeros to the decimal places to assist in lining up the numbers correctly. In the following examples, the zeros shown in bold have been added:

```
  500.32        500.00
+ 100.30      - 100.30
--------      --------
  600.62        399.70
```

Multiplying and Dividing Decimals

Multiplying decimals is almost the same as multiplying whole numbers, except you must also determine where to place the decimal point in the product. When multiplying, simply add the number of digits to the right of the decimal in both numbers. This number will tell you how many decimal places are required in the answer. For example, multiply 12.76 by 15.765. Because there are five decimal places in total in both numbers, you must move the decimal five places to the left in the product. Your answer of 20,116,140 will become 201.1614:

```
  15.765
 ×12.76
 201.1614
```

When you are dividing decimals, you want to eliminate the decimal from the divisor (4.5 in our example below). For example, divide 90 by 4.5:

$$4.5\overline{)900.} \; = \; 45\overline{)900}$$

In this example, the decimal point was moved enough places to the right to make the divisor not have a decimal. The number of places you move the decimal in the divisor is the same number of places you move the decimal in the dividend (90 in our example above). What started as 90 divided by 4.5 became 900 divided by 45, which equals 20.

Percent

Percent means a number out of 100. For example, 5% means 5 out of 100. You might be asked to solve three different types of percentage problems. These include *finding a percentage of a number*, *finding the percentage of an unknown number*, and *finding a number using a percentage of another number*. You can do this by using either an equation or a proportion.

Example 1: Finding a Percentage of a Number

30% of 120 is what number?

To solve by using an equation, you would change 30% to a decimal, and then multiply by 120.

$.30 \times 120 = 36$

To solve by using a proportion, set up the proportion and use cross-products to solve.

$$\frac{30}{100} = \frac{x}{120}$$

$30 \times 120 = 100x$

$3,600 = 100x$

$$\frac{3,600}{100} = x$$

$36 = x$

Example 2: Finding the Percentage of an Unknown Number

45% of what number = 135?

To solve by using an equation, you would change 45% to the decimal .45 and set up this equation, in which x = the number, 45% of which is equal to 135:

$.45x = 135$

To solve, divide 135 by .45, or

$$\frac{135}{.45} = x$$

$x = 300$

To solve by using a proportion, set up the proportion, and then use cross-products to solve.

$$\frac{45}{100} = \frac{135}{x}$$

$100 \times 135 = 45x$

$13500 = 45x$

$$\frac{13500}{45} = x$$

$300 = x$

Example 3: Finding what percentage one number is of another number.

What percentage of 50 is 60?

To solve by using an equation, set up the equation:

$x \times 50 = 60$

$x = \frac{60}{50}$

$x = 1.2$

Because the question asks what percentage, you would need to change the decimal from 1.2 to 120%.

To solve by using a proportion, set up the proportion, and then use cross-products to solve.

$$\frac{x}{100} = \frac{60}{50}$$

$100 \times 60 = 50x$

$6000 = 50x$

$\frac{6000}{50} = x$

$120 = x$

Converting To and From Decimals

Decimals can be converted to percents and fractions and vice versa. You are likely to encounter an exam question that requires you to convert a decimal to another format. Therefore, you should be familiar with the topics discussed in the next sections.

Converting a Decimal to a Percent

A decimal can be converted to a percent by multiplying it by 100. The shortcut for multiplying by 100 is to move the decimal point two places to the right. Sometimes you might have to add zeros.

Example 1: Change .23 to a percent.

.23 × 100 = 23. Then, add the percent sign for 23%.

Using the Shortcut Method:

Start with .23 and move the decimal point two places to the right to get 23. Then, add the percent sign for 23%.

Example 2: Change .6 to a percent.

.6 × 100 = 60. Then, add the percent sign for 60%. (Notice that one zero had to be added.)

Using the Shortcut Method:

Start with .6 and move the decimal point two places to the right to get 60. Then, add the percent sign. Again, to get the second place, you had to add a zero.

Converting a Percent to a Decimal

A percent can be converted to a decimal by dividing by 100 and dropping the percent sign (%). The shortcut for dividing by 100 is to move the decimal point two places to the left. As you did earlier, sometimes you might have to add zeros to get the decimal. Let's look at two examples that demonstrate this.

Example 1: Change 50% to a decimal.

$50\% = \frac{50}{100} = .5$

Using the Shortcut Method:

Start with 50 and move the decimal point two places to the left to get .50. Then, you can drop the zero on the end and the % sign to get 50% = .5.

Example 2: Change 5% to a decimal.

$$5\% = \frac{5}{100} = .05$$

Using the Shortcut Method:

Start with 5, move the decimal point two places to the left, drop the % sign, and you get .05. Notice that you have to add the zero before the 5.

Converting a Fraction to a Decimal

Converting a fraction to a decimal requires division. To make the conversion, you must divide the numerator by the denominator. For example, to convert the fraction of $\frac{5}{8}$ to a decimal, simply divide 5 by 8 to get an answer of 0.625.

Converting a Decimal to a Fraction

A decimal can also be converted to a fraction. One very important point to keep in mind is that the fraction should be written in the lowest terms (in other words, reduce the fraction). Let's take a look at an example of converting a decimal of 0.35 to a fraction.

First of all, you must recognize that 0.35 is equal to 35 hundredths, so you can write 0.35 as $\frac{35}{100}$. Now that we have a fraction, it must be reduced to its lowest terms, which would be $\frac{7}{20}$.

Equations

An *equation* is a mathematical sentence with an equals sign. An equation states that two expressions are equal.

When *solving* an equation, you are finding the value of the variable that makes the sentence true. This is called the *solution*. The goal of solving an equation is to *isolate* the variable, or to get the variable on one side of the equals sign and the numbers on the other side. To *isolate* the variable, *inverse operations* will be used; addition and subtraction are inverse operations. Multiplication and division are inverse operations.

Remember, whatever you do to one side of an equation, you must also do to the other side of the equation. This is called the *property of equality*. Let's look at some examples in Table 1.2.

Table 1.2 Examples of Inverse Operations	
Inverse operations with subtraction	$x + 4 = 8$
	$x + 4 - 4 = 8 - 4$
	$x = 4$
Inverse operations with addition	$y - 8 = 20$
	$y - 8 + 8 = 20 + 8$
	$y = 28$
Inverse operations with division	$-2a = 24$
	$\dfrac{-2a}{-2} = \dfrac{24}{-2}$
	$a = -12$
Inverse operations with multiplication	$\dfrac{h}{5} = -10$
	$5 \times \dfrac{h}{5} = -10 \times 5$
	$h = -50$

Two-Step Equations

A two-step equation is an equation that involves two operations. Step 1 is always to add or subtract. Step 2 is always to multiply or divide. Let's look at examples of these concepts:

Example 1: Given the equation $2x + 8 = 12$, use the following steps to solve for the variable x:

$$2x + 8 = 12$$
$$2x + 8 - 8 = 12 - 8$$
$$2x = 4$$
$$\frac{2x}{2} = \frac{4}{2}$$
$$x = 2$$

Step 1 will be to subtract 8 from both sides. To "undo" the addition, use subtraction. Step 2 will be to divide both sides by 2 to isolate the variable. The solution for x is 2.

Example 2: Given the equation $\frac{x}{3} - 7 = 13$, use the following steps to solve for the variable x:

$$\frac{x}{3} - 7 = 13$$

$$\frac{x}{3} - 7 + 7 = 13 + 7$$

$$\frac{x}{3} = 20$$

$$\frac{x}{3} \times 3 = 20 \times 3$$

$$x = 60$$

Step 1 is to add 7 to both sides. To "undo" the subtraction, use addition. Step 2 is to multiply both sides by 3 to isolate the variable. The solution for x is 60.

Multistep Equations

On the exam, you might be asked to solve some multistep equations. A *multistep equation* is an equation that involves more than two steps. Any multistep equation simplifies to a two-step equation. Here is a list of some steps you might need to take to get to the two-step equation:

1. Use the distributive property to remove parentheses.

2. Use the addition or subtraction property of equality to move the variable terms to one side of the equals sign.

3. Combine like terms.

Let's look at some examples to help you understand this better.

Given the equation $2(8 + x) = 22$, solve for the variable x. The following steps demonstrate this:

$$2(8 + x) = 22$$
$$2 \times 8 + 2 \times x = 22$$
$$16 + 2x = 22$$
$$16 - 16 + 2x = 22 - 16$$
$$2x = 6$$
$$\frac{2x}{2} = \frac{6}{2}$$
$$x = 3$$

In the preceding example, you first have to use the distributive property on the portion of the equation $2(8 + x)$, leading to the expression $2 \times 8 + 2 \times x = 22$. Combining like terms, you get $16 + 2x = 22$. From there, you subtract 16 from both sides; $16 - 16 + 2x = 22 - 16$. This results in $2x = 6$. The next step requires you to divide both sides by 2:

$$\frac{2x}{2} = \frac{6}{2}$$

The solution is $x = 3$.

Let's look at the equation $3x + 4x = 28$. Following similar procedures as used previously, the solution will be $x = 4$, as seen next:

$$3x + 4x = 28$$
$$7x = 28$$
$$\frac{7x}{7} = \frac{28}{7}$$
$$x = 4$$

Some equations have variables on both sides of the equals sign. An example of this is $6x + 3 = 8x - 21$. To solve, first choose a side for the variable terms. Subtracting $6x$ from both sides will put the variable on the right side of the equals sign, as seen with $6x - 6x + 3 = 8x - 6x - 21$. This leaves you with $3 = 2x - 21$. Next, add 21 to both sides ($3 + 21 = 2x - 21 + 21$) to isolate $2x$ on one side of the equals sign. This leaves you with $24 = 2x$. Divide both sides by 2 ($\frac{24}{2} = \frac{2x}{2}$) and your solution is $x = 12$. The fully worked equation looks like this:

$$6x + 3 = 8x - 21$$
$$6x - 6x + 3 = 8x - 6x - 21$$
$$3 = 2x - 21$$
$$3 + 21 = 2x - 21 + 21$$
$$24 = 2x$$
$$\frac{24}{2} = \frac{2x}{2}$$
$$x = 12$$

Exponents and Square Roots

Exponents and square roots are other forms of mathematical notations you will see on the PRAXIS exam. Let's review what they are and how they are used.

Exponents

Exponential notation is useful in situations where the same number is multiplied repeatedly. The number being multiplied is called the *base*, and the *exponent* tells how many times the base is multiplied by itself.

For example, 4^6 may also be represented with the following equation: $4 \times 4 \times 4 \times 4 \times 4 \times 4 = 4^6 = 4,096$.

The base in this example is 4, and the exponent is 6.

Consider the following example: $0.5^3 = 0.5 \times 0.5 \times 0.5 = 0.125$. Notice that the base number does not have to be a whole number. The base may be a decimal.

 A number with an exponent of 2 is referred to as the *square* of a number. The square of a whole number is known as a perfect square. The first 15 perfect squares are 1, 4, 9, 16, 25, 36, 49, 64, 81, 100, 121, 144, 169, 196, and 225.

A number with an exponent of 3 is referred to as the *cube* of a number. The cube of a whole number is known as a perfect cube. The numbers 1, 8, 27, 64, and 125 are all perfect cubes.

Square Roots

Finding the square root ($\sqrt{}$) of a number is the inverse of squaring a number. For example, $2 \times 2 = 4$, so $\sqrt{4} = 2$. This is the *positive root*, sometimes called the *principal root*. You can have a negative root, such as with $-2 \times -2 = 4$, so $\sqrt{4} = -2$, but this is usually not given.

Finding Square Roots That Are Not Perfect Squares

To find the value of $\sqrt{}$ that is not a perfect square, use the number line to help estimate. For example, let's estimate $\sqrt{38}$.

Use estimations with square roots that are perfect squares to estimate what $\sqrt{38}$ will be. You see that $\sqrt{36}$ and $\sqrt{49}$ have perfect squares with 6 and 7:

$$6 \rule{3cm}{0.4pt} 7$$
$$\sqrt{36} \rule{3cm}{0.4pt} \sqrt{49}$$

Because $\sqrt{38}$ is closer to $\sqrt{36}$ than $\sqrt{49}$, $\sqrt{38}$ is approximately 6.

Simplifying Square Roots

To simplify numbers under the $\sqrt{}$ symbol, rewrite the number under the $\sqrt{}$ as the product of a perfect square and another factor. Take the square root of the perfect square and leave the other factor under the $\sqrt{}$. Let's look at some examples.

In example 1, simplify $\sqrt{60}$. The number 60 is rewritten as the product of a perfect square, 4, and another factor, 15, as seen with $2 \times \sqrt{15}$ ($\sqrt{4} = 2$ and $\sqrt{15}$). Notice that $\sqrt{15}$ is not a perfect square, so it stays under $\sqrt{}$. Therefore, you get an answer of $2 \times \sqrt{15}$. The following shows the fully worked problem:

$$\sqrt{60}$$

$$\sqrt{60} = \sqrt{4} \times \sqrt{15}$$

$$\sqrt{4} = 2\sqrt{15}$$

$$2 \times \sqrt{15}$$

For example 2, simplify $\sqrt{125}$. In this case, 125 is rewritten as the product of a perfect square, 25, and another factor, 5. Specifically, $\sqrt{125} = \sqrt{25} \times \sqrt{5}$ for a solution of $5 \times \sqrt{5}$. You see that $\sqrt{25} = 5$, but $\sqrt{5}$ is not a perfect square, so it stays under $\sqrt{}$. The fully worked problem is as follows:

$$\sqrt{125}$$

$$\sqrt{125} = \sqrt{25} \times \sqrt{5}$$

$$5 \times \sqrt{5}$$

Inequalities

An *inequality* is a mathematical expression of the relationship between two quantities that are not equal.

Inequality symbols include

< less than

> greater than

≠ not equal

≤ less than or equal to

≥ greater than or equal to

A *solution* to an inequality is any value that makes the sentence true. For example, the solutions for $y > 5$ are any numbers that are greater than 5.

You might be asked whether a number is a solution. For example, is 9 a solution of $x < 9$? The correct response is **no**; 9 is *not less* than 9.

Is 9 a solution of $x \leq 9$? The correct response is **yes**; 9 is *equal* to 9.

A number line is used to graph solutions of inequalities because a solution is not just one number. When graphing the solution of an inequality, one decision that must be made is whether to use an open or closed circle.

Example 1: Graph $x > 2$

The open circle means that 2 is excluded from the solution set—2 is not a solution. The shading is used to show all the numbers that are a part of the solution set.

Example 2: Graph $x \geq 2$

The closed circle means that 2 is included in the solution set—2 is a solution. Again, the shading indicates where the solutions are.

Solving Inequalities

Solving an inequality is similar to solving an equation. Inverse operations are performed to isolate the variable.

Example 1:

$x + 2 \geq 4$—Subtract 2 from both sides of the inequality.

$x + 2 - 2 \geq 4 - 2$

$x \geq 2$ —All numbers greater than or equal to 2 are solutions.

After an inequality is solved, the solutions are shown on a number line.

$$\longleftarrow \!|\!\!-\!\!|\!\!-\!\!|\!\!-\!\!|\!\!-\!\!|\!\!-\!\!|\!\!-\!\!|\!\!-\!\!|\!\!\longrightarrow$$
$$\text{-2 -1 0 1 2 3 4 5}$$

Example 2:

$9 < y - 4$—Add 4 to both sides of the inequality.

$9 + 4 < y - 4 + 4$

$13 < y$—All numbers greater than 13 are solutions.

$$\longleftarrow \!|\!\!-\!\!|\!\!-\!\!|\!\!-\!\!|\!\!-\!\!|\!\!-\!\!|\!\!-\!\!|\!\!-\!\!|\!\!\longrightarrow$$
$$\text{8 9 10 11 12 13 14 15 16}$$

Just as in the equation examples, you might have to solve a two-step inequality, as seen in examples 3, 4, and 5.

Example 3:

$12 + 2x < 48$—Step 1 is to subtract 12 from both sides.

$12 - 12 + 2x < 48 - 12$

$2x < 36$—Now, step 2: Divide both sides by 2.

$$\frac{2x}{2} < \frac{36}{2}$$

$x < 18$—All numbers less than 18 are solutions.

$$\longleftarrow \!|\!\!-\!\!|\!\!-\!\!|\!\!-\!\!|\!\!-\!\!|\!\!-\!\!|\!\!-\!\!|\!\!-\!\!|\!\!\longrightarrow$$
$$\text{14 15 16 17 18 19 20 21 22 23}$$

If an inequality is to be solved by multiplying or dividing *both* sides of the inequality by a negative number, the inequality *symbol must be reversed*.

Example 4:

$-2x < 8$—To solve, divide both sides by -2.

$$\frac{-2x}{-2} < \frac{8}{-2}$$

$x > -4$—Notice that the inequality symbol has been reversed. The solutions are all numbers greater than -4.

Example 5:

$$\frac{x}{-6} > 1$$

To solve, multiply both sides by -6.

$$(-6)\frac{x}{-6} > 1(-6)$$

$x < -6$—Notice that the inequality symbol has been reversed. The solutions are all numbers less than -6.

Geometry

Be prepared to encounter exam questions that test your knowledge about different aspects of geometry. Before you tackle the exam, you should have a good understanding of the following geometry topics, all of which are discussed in the sections that follow:

➤ Angles

➤ Lines

➤ Triangles

➤ Circles

➤ Volume

➤ Surface area

Angles

An angle is formed when two rays intersect at a point called the *vertex*. Angles are most commonly measured in degrees. Angles are classified by their measures (see Table 1.3).

In Figure 1.3, $\overrightarrow{AB}$ intersects $\overrightarrow{AC}$ at point A. A is the vertex of the angle. The name of the angle is either ∠BAC or ∠CAB.

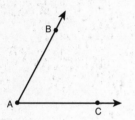

Figure 1.3 *n* is the angle between lines AB and AC.

The most commonly used unit to measure the size of an angle is called a *degree*. The symbol ° is used to indicate degrees. How big is a degree? A full circle is made up of 360 degrees. A semicircle has 180 degrees, and half of that—a quarter of a circle—has 90 degrees. Figure 1.4 shows a perfect 90° angle between lines A and B.

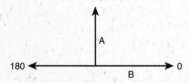

Figure 1.4 A right angle.

Now that you are familiar with the basic definition of an angle, let's take a look at the different types of angles you are likely to encounter on the PRAXIS math exam.

Types of Angles

Angles can range from 0 degrees to 360 degrees. There are basically four main types of angles, which are summarized in Table 1.3.

Table 1.3 Types of Angles		
Type of Angle	**Description**	**Diagram**
Acute angle	An angle that is less than 90 degrees.	
Straight angle	An angle that is 180 degrees.	
Obtuse angle	An angle between 90 degrees and 180 degrees.	
Right angle	An angle that is 90 degrees.	

Complementary Angles

Two angles are *complementary* if their sum equals 90 degrees. The two angles do not have to be adjacent angles. Note the examples:

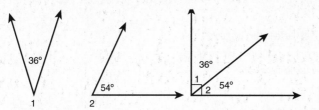

$m\angle 1 + m\angle 2 = 90°$

$36° + 54° = 90°$

$\angle 1$ and $\angle 2$ are complementary.

Supplementary Angles

Two angles are *supplementary* if their sum equals 180 degrees. Again, the two angles do not have to be adjacent. See the following examples:

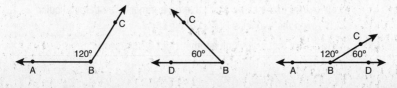

$m\angle\text{ABC} + m\angle\text{CBD} = 180°$

$120° + 60° = 180°$

$\angle\text{ABC}$ and $\angle\text{CBD}$ are supplementary.

Vertical Angles

Vertical angles are formed when two lines intersect. See the following example:

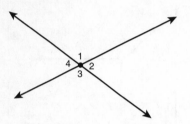

$\angle 1$ and $\angle 3$ are a pair of vertical angles.

$\angle 2$ and $\angle 4$ are a pair of vertical angles.

Vertical angles are congruent, which means they have equal measures.

$\angle 1 \cong \angle 3$ or $m\angle 1 = m\angle 3$

Be aware of the following symbols:

$\cong$ is the symbol that means congruent.

m stands for "measure of."

Lines

Lines are determined by two points. Lines do not end. They continually extend in both directions. Lines may be *perpendicular*, *parallel*, or *intersecting*. Table 1.4 outlines the differences between these relationships.

Table 1.4 Types of Lines	
Type of Line	**Description**
Perpendicular	Two lines that meet at a right angle.
Parallel	Two lines in the same plane that do not meet. The perpendicular between the two lines is always the same.
Intersecting	Two lines that cross one another (that is, intersect).

Lines can be represented by the formula: $y = mx + b$. The (x,y) coordinate is called the *ordered pair*. The m is the slope of the line and the b is the y-intercept; you'll learn more about y-intercept in a few moments.

It is a three-step process to calculate the line formula. The first step is to calculate the slope between two points on the line.

m = slope of the line

m = rise/run

$m = (y2 - y1) / (x2 - x1)$

The second step is to determine the *y-intercept*. The *y-intercept* is where the line crosses the y-axis.

The final step is to take the results and put them into the formula of the line.

Circles

A *circle* is a closed plane curve in which every point is equidistant from its center. Several definitions that you should be familiar with will be covered in greater detail in the following material.

➤ *Circumference*—The distance around a circle.

➤ *Diameter*—A straight line from one point on a circle through the center of the circle to the opposite point.

➤ *Radius*—The distance from the center of the circle to any point on it.

➤ *pi* (π)—The number that is equal to the circumference divided by the diameter (3.141592...).

Radius and Diameter

The *radius* of a circle is a line segment that has one endpoint on the circle and the other endpoint at the center of the circle. One circle has many radii (the plural of radius), each of which has the same length. See the following example:

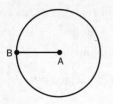

As you can see, $\overline{AB}$ is the radius.

The *diameter* of a circle is a segment with endpoints on the circle that passes through the center of the circle. One circle has many diameters. See the following example:

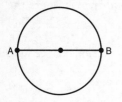

In any circle, two times the length of the radius equals the length of the diameter. Another way to state that is $\frac{1}{2}$ the length of the diameter equals the length of the radius. As you see in this example, $\overline{AB}$ is the diameter.

Circumference

The *circumference* of a circle can also be calculated using the radius or the diameter. The formula for calculating circumference using the diameter is $\pi \times$ diameter ($C = \pi d$). For example, if the diameter of a circle is 4, the circumference is $3.14 \times 4 = 12.56$. Using the radius, the formula for calculating circumference is $2(\pi \times \text{radius})$. If the radius of a circle is 3, the circumference is $2(3.14 \times 3) = 18.84$.

Area

The *area* of a figure refers to the number of squares required to cover it completely, like tiles on a floor. Area is measured in *square units*. When calculating area, there are several formulas to remember, depending on the shape of the object. Table 1.5 outlines the most common shapes and the formulas to calculate the area for them.

Table 1.5	Formulas to Calculate Area
Object	**Formula**
Square	Length × width
Rectangle	Length × width
Parallelogram	Base × height
Trapezoid	Height/2(base1 + base2)
Circle	π × radius²
Triangle	$\frac{1}{2}$ (base × height)

Area of a Square

The area of a square equals side length times side length. Because each side of a square is the same length, it can simply be the length of one side squared.

If a square has one side with a length of 4 inches, the area would be 4 inches times 4 inches, or 16 square inches. (In this case, square inches can also be written as 4^2.) The following is a graphical depiction of this:

$$\text{Area} = s^2 = 4^2 = 16 \text{ in}^2$$

 Be sure to use the same units for all measurements.

Area of a Rectangle

The area of a rectangle is the length on the side times the width. If the width is 4 inches and the length is 6 feet, what is the area? For example:

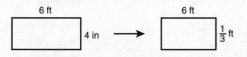

Notice that the units of measurement are different, so you cannot simply multiply 4 times 6. To find the correct answer, you must convert the numbers so that they are using the same unit of measurement. For example, 4 inches is the same as $\frac{1}{3}$ feet. The area is $\frac{1}{3}$ feet × 6 feet = 2 square feet or 2 sq. ft., or 2 ft².

Area of a Circle

The area of the circle can be calculated using the radius of the circle. The formula to calculate the area of a circle is π × radius².

Triangles

A *triangle* is a geometric figure consisting of three points, or *vertices*, which are connected with line segments called *sides*. When one of the angles of a triangle is a right angle, we call it a *right triangle*, as shown in Figure 1.5.

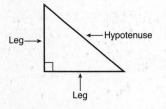

Figure 1.5   A right triangle.

As you can see in the figure, the *hypotenuse* is the side opposite of the right angle. It is also the longest side. The other sides of the triangle are called *legs*.

Pythagorean Theorem

The Pythagorean theorem is a statement about triangles containing a right angle. The Pythagorean theorem states the following:

The sum of the squares of the lengths of the legs of a right triangle is equal to the square of the length of the hypotenuse.

If a and b are the legs of a right triangle and c is its hypotenuse, then $a^2 + b^2 = c^2$. Figure 1.6 illustrates the Pythagorean theorem.

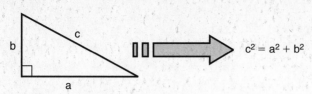

Figure 1.6   The Pythagorean theorem.

According to the Pythagorean theorem, the sum of the areas of squares A and B is equal to the area of square C. The area of square A = a^2, the area of square B = b^2, and the area of square C = c^2. Therefore, the Pythagorean theorem is stated $a^2 + b^2 = c^2$. The following is an example:

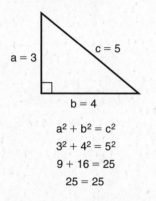

$$a^2 + b^2 = c^2$$
$$3^2 + 4^2 = 5^2$$
$$9 + 16 = 25$$
$$25 = 25$$

You might be asked to use the Pythagorean theorem to solve for a missing side length of a right triangle. Remember, the Pythagorean theorem applies *only* to *right* triangles.

Example 1: Find the length of the hypotenuse in the following triangle:

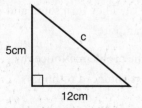

The following example demonstrates how to solve this:

$a^2 + b^2 = c^2$

$5^2 + 12^2 = c^2$

$25 + 144 = c^2$

$169 = c^2$

$\sqrt{169} = c$

$13 = c$

Example 2: Find the length of the leg.

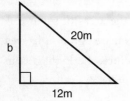

To solve for b:

$a^2 + b^2 = c^2$

$12^2 + b^2 = 20^2$

$144 + b^2 = 400$

$b^2 = 400 - 144$

$b^2 = 256$

$b = \sqrt{256}$

$b = 16$

You might be asked to solve a word problem in which the situation can be modeled by a right triangle. That is when you would use the Pythagorean theorem.

Example 1: Two hikers leave camp and hike 3 km east. They turn south and continue hiking 4 km. How far are they from the campsite?

To solve this, begin by drawing a picture to model the problem. Notice that, in the drawing, the length of the hypotenuse is what you need to find:

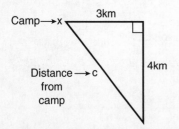

To solve this problem and find the distance to camp, use the following:

$a^2 + b^2 = c^2$

$3^2 + 4^2 = c^2$

$9 + 16 = c^2$

$25 = c^2$

$\sqrt{25} = c$

$5 = c$

As you can see, they are 5 km from the campsite.

Volume

Volume is the measure of the amount of space occupied by an object. To calculate an object's volume, you must know which formula to use. Table 1.6 lists the volume formulas for various objects.

Table 1.6 Formulas to Calculate Volume	
Object	**Formula**
Cube	Length × width × height
Rectangular Prism	Length × width × height
Cylinder	Base × height
	Base = π radius^2
Pyramid	$\frac{1}{3}$(base × height)
Cone	$\frac{1}{3}$ base × height
Sphere	$(\frac{4}{3})\pi$ radius^3

Volume of a Cube

Volume is measured in cubic units. The volume of a figure is the number of cubes required to fill it completely, like blocks in a box.

The volume of a cube = length × width × height. Because each side of a square is the same, the volume can simply be the length of one side cubed. See the following example:

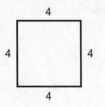

If a square has one side with a length of 4 inches, the area would be 4 inches times 4 inches times 4 inches, or 64 cubic inches. This quantity can also be written as 64 in³.

Be sure to use the same units for all measurements. You cannot multiply feet times inches times yards and still come up with the correct answer.

Measuring the Volume of a Rectangular Solid

The volume of a rectangular solid is equal to the length of the side times the width times the height. If the width is 4 inches, the length is 1 foot, and the height is 3 feet, what is the volume?

Because you cannot simply multiply 4 inches times 1 foot times 3 feet to get 12, you will need to convert all the sides to use the same unit of measurement. For example, 4 inches is equal to $\frac{1}{3}$ foot. You can then calculate the volume by multiplying $\frac{1}{3}$ foot times 1 foot times 3 feet, which equals 1 cubic foot, 1 cu. ft., or 1 ft³.

Measuring the Volume of a Cylindrical Solid

The volume of a cylindrical solid is equal to π times the square of the radius of the circle at the cylinder's base, times the height of the cylinder. Written as a formula, this is $V = \pi r^2 h$.

Surface Area

Surface area is the sum of the areas of all the shapes that cover the surface of the object. Table 1.7 lists the surface area formulas for several objects.

Table 1.7 Formulas to Calculate Surface Area	
Object	**Formula**
Cube	$6 \times$ length $\times$ width
Rectangular solid	$2(\text{length} \times \text{width}) + 2(\text{length} \times \text{height}) + 2(\text{width} \times \text{height})$
Cylindrical solid	$2\pi r^2 + 2\pi rh$ (where r = radius and h = height)

Graphs and Tables

On the PRAXIS math exam you will be asked to interpret data found within graphs and data tables. There are four main types of graphs with which you need to be familiar:

➤ Pie charts (also known as circle graphs)

➤ Bar graphs

➤ Line graphs

➤ XY plots

Pie Charts (or Circle Graphs)

Pie charts provide a clear, visual representation of the relationship between the various parts of a data set. The pie represents a complete set of data, and each slice represents a distinct part (or subset) of that data. For example, the following pie chart depicts how a government spent its annual budget during a year. As you can see from the chart, the majority of the budget was spent on transportation. Note that a circle graph usually uses percentages in its views. As seen in this example, the health, education, transportation, and tourism slices are certain percentages of the whole. The sum of all the percentages must equal 100 percent.

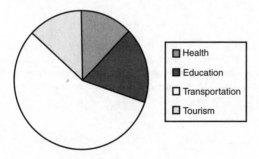

Bar Graphs

Bar graphs are normally used to make comparisons. The following bar graph makes a comparison between the amounts of rainfall that occurred each season.

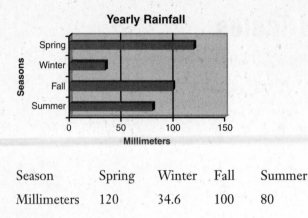

Season	Spring	Winter	Fall	Summer
Millimeters	120	34.6	100	80

Line Graphs

Line graphs are similar to bar graphs. Line graphs show a change over a period of time. They also show the relationship between two different variables. As you can see, the following line graph shows how the daily temperature changed during one week.

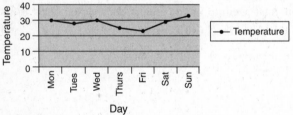

Graphs and charts usually include legends, also known as *keys*, which tell which data set is indicated by which bar, line, or slice in the graph. Make sure you use this information to help interpret the data. Also, read any graph questions very carefully so you know exactly what it is you are being asked.

XY Plots

An XY plot is often used to display scientific data. This type of graph displays the relationship between two variables. Here's an example of an XY plot.

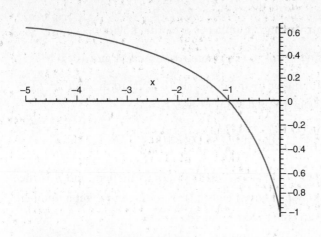

Interpreting Tables

As you can see from the examples included throughout this chapter, tables are a great way to organize and present data. Tables can range in size from simple, with only two columns, to extremely complex. You need to be able to look at a table and interpret the data. You can usually get an idea of the information within a table by looking at the table description as well as the table headings. Again, when it comes to the exam, be sure you know what the question is asking before you begin interpreting the data within a given table.

Scientific Notation

Scientific notation is a shortcut for writing very large or very small numbers. Because our number system is based on powers of 10, this idea is used in scientific notation.

A number is in scientific notation if the first factor is a number between 1 and 10 and the second factor is a power of 10. Let's explore several examples of how to work with scientific notation.

Example 1: 3×10^4 is a number written in scientific notation. The first factor is 3, a number between 1 and 10. The second factor is 10^4, a power of 10. So, $3 \times 10^4 = 3 \times 10,000 = 30,000$.

There are two rules for writing a number in scientific notation:

1. Relocate the decimal point to get a number between 1 and 10.

2. Multiply that number by the power of 10 equal to the number of places you moved the decimal point in step 1.

Example 2: $700,000,000 = 7.0 \times 10^8$ or just 7×10^8

Notice that the decimal point moved eight places to the left, and 8 is the exponent. The decimal point moved eight places to the left to get a number between 1 and 10. Seven is between 1 and 10.

Example 3: $604,000,000,000 = 6.04 \times 10^{11}$

The decimal point moved 11 places to the left, and 11 is the exponent. The decimal point moved 11 places to the left to get a number between 1 and 10. 6.04 is a number between 1 and 10.

Example 4: $.00000065 = 6.5 \times 10^{-7}$

The decimal point moved seven places to the right, and 7 is the exponent. The exponent is negative because the original number was less than 1. The decimal had to move seven places to the right to get a number between 1 and 10. 6.5 is a number between 1 and 10.

Example 5: $.000789 = 7.89 \times 10^{-4}$

The decimal point moved four places to the right, and 4 is the exponent. The exponent is negative because the original number was less than 1. The decimal had to move four places to the right to get a number between 1 and 10. 7.89 is a number between 1 and 10.

Standard form refers to the process of taking a number written in scientific notation and writing a "normal," or standard, number. On the exam, you might be asked to perform both tasks.

Example 6: Write 3.86×10^{13} in standard form.

This means that the decimal point will be moved 13 places to the right to get $38,600,000,000,000$. The decimal point has to be moved to the right to get a very large number. Because the exponent is positive, the number in standard form is a number larger than one.

Example 7: Write 4.8×10^{-4} in standard form.

This means that the decimal point will be moved four places to the left to get .00048. The decimal point has to be moved to the left to get a very small number. Because the exponent is negative, the number in standard form is a number less than one.

Probability

Probability is the likelihood that an event will occur. Theoretical probability is defined as

$P(\text{event}) = \dfrac{\text{number of favorable outcomes}}{\text{number of possible outcomes}}$

Let's look at some examples of probability:

Example 1: A coin

Event	Flipping to get heads
Favorable outcome	Coin lands heads
Possible outcomes	Heads or tails

In this probability formula, the probability of the coin landing heads on any coin toss is

$P(\text{heads}) = \dfrac{1}{2}$

A number cube (die) is often involved in probability questions. Remember that a cube has six sides, so the possible outcomes will be 6. Refer to examples 2–5.

Example 2: $P(\text{rolling an odd number}) = \dfrac{3}{6} = \dfrac{1}{2}$

Example 3: $P(4) = \dfrac{1}{6}$

Example 4: $P(\text{number greater than } 7) = \frac{0}{6} = 0$

This is an impossible event. On a game cube, there are no numbers greater than 7. The probability of all impossible events is zero.

Example 5: $P(\text{number less than } 7) = \frac{6}{6} = 1$

When the probability equals 1, the event is certain to occur. On the game cube, all numbers are less than 7, so you are certain to roll a number less than 7.

ALERT | Probability answers will always be 0, 1, or a fraction between 0 and 1.

Measurement

Measurement can be classified as two specific formats, the *English system (customary)* and the *metric system*. The following sections outline the standard units of measure with both systems. You should be able to convert the units within each system and also convert units between systems.

English System of Measurement (Customary Units)

The English system of measurement is the measurement system generally used in the United States, so this is the system you might be most familiar with. Table 1.8 shows the English system's units of length, weight, and volume. It also provides conversion factors for each unit, which you will need to use when doing conversion problems.

Table 1.8 English Measurement Units	
Length units	1 mile = 5,280 feet (ft)
	1 mile = 1,760 yards (yd)
	1 yard = 3 ft.
	1 foot = 12 inches (in)
Weight units	1 ton = 2,000 pounds (lbs)
	1 pound = 16 ounces (oz)
Volume units	1 gallon(gal) = 4 quarts (qt)
	1 quart = 2 pints (pt)
	1 pint = 2 cups (C)
	1 C = 8 oz

Converting Units of Measurement in the English System

To convert one unit to another, you will need to know the conversion factor. The units seen in Table 1.8 are used as conversion factors to solve problems of this type. Let's do some sample problems to practice conversion.

Example 1: To convert 4 feet to inches, multiply 4 times 12 (the number of inches in a foot), which equals 48 inches. In this example, you went from a larger unit to a smaller unit, so you needed to multiply. If you must convert from a smaller unit to a larger unit, division is needed, as shown in example 2.

Example 2: To convert 8,000 pounds to tons, you divide $\frac{8,000}{2,000} = 4$ tons.

Metric System

The metric system is the measurement system most often used outside the United States. There are three basic units in the metric system:

➤ *Meter* (length)

➤ *Gram* (mass)

➤ *Liter* (volume)

The metric system is based on prefixes that are units of 10. See Table 1.9.

Table 1.9	The Metric System Prefixes		
Prefix	**Symbol**	**Factor Number**	**Factor Word**
Kilo	k	1,000	Thousand
Hecto	h	100	Hundred
Deca	da	10	Ten
Deci	d	0.1	Tenth
Centi	c	0.01	Hundredth
Milli	m	0.001	Thousandth

Conversion of Metric Units

To convert one metric unit to another, you must decide whether you are going from a *larger unit to a smaller unit* or from *a smaller unit to a larger unit*.

If you are going from a larger unit to a smaller unit, you will need to *multiply*. Multiplying moves the decimal point to the right, and you will need to know how many places to move the decimal point. Let's look at the following example to understand this:

Example 1: Convert 6 kilograms to grams. This involves converting from a larger unit to a smaller unit, so you will need to multiply (move the decimal point to the right). Table 1.9 indicates that the prefix *kilo* means 1,000. Therefore, multiply 6 times 1,000, which equals 6,000. That is the same as moving the decimal point three places to the right to get 6,000, as seen in this example:

6.000.
<small>1 2 3</small>

If you are moving from a smaller metric unit to a larger metric unit, you need to *divide*. Dividing moves the decimal point to the *left*. Consider the following example:

Example 2: Convert 80 milliliters to liters.

This involves converting from a smaller unit to a larger unit, so you will need to divide (move the decimal point to the left). Table 1.9 indicates that the prefix *milli* means one-thousandth (.001). Therefore, divide 80 by 1,000, which equals .08. This is the same as moving the decimal point three places to the left. Note the following example:

(Add zeros when there are no existing numbers.)

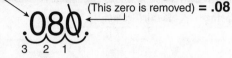

(This zero is removed) **= .08**

Conversion from Metric to English and from English to Metric

Use Table 1.10 to convert measurements from the metric system to the English system and Table 1.11 to convert from English to metric. For example, looking at Table 1.10, if you had 5 meters, you would multiply that by 39.37 to determine the number of inches.

Table 1.10 Conversion from Metric to English System		
Metric System	**Conversion Factor**	**English System**
centimeter	0.03281	foot
centimeter	0.3937	inch
cubic meter	35.314	cubic foot
kilometer	0.6214	mile
meter	3.2808	foot
meter	39.37	inch
meter	0.0006214	mile
meter	1.0936	yard
millimeter	0.0394	inch
liter	2.1134	pint (liquid)
liter	1.0567	quart

Table 1.11 Conversion from English to Metric System		
English System	**Conversion Factor**	**Metric System**
foot	0.3048	meter
inch	2.54	centimeter
inch	25.4	millimeter
mile	1.6093	kilometer
yard	0.9144	meter
gallon (liquid)	3.7854	liter

(continued)

Table 1.11 Conversion from English to Metric System *(continued)*		
English System	**Conversion Factor**	**Metric System**
quart (liquid)	.94635	liter
pint (liquid)	.47318	liter
pint (dry)	.55061	liter

Be sure you are familiar with some of the more common conversion units. You will more than likely encounter at least one math question that requires you to convert one form of measurement to another. Note that the conversion factors are approximate and that you don't need to remember all their decimal places. Use rounding as appropriate to estimate the answers to any conversion problems on the exam.

Exam Prep Questions

1. Round 19,723 to the nearest thousands place.
   - ❑ A. 20,000
   - ❑ B. 19,000
   - ❑ C. 18,000
   - ❑ D. 19,700

2. Round 846,549 to the nearest hundreds place.
   - ❑ A. 850,000
   - ❑ B. 840,000
   - ❑ C. 847,000
   - ❑ D. 846,500

3. What is the square root of 64?
   - ❑ A. 5
   - ❑ B. 8
   - ❑ C. 7
   - ❑ D. 9

4. What is the square root of 10?
   - ❑ A. 5.00
   - ❑ B. 2.20
   - ❑ C. 3.16
   - ❑ D. 4.22

5. Reduce the fraction $\frac{24}{36}$.
   - ❑ A. $\frac{2}{3}$
   - ❑ B. $\frac{4}{6}$
   - ❑ C. $\frac{3}{6}$
   - ❑ D. $\frac{2}{4}$

6. Which of the following fractions is not equivalent to $\frac{2}{3}$?
   - ❑ A. $\frac{4}{6}$
   - ❑ B. $\frac{12}{18}$
   - ❑ C. $\frac{10}{15}$
   - ❑ D. $\frac{6}{12}$

7. $2^2 \times 2^3 = ?$
   - ❑ A. 32
   - ❑ B. 48
   - ❑ C. 56
   - ❑ D. 64

8. $4.76 \times 10^6 = ?$
  - ❑ A. 476,000
  - ❑ B. 4,760,000
  - ❑ C. 47,600,000
  - ❑ D. 476,000,000

9. Over the duration of an entire work week (Monday–Friday), Felicia spent a total of $29.95. One-third of this was for fuel. The remaining amount was for lunch. What was the average amount she spent each day on lunch?
  - ❑ A. $5.50
  - ❑ B. $5.25
  - ❑ C. $4.00
  - ❑ D. $3.75

10. Which of the following ratios is equivalent to 24:20?
  - ❑ A. 48:30
  - ❑ B. 96:80
  - ❑ C. 6:4
  - ❑ D. 120:140

11. Felicia rode her bike for a total of 5 hours and traveled 30 miles. What was her average rate of speed?
  - ❑ A. 6 miles per hour
  - ❑ B. 10 miles per hour
  - ❑ C. 150 miles per hour
  - ❑ D. 35 miles per hour

12. On the first day of his road trip, Conroy drove his car at an average of 45 miles per hour (mph) for 8 hours. How far did he drive that day?
  - ❑ A. 360 miles
  - ❑ B. 135 miles
  - ❑ C. 405 miles
  - ❑ D. 300 miles

13. Change 4.76% to a decimal.
  - ❑ A. 0.0476
  - ❑ B. 0.476
  - ❑ C. 4.76
  - ❑ D. 0.00476

14. Which of the following correctly represents 32% as a fraction reduced to its lowest terms?

    ❏ A. $\frac{32}{100}$

    ❏ B. $\frac{16}{50}$

    ❏ C. $\frac{8}{25}$

    ❏ D. 32

15. A swimming pool measures 12 ft. wide × 10 ft. deep × 12 ft. long. If the pool is filled all the way to the top, what is the volume of the water in it?

    ❏ A. 120 ft. cubed
    ❏ B. 1200 ft. cubed
    ❏ C. 1400 ft. cubed
    ❏ D. 1440 ft. cubed

16. A piece of bread contains approximately 120 calories. Felicia eats two pieces of bread on Monday, one piece on Wednesday, and half a piece on Friday. How many calories did she consume from the bread in one week?

    ❏ A. 240
    ❏ B. 360
    ❏ C. 420
    ❏ D. 480

17. $(a^2)(a^3)(a^n) = a^9$

    What is the value of n in this equation?

    ❏ A. 2
    ❏ B. 3
    ❏ C. 4
    ❏ D. 5

18. Put 18,000,000 in scientific notation.

    ❏ A. 18×10^6
    ❏ B. $.18 \times 10^8$
    ❏ C. 1.8×10^6
    ❏ D. 1.8×10^7

19. The measure of angle A is 120 degrees. What is the measure of angle B?

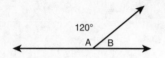

❑ A. 40 degrees
❑ B. 45 degrees
❑ C. 50 degrees
❑ D. 60 degrees

20. A circle has a diameter of 12 cm. What is its circumference, rounded to the nearest tenth?
❑ A. 12.4 cm
❑ B. 37.7 cm
❑ C. 28.9 cm
❑ D. 24 cm

21. A circle has a radius of 8. What is the diameter of the circle?
❑ A. 16
❑ B. 25.1
❑ C. 32
❑ D. 64

22. A bag contains four yellow, two red, and three green marbles. Find the probability of drawing a red marble if one marble is drawn at random.
❑ A. $\frac{2}{9}$
❑ B. $\frac{4}{9}$
❑ C. $\frac{1}{3}$
❑ D. $\frac{2}{5}$

23. Solve for x. $3x - 7 = 35$
❑ A. $x = 7$
❑ B. $x = 14$
❑ C. $x = 12$
❑ D. $x = 9\frac{1}{3}$

24. $-39 + -62 = ?$
❑ A. 101
❑ B. 23
❑ C. -101
❑ D. -23

25. Solve for x: $4 + x \leq 7$

   ❑ A. $x < 11$
   ❑ B. $x \leq 11$
   ❑ C. $x \leq 3$
   ❑ D. $x \geq 3$

26. $(6 \times 10^4)(4 \times 10^5) = ?$

   ❑ A. 2.4×10^{10}
   ❑ B. 24×10^{20}
   ❑ C. 10×10^{20}
   ❑ D. 10×10^9

27. Felicia is painting one side of her fence. A single can of spray paint will cover 300 square feet. Her fence is 6 feet tall and 300 feet long. How many cans of spray paint does she need?

   ❑ A. 3
   ❑ B. 4
   ❑ C. 5
   ❑ D. 6

28. If $m\angle A = 36°$ and $m\angle B = 54°$, then $\angle A$ and $\angle B$ are called what kind of angles?

   ❑ A. Complementary
   ❑ B. Supplementary
   ❑ C. Vertical
   ❑ D. None of the above

29. FKB Car Dealership sold 10,000 vehicles in 2003. How many vans were sold during that year?

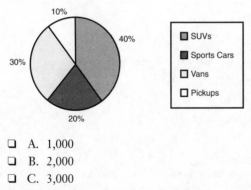

   ❑ A. 1,000
   ❑ B. 2,000
   ❑ C. 3,000
   ❑ D. 6,000

30. The following line graph displays weight gain for John and Mary. How much weight did John gain in the first six months?

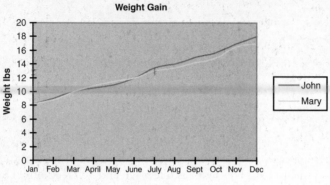

Weight Gain

❑ A. 4 pounds 8 ounces
❑ B. 3 pounds
❑ C. 10 ounces
❑ D. 5 pounds 2 ounces

31. $(x^3)^3 = ?$
❑ A. $3x$
❑ B. x^3
❑ C. x^6
❑ D. x^9

32. $(a^3b^7)^6 = ?$
❑ A. a^9b^{13}
❑ B. a^9b^{42}
❑ C. $a^{18}b^{42}$
❑ D. $a^{18}b^{13}$

33. John had the following test scores throughout the year:

75, 69, 88, 92, 69, 73, 82, 97, 71

69, 69, 71, 73, 75, 82, 88, 92, 97

What was his median test score?
❑ A. 75
❑ B. 80
❑ C. 69
❑ D. 97

Exam Prep Answers

1. Answer A is correct. The 7 in the hundreds place means you must round up. The answer becomes 20,000 when you round up the number 9, which is in the thousands place. Therefore, answers B, C, and D are incorrect.

2. Answer D is correct. Because the four is in the tens place, you do not round up—you just change the last two digits to zeros. The answer then becomes 846,500. Therefore, answers A, B, and C are incorrect.

3. Answer B is correct. The square root of 64 is 8. The square root of a number is that number times itself, and 8×8 equals 64. Therefore, answers A, C, and D are incorrect.

4. Answer C is correct. There is no perfect square for 10. An accurate square root for 10 is 3.16. You can find the answer by approximating between the square root of two whole numbers that have perfect squares, as you saw earlier in the chapter. Therefore, answers A, B, and D are incorrect.

5. Answer A is correct. The fraction can be reduced to $\frac{2}{3}$ by dividing the numerator and denominator by 12 (the greatest common factor [GCF]). Therefore, answers C and D are incorrect. Answer B is incorrect because this fraction can be further reduced.

6. Answer D is correct. The fraction $\frac{6}{12}$ is not equivalent to $\frac{2}{3}$. The remaining options are equivalent. Because the question asked which fraction is not equivalent, answers A, B, and C are incorrect.

7. Answer A is correct. The answer to the equation is 32. You can find the answer by adding together the exponents to get 2^5, which is equal to 32. This is possible because both exponents being multiplied have the same base: 2. Another way of solving this problem is to find the value of each exponent separately and then to determine their product: $2^2 \times 2^3 = 4 \times 8 = 32$. Therefore, answers B, C, and D are incorrect.

8. Answer B is correct. The answer to the equation 4.76×10^6 is 4,760,000. Therefore, answers A, C, and D are incorrect.

9. Answer C is correct. You can use approximation to solve this problem. $29.95 is approximately equal to $30. If Felicia spent one-third of this amount on fuel, that means she spent $30 \times \frac{1}{3} = \$10$ on fuel. The question tells you that she spent the remaining amount ($30 – $10 = $20) on lunch. Now, to find the correct answer for the average amount Felicia spent on lunch each day during her Monday–Friday work week, divide the total amount spent on lunch by the number of days she bought lunch: $20 / 5 days = $4 per day. Felicia spent an average of

$4.00 a day on lunch. A third of the money was spent on fuel. This leaves $20.07. The average work week is 5 days. You can find the answer by dividing $20.07 by 5. Therefore, answers A, B, and D are incorrect.

10. Answer B is correct. The answer of 96:80 is an equivalent ratio to 24:20. To see this, simply multiply both 24 and 20 by 4, and you get an equivalent ratio of 96:80. Therefore, answers A, C, and D are incorrect. These are not equal ratios.

11. Answer A is correct. You can find the rate using the following formula: rate = distance ÷ time. 30 divided by 5 equals 6. Therefore, answers B, C, and D are incorrect.

12. Answer A is correct. You can find the distance traveled using the following formula: distance = rate × time. 45 mph × 8 hours = 360 miles. Therefore, answers B, C, and D are incorrect.

13. Answer A is correct. The decimal value of 4.76% is 0.0476. You can find the answer by multiplying 4.76 by 0.01 (that is, by moving the decimal point two places to the left and dropping the % sign.) Therefore, answers B, C, and D are incorrect.

14. Answer C is correct. $\frac{8}{25}$ is the fractional value for 32%. You can find the answer by converting the percent to a fraction and reducing it to lowest terms. Therefore, answers A, B, and D are incorrect.

15. Answer D is correct. You can find the answer using the following formula: L × W × H. The volume of the pool is 1440 ft. cubed. Therefore, answers A, B, and C are incorrect.

16. Answer C is correct. Felicia consumed 420 calories from the bread in one week. Simply multiply 120 by 3.5 to find the answer. Therefore, answers A, B, and D are incorrect.

17. Answer C is correct. The correct value of n is 4. Therefore, answers A, B, and D are incorrect.

18. Answer D is correct. The first factor in A and B is not a number between 1 and 10. C has the wrong exponent.

19. Answer D is correct. To correctly solve this problem, you must recognize that angles A and B are supplementary, which means they add up to 180 degrees. Therefore, the measure of angle B is 60 degrees. You can find the answer by subtracting 120 from 180. Therefore, answers A, B, and C are incorrect.

20. Answer B is correct. You can find the circumference of a circle by multiplying the diameter by 3.14. 12 cm multiplied by 3.14 equals 37.7 cm. Therefore, answers A, C, and D are incorrect.

21. Answer A is correct. You can find the diameter of a circle by multiplying the radius by 2. Therefore, answers B, C, and D are incorrect.

22. Answer A is correct. There are two red marbles out of nine marbles. Therefore, answers B, C, and D are incorrect.

23. Answer B is correct. To solve for x, you must isolate the variable x and solve, like this:

$3x - 7 = 35$

$3x - 7 + 7 = 35 + 7$

$3x = 35 + 7$

$3x = 42$

$x = \dfrac{42}{3}$

$x = 14$

Double-check your solution by plugging 14 back into the original equation in the place of x, and you will see that this makes the equation true. Therefore, answers A, C, and D are incorrect.

24. Answer C is correct. Adding together two negative numbers will result in a negative answer. Therefore, answers A, B, and D are incorrect.

25. Answer C is correct. Subtract 4 from both sides and don't reverse the symbol. Therefore, answers A, B, and D are incorrect.

26. Answer A is correct. The answer to the equation is 2.4×10^{10}. Remember to add (not multiply) the exponents. Therefore, answers B, C, and D are incorrect.

27. Answer D is correct. To find the answer, first calculate the square footage that needs to be painted: 6 ft. × 300 ft. = 1,800 ft.^{2}. Next, divide 1,800 ft.^{2} by the number of ft.^{2} covered by one can of paint to find the total number of cans required to do the job:
1,800 ft^2 ÷ (300 ft^2/can) = 6 cans
Therefore, answers A, B, and C are incorrect.

28. Answer A is correct because 36° + 54° = 90°. Two angles whose sum is 90 degrees are called *complementary angles*. Therefore, answers B, C, and D are incorrect.

29. Answer C is correct. From the graph you can see that 30% of the vehicles sold during 2003 were vans. There were a total of 10,000 vehicles sold during this year. You can find the answer by multiplying 10,000 by 0.30. Your answer is then 3,000. Therefore, answers A, B, and D are incorrect.

30. Answer A is correct. Over the first six months, John gained a total of 4 pounds 8 ounces. You can find the answer by using the data in the line graph. Simply determine how much weight he gained each month and add the values together. Therefore, answers B, C, and D are incorrect.

31. Answer D is correct. When there is an exponent within a parentheses with an exponent, you can find the answer by multiplying the exponents. $3 \times 3 = 9$. As such, the correct answer is x^9. Therefore, answers A, B, and C are incorrect.

32. Answer C is correct. You can find the answer by multiplying the exponents. You must multiply the exponent 3 by the exponent 6, as well as the exponent 7 by the exponent 6. Your answer then becomes $a^{18}b^{42}$. Therefore, answers A, B, and D are incorrect.

33. Answer A is correct. The median is the middle value in a list. When you arrange the numbers in order, you can see that because there are an even number of test scores (18) in the list, there is no single "middle number." Therefore, you must take the average of the two numbers on either side of the middle. In this case, the numbers 75 and 75 are the middle two values in the list.

    69 69 69 69 71 71 73 73 **75 75** 82 82 88 88 92 92 97 97

    Averaging 75 and 75, you get 75: $(75 + 75) \div 2 = 150 \div 2 = 75$. Therefore, answers B, C, and D are incorrect.

PRAXIS I Reading

Terms you'll need to understand:

✓ Main idea
✓ Supporting idea
✓ Context clues
✓ Antonym
✓ Synonym
✓ Substitution
✓ Fact
✓ Opinion

Techniques you'll need to master:

✓ Identify the main idea of a passage
✓ Identify the main idea when it is implied
✓ Identify the meaning of words as they are used in the context of a specific reading passage
✓ Identify the supporting ideas within a passage
✓ Determine the strengths and weaknesses of an argument
✓ Determine the relevance of evidence presented in a passage
✓ Use context clues to figure out the meaning of a word within its context
✓ Identify fact versus opinion

The Pre-Professional Skills Test (PPST) in reading is designed to measure your ability to understand, analyze, and evaluate a written passage. This test includes a total of 40 questions, and you have 60 minutes in which to answer them.

The format for this test is multiple choice. The questions on the test consist of a reading passage followed by possible answers (depending on what the question is asking you to do). Some of the reading passages may be short statements that consist of one or two sentences, whereas some are longer. The longer passages are approximately 200 words in length. The shorter ones are in the range of 100 words.

The PPST in reading is broken down into two objectives:

➤ Literal comprehension

➤ Critical and inferential comprehension

The literal comprehension questions will test your ability to understand what you have read. The literal comprehension questions can be further broken down into four categories of question types:

➤ Main idea questions

➤ Supporting idea questions

➤ Organization questions

➤ Vocabulary questions

Questions based on critical and inferential comprehension will test your ability to evaluate a reading selection and its message. You can expect to encounter argument evaluation questions, inferential reasoning questions, and generalization questions.

 The computer-based version of the PRAXIS reading exam contains 46 questions, as opposed to 40 on the paper-based test. However, you have 75 minutes to complete the computer-based test.

Understanding What You Read

Achieving success on the PRAXIS reading exam will be dependent upon your ability to understand what you read. The following sections will look at how you can improve your reading skills to ensure success on the exam.

When you are reading passages on the PRAXIS reading exam, remember to read literally instead of critically.

Identifying the Main Idea

Every passage has a *main idea*. One expectation for taking the PRAXIS reading exam is that you will be able to identify the main idea within a given reading passage.

The multiple-choice questions will ask you to identify the correct sentence that states the main idea. Some questions might require you to first determine the main idea and then choose which sentence is closest in meaning to the main idea (instead of choosing the exact sentence from the passage).

The main idea of a reading passage is the message the author is trying to give about the topic. Sometimes the main idea is easily identifiable and is stated directly in the text (normally at the beginning of the passage or in the concluding paragraph).

Unfortunately, however, the main idea of a passage is not always directly stated, making it more difficult to determine what it is. In such situations, the main idea for the passage is implied, not directly stated. So, how can you find the main idea if it is not directly stated? You can use the following strategies to figure out the main idea that is being implied:

➤ Look for sentences that provide examples about the topic. This can lead you to the main idea of the passage.

➤ The main idea may be introduced through examples or facts given in the opening paragraph that relate to the topic.

Be prepared to encounter reading passages in which the main idea is not clearly or directly stated.

For example, let's take a look at two different passages. Both passages have the same main idea. In the first passage, the main idea is clearly stated in the first sentence. In the second passage, the main idea is implied through a variety of examples.

Example 1

Home computers are used for a variety of different tasks. Some people use their computers to play multimedia games or simple games such as Solitaire. Home computers can also be used for managing finances. You can use your computer to pay bills and perform bank transactions. Another use for home computers is online communication. If your computer is connected to the Internet, it can be used for chat and email. Finally, many people use their home computers for performing other tasks such as word processing and digital imaging.

Example 2

Now, let's talk about guidelines for a minute. For a standard user account, be it a local access or domain account, passwords should never be written down. This provides the greatest amount of security. The Administrator account password, however, is a different story. First of all, the appropriate individual user accounts should be placed in the Administrators group, and these administrators should be instructed to perform administrative duties from those accounts rather than the Administrator account. The general rule should be that no one logs in using the Administrator account. Auditing can be enabled to report instances when this happens. If this rule is enforced, those audit logs will tell you either (a) when someone breaks the rule, (b) when an emergency or configuration issue arises requiring legitimate usage of the Administrator account, or (c) when someone has hacked into your system. After auditing has been enabled, the Administrator account password should be written down and hidden somewhere that is secure and safe. At least two people in the company should remember this account password for emergency purposes, but the fewer people who are aware of the password, the more secure the system becomes. The reasoning behind all of these precautions is that when hackers obtain access to your system or network, they always go for the Administrator account access first because it has nearly universal control over everything. If you effectively lock down the account in this way, the hackers' lives become more difficult. If you're lucky, they won't be willing to invest the extra time necessary to circumvent these tactics, and they'll give up before causing harm.

Identifying the Purpose

People write for a reason, whether it is to inform or entertain readers. The purpose of a passage identifies why it has been written. For the PRAXIS reading exam, you should be able to determine an author's purpose for writing a passage. There are basically four different reasons for writing:

➤ *To entertain*—The writer uses humor or some other technique to amuse the reader.

➤ *To describe something*—The writer gives the reader information.

➤ *To explain something*—The writer explains something to the reader, such as how to perform a specific procedure.

➤ *To persuade*—The writer attempts to convince the reader that the opinion in the essay is true.

Fact Versus Opinion

Be prepared to encounter test questions that require you to determine which statements from a passage are fact and which ones are opinion.

Factual statements are those that can be proven. *Opinions*, on the other hand, are those statements that describe how someone thinks or feels about a particular topic and therefore cannot be proven. You can look for various context clues to help determine whether a statement is a fact or an opinion. Statements that are opinions will often contain words such as *think* and *feel*, whereas factual statements will not include any ambiguous words that can be interpreted to mean different things by a reader.

Vocabulary

The PRAXIS reading test will test your knowledge of vocabulary. More specifically, you will be expected to have the skills to identify the meaning of a specific word as it is used within the context of a reading passage. Although this might seem simple, these types of questions can in fact be very difficult. You might know the common definition of a word, but the word's meaning can change based on the context in which it is used. Before taking the PRAXIS reading test, you should have experience using context clues.

NOTE   *Context clues* can be used to determine the meaning of a word within a specific context. The context includes the other words and sentences surrounding a particular word. You can gather clues from the context to figure out the meaning of a word.

Context Clues

Using vocabulary in context is important because it allows you to read without having to continually look up the meanings of words in a dictionary. It's also important for answering vocabulary questions on the PRAXIS exam.

You can watch for different types of context clues that can help you determine what the meaning of a word is. These include

➤ Synonyms

➤ Antonyms

➤ Examples

➤ General sense and knowledge

➤ Substitution

➤ Inference

Synonyms

A *synonym* is a word that has the same meaning as another word. Sometimes a sentence may include a synonym for the word you need to define. Take the following sentence as an example. What is the meaning of the word *dissipate*?

The evening storm did not *dissipate* until early morning when the clouds broke up and disappeared.

You can use context clues within the sentence to determine the meaning. By reading the entire sentence, you can deduce that the words *broke up* and *disappeared* are synonyms for the word *dissipate*. Therefore, the meaning of the word in this particular sentence is "break up and disappear."

 Watch out for synonym clues within a sentence to figure out the meaning of a word. Synonym clues can be indicated by expressions including *such as, or, that is, in other words,* and so on. Also look for punctuation clues such as commas, dashes, parentheses, and colons.

Antonyms

An *antonym* is a word that has the opposite meaning of another word. A sentence may contain an antonym for the word you are trying to define. For example, the following sentence contains an antonym for the word *loquacious*:

During class the young girl was silent; however, she was *loquacious* on the playground.

As you can see from the example, an antonym for the word *loquacious* has been embedded in the sentence, thereby enabling you to unlock the meaning of the word.

Antonym clues can include phrases and words such as *but, although, though, while, however, on the other hand, unlike, except, while, unless,* and so on.

Examples

Sometimes you will be able to unlock the meaning of a word through examples. A writer might provide an example of the word in context. For example:

The fans wreaked *havoc* after the game by throwing food and chairs, smashing windows, and yelling profanity.

From the examples provided in the sentence, you can easily unlock the meaning of the word *havoc*.

General Sense and Knowledge

Sometimes you will have to resort to your own general sense and knowledge of a topic to determine the meaning of a word within a specific context. In such situations, try to recall any prior knowledge or any personal experiences you may have with the topic at hand to unlock the meaning of the word.

Substitution

Substitution is another context clue that you can use to unlock the meaning of a word within a specific context. When you are asked to identify the meaning of a term, reread the sentence and substitute another word that may make sense for the unknown word. Take the following sentence as an example:

By the end of winter, the *mass* of firewood used to heat the house was starting to dwindle.

If you have to unlock the meaning of the word *mass* in the preceding sentence, try substituting the term with another word that might make sense, such as *supply, stockpile,* or *hoard*.

Inference

In some cases, information will not be clearly stated but will be implied or inferred instead. Be prepared to read between the lines with some passages you encounter on the exam.

Inference, or *inferring*, means that you must go beyond what the writer has explicitly stated in the passage and look for those details that are implied or hinted. You might encounter some questions that require you to draw conclusions about what an author is implying.

In such cases, look at the examples and ideas that the author has provided. Chances are that you will be able to infer what the author is implying. Also, use your general sense about the topic to infer meaning.

Reading Strategies

As already mentioned, the PRAXIS reading exam is timed. You only have 60 minutes to answer a total of 40 questions (75 minutes to answer 46 questions if you are taking the computer-based version). So, you will need to fine-tune your reading skills to ensure that you can correctly answer the given number of questions in the given amount of time. The following section will provide you with some useful test-taking tips to help you pass the exam. These include

➤ Skimming passages

➤ Prereading questions

➤ Locating information

➤ Eliminating answers

To put them all together, here are some recommended steps for tackling the reading passages and questions:

1. Skim the passage.

2. Read the questions carefully.

3. Read the entire passage from start to finish.

4. Tackle the general questions first.

5. Locate the section of the passage containing the answer.

6. Eliminate answers. Answer the question.

Skimming

Instead of jumping right in initially and reading the passage word for word, you should skim over it first to get an idea of what the author is writing about. You can usually get a good idea of what a passage is about by reading the introductory and concluding paragraphs, as well as the first sentence of each paragraph within the body. When you've done a quick skim of the passage, go back and read it in its entirety.

Reading a passage in its entirety first is kind of like going in blind. You'll find it much easier to understand a passage if you skim over it first to get a grasp of the main idea. You'll also find it much easier to answer the questions if you know what the questions are asking before you read a passage.

Prereading Questions

Instead of reading the entire passage first, preread the questions before you read the passage. This way, you will have an idea of what you will be looking for. You can then actively keep an eye out for the information and key words in the questions as you are reading through the passage.

Locating Information

Depending on the length of the passage, locating the information that is relevant to the question can be difficult. Also remember that you are on a time constraint, so you need to locate relevant information efficiently, instead of rereading the entire passage or searching for it randomly.

The question will likely give you clues as to where in the passage you should begin looking for the correct answer. Use these clues to make more efficient use of your time and quickly locate the correct answer within the passage.

When you read the questions, pick out the key words or phrases and locate them within the passage. You will more than likely find the correct answer to the question nearby. Conversely, if you reread the entire passage when you attempt to answer each question, chances are you will not have enough time to complete the entire exam.

For example, if a question asks when the Immigration Restriction Act was passed, skim the passage looking for the key words *Immigration Restriction Act*.

Some questions may not repeat the key words and phrases exactly as they appear in the passage. Of course, this makes finding the answer a little more difficult. In such cases, skim the passage for key words and phrases that have similar meanings.

Using "paragraph focus" is a good way of locating the correct answer to a question instead of having to reread an entire passage.

Eliminating Answers

So, you've skimmed the passage and found the paragraph that references the key words in the question. Your next step is to begin looking at the possible answers. (Each question should have a total of four or five possible options.) Use the process of elimination to begin narrowing down the choices.

With most multiple-choice questions, two or three of the options can usually be eliminated right away, leaving you with two or three possible choices. Reread each answer carefully. Often, answers may sound the same but a slight change in the wording makes them different. Here are some tips you can use when eliminating possible answers:

➤ When trying to identify the correct answer, try looking for key words that appear in the question as well as the answer.

➤ For questions using the word *except*, cross off all those options that do not meet the exception.

➤ Use contextual clues found within the question to eliminate answers.

➤ Eliminate any answers that are worded similarly. If one answer is incorrect, chances are another answer meaning the same thing is incorrect as well. Therefore, eliminate it to avoid confusion.

➤ Look for definitions within the available options. For example, if a question asks, "Why are rattlesnakes described as dangerous?" look for answers that define or provide examples of the word *dangerous*.

➤ For factual questions, eliminate any answers that contain ambiguous wording. Remember, facts can be proven.

Exam Prep Questions

1. The young child was enamored with his new birthday present.

   The word *enamored* means

   ❏ A. Happy
   ❏ B. Captivated
   ❏ C. Confused
   ❏ D. Distraught

2. Some people think that the real issue behind cigarette smoking is discrimination, and discussing the dangers of smoking only obscures the real issue.

   The word *obscures* means

   ❏ A. Conceals
   ❏ B. Undermines
   ❏ C. Makes more obvious
   ❏ D. Makes evident

3. The security guard's countenance deterred any rowdiness at the game.

   The word *countenance* means

   ❏ A. Presence
   ❏ B. Absence
   ❏ C. Expression
   ❏ D. Tolerance

4. The students displayed a heedless attitude toward the substitute teacher in their classroom.

   The word *heedless* means

   ❏ A. Careful
   ❏ B. Without regard
   ❏ C. Respectful
   ❏ D. Polite

5. Before the final game, the coach used many tactics to instill the hope in his players that winning was possible.

   The word *instill* means

   ❏ A. Inspire
   ❏ B. Discourage
   ❏ C. Dampen
   ❏ D. Dishearten

6. It's not what you know—it's who you know, or so the saying goes. What we know can get us very far in the world, but sooner or later, we all have to accomplish something that we don't have the skills to do ourselves. Whether it's at work, at home, or at play, eventually there's a task or chore that we need someone to do for us. It can be anything from finding a Flash programmer/designer to unloading sheets of plywood from the minivan.

Every day, we rely on others to do specialized tasks that we can't do for ourselves: sales reps, service providers, lawyers, doctors, childcare providers, and contractors. We use phones, email, and word of mouth to communicate recommendations and referrals in hopes of finding the right person to meet our need. Sooner or later, we all need to tap into our people network to find friends to help us get by.

Six Degrees of Separation

Social networks are based on the work of Stanley Milgrim. In 1967, he sent packages to randomly selected people in Omaha, Nebraska— asking them each to mail the package back to a stockbroker in Boston. They were asked to pass it along to someone they thought was better able to find the target. Milgrim found that on average only six acquaintances were needed for the package to find its target. Hence, the six degrees of separation are commonly understood as the number of people between us and an unknown acquaintance. (This concept was also popularized with the *Six Degrees of Kevin Bacon*, a game in which contestants try to connect Kevin Bacon to another actor by listing the movies they have in common.)

In 1998, researchers at Columbia University attempted to re-create Milgrim's findings online by asking people to forward an email to someone more likely to be an acquaintance of the target. The average chain was completed in about six hops (five if the source and target person were in the same country). However, only 384 of the more than 24,000 chains were completed. The researchers' small-world hypothesis held up in the digital age, but only when the source believed in the strength of his network and was motivated to proceed. There are many venues in which to network and build networks, but the sources in Columbia's study needed to believe in the probability of success to complete their action in the chain. In other words, just building it doesn't mean they will come. Several online social networks have already discovered that to their chagrin and have gone out of business—but many still remain.

What is the main idea of this passage?

❑ A. Social networks are based on the work of Stanley Milgrim.

❑ B. It's difficult to tap into our people network.

❏   C.   Online social networks are another venue for tapping into our people network.

❏   D.   Columbia University performed a study about online social networks.

7. Troubleshooting is solving a problem. It doesn't matter whether it's a computer problem or a car problem: It's still troubleshooting. Many of the same concepts of troubleshooting can be used not just to figure out solutions, but also to anticipate the actions and motivations of people, corporations, and even the government. Here's the number one rule for troubleshooting: Use the scientific method.

The scientific method is basically this: You have a problem or need to find out some information. First, you come up with what's known as a theory, or an idea of what the solution might be. Then, you come up with a test to see whether your theory is correct. If it's correct, great… fix the problem. If it's wrong, you've eliminated one theory, and you go back to step one and formulate a new theory based on the new information that you have. This is also known as the *process of elimination*. We put this phrase in italics because this is really the core of the scientific method.

Here's a very simple example of how the process of elimination works: The server is running slowly. The problem could be heat, humidity, RAM, electrical problems, cables, cockroaches (yes, the little buggers actually love electrical equipment), the hard disk, the processor, a program on the server, the network, the network hub, the router, the number of users on the network, the time of day (in conjunction with the number of users on the network), or the number of network requests. The list goes on and on and on. Immediately, you could probably eliminate the possibility of heat, humidity, electrical problems, and cockroaches by simply going into the room and noticing that it's cool and dry, the other systems are working fine, the external cables are well-seated and intact (ensuring against rats and the boss's Pomeranian puppy), and nothing is skittering around on the floor or oddly in the machine. From there, you have the hard disk, RAM, the processor, programs, and network-related stuff.

What is the main idea of the passage?

❏   A.   The scientific method of troubleshooting uses the process of elimination.

❏   B.   Computers cause a lot of problems.

❏   C.   Formulate a theory and then test the theory.

❏   D.   Troubleshooting is solving a problem.

8. When the daunting task of rebuilding a power user's system is at hand, Windows XP supplies a utility to back up customized settings called the Save My Settings Wizard. The utility is great for default user settings, custom templates, and custom toolbars, but what about add-ins? Beware of power users who have a programming background or users who currently use files that contain macros.

For example, application developers can write an Excel macro to control the most important component of Microsoft Word, its automation server. Excel would be acting as the client application and Word as the server application. You can also write Visual Basic applications that control Excel. The process of one application controlling another is referred to as *automation*, formerly *OLE Automation*.

Automation allows you to develop complex macros that have the ability to control objects from a variety of applications. This is a powerful tool when creating application files. It allows the user to interact with multiple applications, such as Access, and not even realize that interaction is occurring. Automation displays a seamless interface for the end user.

Typically, automation occurs in complex documents, which assists the end user in the long run but can make the IT technician's job a little more challenging. For example, if a developer has Access installed on her system and is using the Access database behind the scenes to populate an Excel application, the end user could be unaware of the interaction with the Access database. If the end user does not know that Access is necessary and the application is not reinstalled on his system, the Excel file will not run properly. When the macro is executed, it will generate an error message and will stop executing when it tries to locate the library file for the Access application.

There are also several popular add-ins that are in use when developing automated mail. For example, Redemption allows you to bypass Microsoft's built-in safety features when working with Outlook VBA projects. You can program automated mail tasks; however, several prompts appear warning you that your address book is being interrogated or that another program is trying to send on your behalf. Redemption is a library file that can be installed and used to program these events instead. It will eliminate these warning messages.

It is the responsibility of the programmer/developer to ensure that the end user can operate the file properly. Before the system was rebuilt it worked, and now it is your job to make it work again. Serious errors will occur if these add-ins or reference library files are missing from a system. Without these reference library files, any file that uses the library files will no longer function properly.

To rectify this problem is quite simple. Reinstall the library file and reactivate the use in the application. To achieve the desired results, start by reinstalling the appropriate library file, and then follow these steps:

1. Open the file that contains the error message about the missing reference library file.
2. Open the Visual Basic Editor (VBE) window. Click the Tools menu, select Macro, and then click the Visual Basic Editor submenu option.

3. Select the References option from the Tools menu.
4. Scroll through the available references until you find the required object library file.
5. Check the box beside the reference.
6. Click OK to close the References dialog box.

After you have completed these steps, execute the macro that had the reference library error message. This should eliminate the problem without modifying the original code. If further problems persist, you should consult the programmer/developer of the application to ensure that the reference library priority is in the correct position in the References dialog box.

What is the main idea of the passage?

❏ A. The Save My Settings Wizard can be used to save customized settings in Windows XP.
❏ B. Automation allows you to develop complex macros.
❏ C. Library files must be reinstalled to eliminate reference errors.
❏ D. Power users like to create files that use macros.
❏ E. Redemption allows you to bypass Microsoft's built-in safety features when working with Outlook VBA projects.

9. The directions in the passage explain how to

❏ A. Reinstall Windows XP
❏ B. Reinstall a library file
❏ C. Use the Save My Settings Wizard
❏ D. Install Redemption
❏ E. Create a macro

10. Australia was emerging as a nation of considerable wealth by 1900. As the nation grew and the economy became stronger, Australia hoped to join Britain's former colonies as a country of great wealth and future potential.

Prior to 1900, most development occurred in the areas of ports, roads, and railways. Because the country relied heavily on the sale of its produce, it would sustain a financial hit if its produce was not able to reach local and overseas markets. As a result, an efficient system for transporting produce was important to the growth of many industries.

Along with developing an efficient transport system, other inventions at the turn of the century also contributed to Australia's wealth. Of these new inventions, one of the most important was the invention of a method for transporting frozen goods. This invention played an important part in strengthening Australia's economy and allowed Australia to sell and transport its primary products to overseas markets.

What is the main idea of the passage?

- ❏ A. The strength of the Australian economy
- ❏ B. The new inventions at the turn of the century
- ❏ C. The development of the Australian economy
- ❏ D. The importance of refrigeration

11. What was the most important invention for Australia?

- ❏ A. Frozen goods
- ❏ B. Stump-pump plow
- ❏ C. Refrigeration
- ❏ D. Transportation

12. Why was the development of transportation important?

- ❏ A. Products needed to reach local and overseas markets.
- ❏ B. To transport frozen goods.
- ❏ C. To open up more land for farming.
- ❏ D. Australia needed to be a nation of considerable wealth.

13. When it came to choosing a leader for Australia, the obvious choices included those men who made significant contributions to the forming of the country's constitution.

One such person was Edmund Barton. He was a lawyer from New South Wales and the prime minister of Australia from 1901 to 1903. His most memorable contributions included the creation of the Australian High Court and the passing of the Immigration Restriction Act in 1901. Edmund Barton was also a protectionist and a member of the Protectionist party, which was very influential until 1910.

Another person involved in the drafting of Australia's constitution was Alfred Deakin. He was a lawyer and journalist from Victoria, who served as prime minister from 1903 to 1910. He is remembered for the Basic Wage Act, which addressed economic concerns; for the formation of the Australian Arbitration Commission; and for establishing the Royal Military College at Duntroon. The Australian Capital Territory was also established while Alfred Deakin was in office.

From 1908 to 1913, Andrew Fisher was the Labor prime minister. Because he was a former coal miner, he was viewed as a representative of the Australian worker. He was best known for the creation of the Commonwealth Bank.

When was Edmund Barton prime minister of Australia?

- ❏ A. 1910
- ❏ B. 1910 to 1913
- ❏ C. 1903 to 1910
- ❏ D. 1905 to 1908
- ❏ E. 1901 to 1903

14. What was passed to address economic concerns?

   ❑ A. Australian Capital territory

   ❑ B. Basic Wage Act

   ❑ C. Australian Arbitration Commission

   ❑ D. Immigration Restriction Act

15. What is the main idea of the passage?

   ❑ A. Many acts were passed during 1901 and 1910.

   ❑ B. Edmund Barton was the most influential man in Australia.

   ❑ C. Several important men made significant contributions to Australia's constitution.

   ❑ D. The influence of the Protectionist party.

16. When was the Immigration Restriction Act passed?

   ❑ A. 1901

   ❑ B. 1903

   ❑ C. 1905

   ❑ D. 1908

17. Pioneer children in the 1800s had a different lifestyle than children growing up today. Children growing up in this generation get to experience many different pleasures. However, for pioneer children, life was very different. It was full of danger, daily chores, and minimal pleasures.

Pioneer families made the grueling trip to the West by wagons. Breakfast was prepared and eaten before sunrise, and then the wagons were loaded. After they began traveling, they only stopped for a few short breaks. At night, when it was too dark to keep going, the wagons would stop for the night, forming a circle for protection. However, the children were still expected to complete their chores before playtime.

The journey west was only the beginning. When a pioneer family arrived, they still needed to clear a piece of land and build a home. The homes were not made of brick and stucco as they are today. Rather, they were made of logs or sod. Children were expected to help with building the home. Daily chores resumed after the home was built. These usually included plowing fields, tending to animals, cooking, and sewing.

However, life was not all work for pioneer children. They did have time to play after their chores were finished. Sunday was also considered a special day of the week. It was the day when neighboring families would get together for picnics and dances after church.

Pioneer children experienced many hardships as they grew up. However, many of these children later made the wild frontier home for their own families.

What is the main idea of this passage?

❏   A.   Pioneer children had a lot of chores to do.

❏   B.   Pioneers traveled all day.

❏   C.   Pioneer families traveled in wagons.

❏   D.   Pioneer children did not lead easy lives.

18. Which detail best supports the main idea of this passage?

❏   A.   Pioneer children had to help build the homestead and do daily chores.

❏   B.   Pioneer families traveled west in wagons.

❏   C.   Pioneer children had a lot of space in which to run and play.

❏   D.   Neighboring families gathered on Sundays.

19. What is the best summary of the third paragraph?

❏   A.   Pioneer families lived in log cabins and sod houses.

❏   B.   Pioneer children were expected to perform daily chores.

❏   C.   Pioneer families cleared a piece of land and built a homestead. Children helped build the homestead as part of daily chores.

❏   D.   Life was not easy for pioneer children.

20. What is the meaning of the word *grueling*?

❏   A.   Easy

❏   B.   Long

❏   C.   Simple

❏   D.   Tough

21. During ancient times, the Veneti occupied the land surrounding Venice. According to common belief, Venice was founded in 452 A.D. when people from numerous cities in northern Italy came to the islands of the lagoon to seek protection from the Teutonic barbarians who invaded Italy during the fifth century. The refugees from northern Italy eventually established their own government. It was headed by tribunes for each of the 12 principal islands. Venice was practically independent, even though it was technically part of the Eastern Roman Empire. Venice was then organized as a republic in 697. The threat of foreign invasion kept the Venetians united, even when there was internal dissension.

Attacks occurred against Venice in 836 and 900 by the Saracens and the Hungarians, respectively. A commercial treaty was signed with the Saracens in 991. The treaty established a policy of trade between the Venetians and the Muslims. Venice soon became the greatest commercial trade center for the East because of the Crusades and the development of trade with the Orient.

In 1204, the Byzantine Empire was partitioned. The republic profited from this and went on to become Europe's strongest political power in the Mediterranean region. Although Venice was technically a republic, it became a firm oligarchy by the end of the thirteenth century.

In what year did the Venetians sign a treaty with the Saracens?

- ❑ A. 452
- ❑ B. 697
- ❑ C. 836
- ❑ D. 991
- ❑ E. 1204

22. In the passage, what is the meaning of the word *dissension*?

- ❑ A. Consent
- ❑ B. Conflict
- ❑ C. Peace
- ❑ D. Hatred
- ❑ E. Harmony

23. Which group attacked Venice in 900?

- ❑ A. Hungarians
- ❑ B. Muslims
- ❑ C. Veneti
- ❑ D. Romans
- ❑ E. Saracens

24. When did the Venetians organize Venice as a republic?

- ❑ A. 452
- ❑ B. 900
- ❑ C. 991
- ❑ D. 836
- ❑ E. 697

Exam Prep Answers

1. Answer B is correct. In the sentence, the word *enamored* means captivated. Therefore, answers A, C, and D are incorrect.

2. Answer A is correct. In the sentence, the word *obscures* means conceals or hides. Answers C and D are incorrect because these words mean the opposite of *obscures*. Answer B is incorrect because *undermines* means to weaken or demoralize.

3. Answer C is correct. In the sentence, the word *countenance* means expression. Answers A and B are incorrect because *countenance* does not mean presence or absence. Answer D is incorrect. Although the word *countenance* can mean to tolerate, that meaning is incorrect for the context in which the word is being used.

4. Answer B is correct. In the sentence, the word *heedless* means without regard. Answer A is incorrect because *heedless* does not mean careful. Answers C and D are incorrect because they are antonyms for the word *heedless*.

5. Answer A is correct. In the sentence, the word *instill* means inspire. Answers B, C, and D are incorrect because they are antonyms for the word *instill*.

6. Answer C is correct. The main idea behind the passage is that online social networks are another means of tapping into our people network. Therefore, answers A, B, and D are incorrect.

7. Answer A is correct. The main idea of the passage is that the scientific method of troubleshooting involves using the process of elimination. Therefore, answers B, C, and D are incorrect.

8. Answer C is correct. The main idea behind the passage is that library files must be reinstalled to eliminate reference errors. Therefore, answers A, B, D, and E are incorrect.

9. Answer B is correct. The steps outlined in the passage explain how to reinstall a library file. Therefore, answers A, C, D, and E are incorrect.

10. Answer C is correct. The main point of the passage is the development of the Australian economy. Therefore, answers A, B, and D are incorrect.

11. Answer C is correct. The passage states that refrigeration was the most important invention for Australia's primary industry. Therefore, answers A, B, and D are incorrect.

12. Answer A is correct. The passage states that the development of transportation was important because products needed to reach local and overseas markets. Therefore, answers B, C, and D are incorrect.

13. Answer E is correct. Edmund Barton was prime minister from 1901 to 1903. Therefore, answers A, B, C, and D are incorrect.

14. Answer B is correct. The passage states that the Basic Wage Act was passed to address economic concerns. Therefore, answers A, C, and D are incorrect.

15. Answer C is correct. The main idea of the passage is that several important men made significant contributions to Australia's constitution. Therefore, answers A, B, and D are incorrect.

16. Answer A is correct. The passage states that the Immigration Restriction Act was passed in 1901. Therefore, answers B, C, and D are incorrect.

17. Answer D is correct. The main idea of the passage is that pioneer children did not lead easy lives. Answers A, B, and C are incorrect. These are supporting ideas.

18. Answer A is correct. The best supporting detail within the passage is that pioneer children had to help build the homesteads along with doing daily chores. Therefore, answers B, C, and D are incorrect.

19. Answer C is correct. The best summary for the third paragraph is that pioneer families cleared a piece of land and built a homestead. Children helped build the homestead as part of daily chores. Therefore, answers A, B, and D are incorrect.

20. Answer D is correct. The word *grueling* means tough or difficult. Answers A, B, and C are incorrect. *Easy* and *simple* are antonyms for the word *grueling*.

21. Answer D is correct. The passage clearly states that the Venetians signed a commercial treaty with the Saracens in 991. Therefore, answers A, B, C, and E are incorrect.

22. Answer B is correct. In the passage, the word *dissension* also means conflict. Therefore, answers A, C, D, and E are incorrect. The word *consent* is an antonym for the word *dissension*.

23. Answer A is correct. The passage clearly states that the Hungarians attacked Venice in 900. Therefore, answers B, C, D, and E are incorrect. The Saracens attacked Venice in the year 836.

24. Answer E is correct. The Venetians organized Venice as a republic in the year 697. Therefore, answers A, B, C, and D are incorrect.

Need to Know More?

 Visit www.ets.org to find specific information about the exam, exam objectives, and sample reading passages.

 Spears, Deanne. *Developing Critical Reading Skills, 6th Edition*. McGraw-Hill, 2002. ISBN 0072491329.

Hancock, Ophelia H. *Reading Skills for College Students, 6th Edition*. Pearson Education, 2003. ISBN 0131772279.

PRAXIS I Writing

Terms you'll need to understand:

✓ Noun
✓ Verb
✓ Adjective
✓ Pronoun
✓ Adverb
✓ Apostrophe
✓ Colon
✓ Semicolon
✓ Comma
✓ Compound word
✓ Idiom

Techniques you'll need to master:

✓ Identify the different parts of a sentence
✓ Understand the different types of sentences
✓ Understand the differences between nouns, verbs, adjectives, adverbs, and pronouns
✓ Identify and correct errors in sentence structure, mechanics, and grammar
✓ Combine words correctly to form compound words
✓ Identify the correct use of punctuation within a sentence
✓ Identify incorrect word usage in a sentence
✓ Identify the improper use of idioms

The writing component of the PRAXIS exam is broken down into two sections: *45 multiple-choice questions* and *one essay question*. This chapter will focus on the multiple-choice writing component of the exam. This part of the PRAXIS exam will test your knowledge of standard English.

The 45 multiple-choice questions are further broken down into two distinct sections: *usage* and *sentence correction*. The grammar usage questions will test your ability to identify different errors in phrases and sentences. The sentence correction questions will test your ability to properly restate a phrase or question if the existing structure is incorrect.

You can expect to encounter approximately 17 questions on grammatical relationships, 17 questions pertaining to structural relationships, and 11 questions on word choice and mechanics.

This chapter will cover grammar and sentence structure. A review of basic grammar skills will be provided, as well as the different types of questions you are likely to encounter. After working through the chapter, you will also be able to identify different types of errors in phrases and sentences.

You will also be expected to identify those sentences and phrases that are considered error-free.

Grammar

Part of the PRAXIS I Writing exam will test your knowledge of basic grammar. You will be expected to be able to identify incorrect uses of grammar within a given sentence or passage. The following sections will look at grammar-related exam topics that you are likely to encounter on the exam. This includes

➤ Nouns

➤ Pronouns

Nouns

I'm sure we are all familiar with the term *noun* because it's a component we learn about in the elementary grades. The definition of a noun is relatively simple. It's defined as a person, place, or thing. Every sentence must contain at least one noun as its subject. For example:

➤ The **car** is blue.

➤ A **whale** is a **mammal**.

 Be prepared to encounter questions asking you to identify the noun that is the subject within a sentence. Because a sentence or phrase can contain more than one noun, only one of the nouns will be listed as a possible answer. Read the sentence carefully, identify all the nouns, and compare them to the given answers.

Proper and Common Nouns

Nouns can be broken down into two different categories: *proper nouns* and *common nouns*. A proper noun is the name of a particular person, place, or thing. For example, *Mrs. Smith*, *California*, and *Felicia* are all examples of proper nouns. The thing to keep in mind with proper nouns is that they are usually capitalized. Common nouns, on the other hand, designate any one of a class of people, places, or things, and they are not capitalized. For example, *dog*, *state*, and *country* are examples of common nouns.

Plural and Possessive Nouns

Nouns can also come in two different forms: *plural nouns* and *possessive nouns*. As the name implies, plural nouns indicate more than one person, place, or thing. A plural noun can be formed by adding the appropriate ending to the noun, such as *s*, *es*, or *ies*. For example, *cars*, *dishes*, and *babies* are plural nouns. Possessive nouns indicate ownership, which is normally formed by adding *'s* to the end of a noun. For example, in the phrases "my grandmother's house" and "my dog's bone," *grandmother's* and *dog's* are possessive nouns.

Pronouns

A *pronoun* is a word that can take the place of a noun. Pronouns include words such as *ours*, *he*, *she*, and *you*. Without pronouns, sentences would have to contain a lot of repeated nouns. For example, consider the following phrases:

➤ My parents sold their house after 25 years. My parents are moving to another city. My parents plan to buy a condo there.

With pronouns, you can eliminate the use of some of the nouns, which will make the sentence much more readable, as in this example:

➤ My parents sold their house. **They** are moving to another city. **They** plan to buy a condo there.

Forms of Pronouns

Pronouns can be subjective, objective, possessive, reflexive, relative, demonstrative, reciprocal, or interrogative. Each different type of pronoun is outlined in the following list. The subjective, objective, and possessive forms of singular and plural pronouns are also summarized in Tables 3.1 and 3.2.

➤ *Subjective pronouns*—A subjective pronoun is the subject in a sentence or phrase. The subject performs the action within the sentence. Subjective pronouns include the words *I, you, he, she, it, we, you,* and *they.*

➤ *Objective pronouns*—An objective pronoun is the direct or indirect object in a sentence or a phrase or is the object of a preposition. Words in this category include *me, you, him, her, it, us, you,* and *them.*

➤ *Possessive pronouns*—This type of pronoun identifies who owns an object. Possessive pronouns include the words *mine, yours, his, hers, its, ours,* and *theirs.*

➤ *Reflexive pronouns*—This type of pronoun is used to reference the subject of a sentence. Such words include *myself, yourself, himself, herself, itself, ourselves, yourselves,* and *themselves.*

➤ *Relative pronouns*—This type of pronoun relates back to a noun that precedes it in the sentence. The relative pronoun acts as the subject or object within a dependent clause. Relative pronouns include words such as *who, whom, whoever,* and *whomever.*

➤ *Demonstrative pronouns*—This type of pronoun is used in place of a person, place, or thing. Demonstrative pronouns include *this, that, those,* and *there.*

➤ *Reciprocal pronouns*—This type of pronoun is used to simplify sentences. Reciprocal pronouns include *each other* and *one another.*

➤ *Interrogative pronouns*—This type of pronoun replaces or stands in place of the answer to a question. Interrogative pronouns include *who, whom, whose, which,* and *what.*

The following sentences provide examples of the different types of pronouns:

1. My parents are going on a vacation. **They** will be gone for two weeks.

2. This book amazed **her**.

3. Felicia bought a new computer and put it in **her** home office.

4. Bob went to the movies, but he went by **himself**.

5. The student **who** won the spelling contest studied for several days.

6. Do these pants go with **this**?

7. For their anniversary, my parents gave **each other** small gifts.

8. Who won the 10-mile bike race?

Table 3.1 The Use of Singular Pronouns				
Person/Gender	**Subjective**	**Objective**	**Possessive**	**Reflexive**
First person male/female	I	me	mine	myself
Second person male/female	you	you	yours	yourself
Third person male	he	him	his	himself
Third person female	she	her	hers	herself

Table 3.2 The Use of Plural Pronouns				
Person/Gender	**Subjective**	**Objective**	**Possessive**	**Reflexive**
First person male/female	we	us	ours	ourselves
Second person male/female	you	you	yours	yourselves
Third person male/female	they	them	theirs	themselves

When trying to determine which pronoun is correct, try repeating each pronoun in the sentence aloud and listening carefully. This is a good way of determining which pronoun is correct. An incorrect pronoun will more than likely sound incorrect when you read the sentence.

Adjectives

An *adjective* is a word that describes or modifies a noun or pronoun. It normally precedes the noun and gives the reader more information about the noun. However, keep in mind that adjectives can also be placed at the end of a sentence or phrase. Adjectives usually make sentences more interesting.

Adjectives are also used for comparison. This is usually done by adding *er* or *est* to the end of the adjective. These are known as *comparative* and *superlative* adjectives, respectively. For example:

➤ My car is **old**.

➤ My parents' car is **older**. (comparative adjective)

➤ My grandmother's car is the **oldest**. (superlative adjective)

 Here is a simple rule for using adjectives. For comparison purposes, you can add *er* or *est* to the end of an adjective. However, if the adjective is more than three syllables long, use the words *more* and *most* for comparison. For example, "My car is **more** reliable than yours."

Also keep in mind that there are some irregular forms of adjectives that do not follow the standard comparative and superlative forms. An example of an irregular adjective is the word *good*. You would not say *gooder* or *goodest*. Instead, you would use the words *better* and *best*. By reading the sentence aloud, you can typically use your ear to determine whether the comparative adjective is correct.

Verbs

A *verb* is a word that expresses the action, event, or state of being in a sentence. For example:

➤ I **am** a teacher.

➤ She **swam** the entire length of the swimming pool.

➤ I **wrote** my English essay.

Verb Tense

Verbs can be used in different *tenses*. The verb tense gives the reader information about when something occurred. Actions or events can occur in the past, present, or future. The following examples show verbs used in different tenses:

➤ I **walk** to school. (present tense)

➤ We **will plan** to go to a movie this evening. (future tense)

➤ We **planned** our winter holiday well in advance. (past tense)

➤ She **swims** in the pool. (present tense)

➤ She **swam** in the pool. (past tense)

➤ She **will swim** in the pool. (future tense)

The common way of changing a verb to past tense is to add *ed* to the end of the word. However, some verbs are irregular and do not follow this rule. For example, the word *ride* is considered irregular because the past tense is *rode*.

Auxiliary Verbs

A verb in a sentence can consist of more than one word. *Auxiliary verbs* are used to help the main verb and give information about when the action or event occurred. The words *will*, *was*, and *have* are used as auxiliary verbs, as in these examples:

➤ I **will run** the marathon.

➤ I **was running** in the marathon.

➤ I **have run** in the marathon.

 The most common auxiliary verbs are the forms of *be*, *have*, and *do*.

Finite, Non-Finite, and Infinitive Verbs

As already mentioned, verbs can be written in the past tense. Any verb that shows tense is known as a *finite* verb; for example, "We rode," "I biked," and "I swam." On the other hand, a non-finite verb does not show tense, such as "to jump" or "jumping."

Non-finite verbs include participles and infinitives. (The participle does not show tense but is used with auxiliary verbs that indicate tense.) Non-finite verbs ending with *ing* are referred to as present participles. For example:

➤ I am **walking** through the park.

➤ I am **baking** a cake for the party.

Non-finite verbs ending in *ed* or sometimes *en* are referred to as past participles. For example:

➤ I have **finished** my homework.

➤ I have **cleaned** the entire house.

➤ I have **eaten** my snack.

An infinitive is a non-finite verb that usually takes the base form of a verb. An infinitive can take two different forms. The base form of the verb can be preceded by the word *to* or the *to* infinitive can precede another verb, as shown in the following examples:

➤ The girls wanted **to swim** in the pool.

➤ We love **to be sitting** by the lake on a hot summer day.

Adverbs

Adverbs are words in a sentence that modify verbs, adjectives, or other adverbs. Adverbs can essentially modify any word except a noun. These words are usually formed by adding *ly* to the end of an adjective; for example, *beautifully*, *happily*, and *quickly*.

Adverbs can modify verbs and adjectives by telling the reader where, when, or how something was done, as seen in the following examples:

➤ I cannot find my car keys; I left them over **there**.

➤ The crowd cheered **loudly**.

➤ **Yesterday** we went to the zoo.

 Watch out for double negatives. A sentence can only contain one negative. For example, the sentence "There wasn't hardly anyone at the concert" contains a double negative.

Adjectives or Adverbs

It can be difficult to distinguish between adverbs and adjectives. Here are some points and rules to help you distinguish between the two.

➤ Many adverbs can be recognized by the *ly* extension at the end of a word. For example:

He spoke **quietly**. (adverb)

He is **quiet**. (adjective)

➤ You cannot use an adverb to modify a noun, as shown in the following examples:

The **quietly** children watched a movie. (incorrect)

The children **quietly** watched a movie. (correct)

➤ If the noun comes before a form of the verb *to be*, the verb is followed by an adjective, not an adverb.

On my way to take the exam, I was **nervously**. (incorrect)

On my way to take the exam, I was **nervous**. (correct)

➤ If a noun is preceded by a verb describing sense or appearance, the verb is followed by an adjective, not an adverb. For example:

My mom seemed to be **unhappyily** today. (incorrect)

My mom seemed to be **unhappy** today. (correct)

➤ If the word being used modifies the verb, an adverb is used.

The children slept **quietly**.

Sentence Structure

Words are grouped together to form sentences. A sentence can be an idea, a statement, a question, a dialogue, and so on. A sentence can even consist of a single word.

The multiple-choice questions that will appear in the writing portion of the PRAXIS exam will test your ability to identify errors in sentence structure; therefore, you should have an understanding of sentences in the English language.

Sentence Types

In its simplest form, a sentence can consist of a single word, such as, "Look!" Every sentence will contain at least one clause. A *clause* contains a subject and a predicate. The subject of the clause tells the reader who or what the sentence is about, and the predicate gives information about what the subject does.

Two different types of clauses can exist in a sentence. An *independent clause* is one that can stand alone within a sentence. A *dependent clause*, or subordinate clause, is one that cannot stand alone, as shown in these examples:

➤ My dog buried his bone. (independent clause)

➤ After he buried his bone (dependent clause)

Now that you are familiar with the parts of a sentence, let's take a look at the different types of sentences:

➤ *Simple sentence*—A simple sentence is one that contains a single independent clause.

➤ *Compound sentence*—A compound sentence consists of two or more independent clauses that are joined using a word such as *and*. These joining words are referred to as *coordinating conjunctions*. For example:

We went out for dinner, **and** later we went to see a late-night movie.

➤ *Complex sentence*—A complex sentence consists of an independent clause and at least one or more dependent clauses. For example:

Because it was raining, we decided not to go to the beach for the day.

Coordination

As already mentioned, clauses can be joined together to form compound and complex sentences. Independent clauses can be joined to form a compound sentence through coordination using any of the following words:

➤ And

➤ Or

➤ Nor

➤ For

➤ But

➤ Yet

➤ So

Subordination

A complex sentence is formed by joining an independent clause and a dependent clause. These clauses are joined through subordination using words such as *although*, *because*, *unless*, *though*, *since*, *which*, *while*, and *that*. If you join two independent clauses through subordination, one of the clauses becomes dependent, as shown in the following examples:

➤ The teacher reviewed the concept of multiplication. The topic was studied a month ago.

➤ **Although** the topic was studied a month ago, the teacher reviewed the concept of multiplication. (subordination)

Capitalization

Another aspect that you may be tested on is *capitalization*. You should be aware of when to capitalize certain words within a sentence. Of course, you may think that this is simple and that all you need to remember is to capitalize the first letter of each sentence. However, as you will see in the following list, there are a number of other rules that apply to capitalization.

When determining when to use capitalization, keep these rules in mind:

➤ Capitalize the first word of each sentence.

➤ Always capitalize the first person singular word *I*.

➤ Capitalize proper nouns including the names of specific people and organizations, places, and in certain circumstances, things.

➤ Relationships should be capitalized when used as proper names, as seen in the following two examples:

We are going to visit **Grandma Mary**.

I bought **Dad** a fishing rod for his birthday.

➤ Always capitalize the specific use of the word *God* and other religious figures.

➤ Geographical locations should be capitalized, as seen in the following example:

The last place I visited was **Chicago, Illinois**.

➤ Do not capitalize directional names when they refer to compass directions. The following examples demonstrate this:

You must turn **west** on Highway 12 to reach your destination.

The school is three miles **south** of our home.

➤ Capitalize the days of the week, months of the year, and holidays. Do not capitalize the seasons unless they are used in a title. Note the following three examples:

I play tennis every **Monday** evening.

We are planning on taking a vacation in **January**.

We are going on a vacation this **winter**.

➤ Capitalize the names of newspapers, magazines, and journals.

➤ Capitalize the names of historical events. For example:

We are studying **World War I** in our class.

Compound Words

Two or more words can be combined to form what is called a *compound word*. This is particularly true of adjectives and nouns.

For example, the words *play* and *house* can be combined to form the compound word *playhouse*. Unfortunately, there is no way to know how to correctly combine all compound words other than consulting a dictionary (or, of course, through memorization).

Be prepared to encounter compound words in this section of the PRAXIS exam. More specifically, be prepared to identify those compound words that are incorrect, such as those containing a hyphen when one is not required.

There are three different forms of compound words: open form, hyphenated form, and closed form.

➤ *Open form*—With this form of compound word, each word is written separately; for example, *school bus*.

➤ *Hyphenated form*—With this form, the words forming the compound word are separated by a hyphen; for example, *merry-go-round*.

➤ *Closed form*—With this form of compound word, the two words are written as one; for example, *stingray*.

One important point to keep in mind when using compound words is that a hyphen is not used if the compound word is made up of a proper noun or a proper adjective. However, if the compound modifier comes before the noun, it is hyphenated. Also, if the compound modifier is placed after the noun, it may not be hyphenated.

When it comes time to take the exam, you will not be permitted to take a dictionary in with you. Therefore, you will have to rely on your own knowledge and skill to determine whether a hyphen is required. Here are a few points to keep in mind that will help you do this:

➤ Determine whether the meaning of the sentence might change if a hyphen is not used.

➤ If a word is added to a past participle that precedes a noun, a hyphen is required; for example, *well-respected professor*.

➤ Hyphens are not required if the compound word is created using *ly*.

Punctuation

Another aspect of the English language and writing (as well as another aspect that you will be tested on) is punctuation. In order to be fully prepared for the writing component of the PRAXIS I exam, you need to be familiar with the different types of punctuation, such as periods and commas, and when each is appropriate.

Commas

A *comma* is a form of punctuation that separates different parts of a sentence into more manageable segments. For example, you can use a comma to separate an introductory clause from the main clause of a sentence. Commas should be used to separate two independent clauses within a sentence.

 An independent clause is one that contains both a subject and a verb and forms a complete sentence; it can stand on its own.

As with most other components of standard English, there are certain rules to follow in deciding when to use a comma and where to place one. These topics will be discussed in the following section.

When to Use Commas

Because many, if not all, of the multiple-choice questions will require you to identify errors within a sentence, you need to know when and how to use commas within a sentence. You can use the points in the following list as a guideline for using commas:

➤ A comma should be placed between two independent clauses that are separated by any of the following words: *but, or, nor, and, for,* and *yet.* If two independent clauses are separated by the word *so,* in which the meaning of *so* is as a result, a comma should be used.

The words in the preceding list are known as *coordinating conjunctions*. When it comes to comma placement, the comma will usually go before the coordinating conjunction. Rarely will the comma appear after. Keep this in mind if you encounter any exam questions that require you to correctly place a comma in a sentence.

➤ If a sentence contains an unessential adjective clause, include commas, as shown in the following example:

Felicia Buckingham, the former principal of the local high school, was head of the school board.

➤ If a sentence includes two or more coordinate adjectives in a row, separate them with a comma, as shown in the following example:

This young man has become an articulate, confident, inquisitive student.

If the adjectives are cumulative, don't separate them.

He bought a small red car.

➤ If a sentence includes a direct quote, place a comma before the quotation marks, as shown in the following example:

Their mother said, "It's time to go to bed."

➤ When a sentence includes a list of three or more items in a row, separate them using a comma. For example:

We went grocery shopping and bought apples, oranges, and bananas.

➤ If a dependent clause precedes an independent clause in a sentence, a comma should be used to separate them. However, the same is not true if an independent clause is followed by a dependent clause. In the following example, only the first sentence requires a comma because the dependent clause precedes the independent clause.

Unless you pay, I am not going to the movies with you.

I am not going to the movies with you unless you pay.

➤ Place a comma after any transition words such as *therefore* and *however*. For example:

We went to the beach for the day. However, it rained all morning.

➤ Commas are also required between a city and state, the date and the year, as well as between a name and a title.

When determining whether commas are necessary, read the sentence to yourself pausing at each comma. If the pauses seem natural when you read the sentence, the commas are more than likely required. If not, the comma placement is incorrect.

Colons and Semicolons

Colons and *semicolons*—they sound similar and look similar, but they each serve a different purpose. The following section will describe each of these punctuation marks. Be sure you know the difference between a colon and a semicolon and when each is appropriate.

Colons

There are several rules as to when colons should be used in a sentence. The most common use for colons is at the end of sentences that introduce a list, such as a list of steps, as shown in the following example:

Use the following steps to open a new Microsoft Word document:

1. Click Start.

2. Point to All Programs.

3. Point to Microsoft Office.

4. Click Microsoft Word.

Semicolons

Semicolons are often referred to as "super commas." Semicolons are used to join together two independent clauses that are not joined together using a coordinating conjunction (such as *but* or *yet*). Another situation in which a semicolon should be used is in place of the word *and* plus a comma. Finally, semicolons are also used between two independent clauses that are joined using a transitional expression.

Transitional expressions can include words such as *therefore, consequently, however, moreover,* and *accordingly.*

The following sentences provide examples of how semicolons should be used:

1. Our dog always gets off her leash; therefore, we had to fence the back yard.

2. The semester was finally finished; we were glad it was spring break.

Apostrophes

Many people get confused as to when an apostrophe is required. However, there are only two rules you need to remember when using apostrophes: *Apostrophes* are used to show possession and omission. Let's take a look at two examples of how apostrophes are used. The first sentence demonstrates how an apostrophe is used to show possession. The second sentence demonstrates how the apostrophe is used for letter omission.

➤ My mother's house is full of antique furniture.

➤ He doesn't know whether he'll be able to make it to the meeting this afternoon.

Other Forms of Punctuation

There are many other forms of punctuation aside from the ones already described. Again, you will need to be able to identify sentences that have incorrect punctuation. Therefore, along with apostrophes, colons, and semicolons, be aware of the following punctuation marks and when to use them:

➤ *Periods*—Periods are the most common form of punctuation. They are used in several different situations. Periods are used to end a sentence, for abbreviations, and for lists beginning with letters or numbers. (For example, a period would precede each number in a numbered list.) A period is also placed before closing quotation marks, as shown in the following example:

The mother said to the boy, "You may not have more ice cream."

➤ *Question marks*—Question marks are used to end a sentence that asks a direct question. However, they are not used for those sentences asking indirect questions, as shown in the following examples:

How many more days are left until spring break?

The woman asked if she could switch seats with the gentleman beside her.

➤ *Quotation marks*—The most common use of quotation marks is to offset text within a sentence, such as dialogue.

The police officer asked, "Can I please see your license and registration?"

Word Confusion

Some words sound the same but are spelled differently and have different meanings. Deciding which word to use can often lead to confusion (hence the title "Word Confusion"). One example is choosing between the words *there*, *their*, and *they're*.

When it comes to the PRAXIS exam, be prepared to encounter some word confusion. For instance, a sentence may contain the word *than* when the correct word that should be used is *then*. An entire chapter or even a small book could be dedicated to word confusion, listing all the words that sound the same but are spelled differently. Table 3.3 lists some of the more common words that often confuse us.

Table 3.3	Examples of Word Confusion
Words	**Description**
Its/it's	Use *it's* to replace *it is* or *it has*. Use *its* to show ownership. For example: **It's** been snowing for three days. I found the marker. Where is **its** lid?
Accept/except	She would **accept** the promotion, **except** someone had to be hired to fill her existing job role.
Their/there/they're	**They're** taking **their** boat down the road to park it over **there**.
Your/you're	**You're** going to have to pack **your** suitcase the night before.
Affect/effect	The doctor informed me that the medicine could have side **effects**, but it didn't **affect** me.
Aid/aide	The job of the teacher's **aide** was to **aid** any students who needed extra help.
Were/we're/where	**We're** going to the lake for the summer. **Where** did you say you **were** going?
That/which	The school **that** my brother used to attend, **which** is across the street from my parents' house, is closing next year.
Break/brake	I had to get the **brake** in my car fixed on my lunch **break**.
Threw/through	I **threw** the baseball **through** the living room window.
Than/then	I had more experience **than** the other candidates. We were going to the beach and **then** to our friend's cabin.
Good/well	My son is a **good** hockey player; he skates **well**.

(continued)

Table 3.3	Examples of Word Confusion *(continued)*
Words	**Description**
Fewer/less	There were **fewer** red ones than green ones. Although I have **fewer** clients now, I still have **less** free time.
Last/recent	On our most **recent** visit to the city, we went to see the **last** concert before the theater was permanently closed.
Right/write	I asked her to **write** down the directions so that I would remember where to turn **right**.
Sense/since	I have a much better **sense** of direction **since** I have been exploring the city.
Anticipate/expect	I am trying to **anticipate** the number of people at the party; I **expect** there will be about 400 guests.
Confident/confidant	She informed her **confidant** of the situation; she was **confident** the information would not be made public.
Now/know/no	After realizing the dangers of it, I **now know** why my parents always said **no** when I asked for a dirt bike.
Passed/past	In the **past**, we would have always **passed** slow drivers on this street.
Quiet/quit/quite	The staff was **quite** shocked and **quiet** when the vice-president announced his intent to **quit** the company.
Precede/proceed	We had to **proceed** with the final speaker because the one who was to **precede** her did not show up.
Later/latter	\We will deal with the **latter** issue at a **later** date.
Which/who	*Which* should only be used when referring to objects. *Who* should be used to refer to people. His cousin, **who** lives in Maine, came to visit. **Which** car do you like?

Idioms

Idioms are often referred to as *slang expressions*. Idioms are simply expressions that have a completely different meaning than the individual words that make up the expression. For example, the phrase *add up* is an idiom that has the meaning of not consistent, as shown in this example:

➤ When I asked the teenagers where they had been, their stories did not **add up**.

The English language has many idioms. Be prepared to identify any errors with idioms for the multiple-choice writing portion of the PRAXIS I exam. To assist you, Table 3.4 lists some of the more commonly used idioms along with their meanings.

Table 3.4 Common Idioms	
Idiom	**Meaning**
As easy as pie	Simple
	The test questions were **as easy as pie**.
Antsy	Restless
	I was getting very **antsy** waiting for the bell to ring.
Beat around the bush	To avoid an issue or a question
	He **beat around the bush** when I asked him where we were going.
The bottom line	The most important piece of information
	The bottom line was that we could not afford a new house.
Far-fetched	Untrue; not believable
	The story he told us about his childhood sounded a little **far-fetched**.
Go with the flow	One step at a time; take things as they come
	We didn't make any definite plans for our vacation. We decided to just **go with the flow**.
Jump the gun	To act hastily
	Jim **jumped the gun** on buying a new television.
Keep an eye on	To watch out for
	The neighbor **kept an eye on** our house while we were away.
Leave well enough alone	Take no action
	Even though her children were once again late for dinner, Mary decided to **leave well enough alone**.
Live and let live	To let others live as they choose
	Even though I was against the move, I decided to **live and let live**.
Make a mountain out of a molehill	To overreact
	My mother tends to **make a mountain out of a molehill** if we are late getting home.

(continued)

Table 3.4 Common Idioms *(continued)*	
Idiom	**Meaning**
Not on your life	Definitely not
	When I asked my friend if she was going to move back home, she said, "**Not on your life**."
Once in a while	Occasionally
	Every **once in a while**, we go to the drive-in.
Rain or shine	No matter what
	We planned on going to the lake **rain or shine**.
Sleep on it	To decide later
	I wasn't sure of my decision yet, so I decided to **sleep on it**.
State of the art	Up-to-date; latest technology
	The new school was **state of the art**.
Under the weather	Ill; not well
	I was feeling **under the weather**, so I decided to take the day off work.

Exam Prep Questions

For questions 1 through 3, identify whether the underlined word is a noun, verb, adjective, pronoun, or adverb.

1. After the show, my cousins and I all went out for a late snack. <u>We</u> ordered desserts and coffee.
   - ❑ A. Noun
   - ❑ B. Verb
   - ❑ C. Adjective
   - ❑ D. Pronoun

2. I watched the cat as she <u>quietly</u> snuck up behind the bird.
   - ❑ A. Verb
   - ❑ B. Adjective
   - ❑ C. Adverb
   - ❑ D. Pronoun

3. The amount of the purchase <u>was calculated</u> in American dollars.
   - ❑ A. Adjective
   - ❑ B. Verb
   - ❑ C. Noun
   - ❑ D. Pronoun

For questions 4 through 7, identify the main verb in each sentence or phrase.

4. During the night, the temperature dropped below the freezing point.
   - ❑ A. During
   - ❑ B. Temperature
   - ❑ C. Dropped
   - ❑ D. Below the

5. The night before the exam, I decided to relax and rest instead of cramming.
   - ❑ A. Decided
   - ❑ B. Relax
   - ❑ C. Rest
   - ❑ D. Cramming

6. The boys threw the baseball through the kitchen window.
   - ❑ A. Boys
   - ❑ B. Threw
   - ❑ C. Baseball
   - ❑ D. Through

7. By the time we left the party, almost everyone had gone home for the evening.
   - ❏ A. Time
   - ❏ B. Party
   - ❏ C. Had gone
   - ❏ D. Home

For questions 8 through 15, identify the incorrect use of commas and other punctuation in the sentence, and then select the answer that corrects the error.

8. The grade one class was not going on a field trip to the museum unless there were enough parent volunteers.
   - ❏ A. class, was
   - ❏ B. trip, to
   - ❏ C. museum, unless
   - ❏ D. No error

9. "The man in the blue jacket," yelled the woman "is the one who tried to grab my purse."
   - ❏ A. man, in
   - ❏ B. blue, jacket
   - ❏ C. woman, is
   - ❏ D. No error

10. In the English class we take this semester, we have been studying nouns, verbs and adjectives.
    - ❏ A. semester we
    - ❏ B. verbs, and
    - ❏ C. in, the
    - ❏ D. No error

11. My grandmother, whom we visit twice a year, was born in Minneapolis Minnesota on May 12, 1937.
    - ❏ A. grandmother whom
    - ❏ B. Minneapolis, Minnesota
    - ❏ C. May, 12
    - ❏ D. No error

12. We went to the new grocery store around the corner from our house to buy bread and milk.
    - ❏ A. new, grocery
    - ❏ B. store, around
    - ❏ C. bread, and
    - ❏ D. No error

13. We went to the grocery store to buy the following items; apples, bananas, oranges, and grapes.
    - ❑ A. store, to
    - ❑ B. items:
    - ❑ C. oranges,
    - ❑ D. grapes?
    - ❑ E. No error

14. Doctor Felicia Zibell who is a chiropractor, helped to relieve most of my back and shoulder pain.
    - ❑ A. Doctor,
    - ❑ B. Zibell,
    - ❑ C. chiropractor;
    - ❑ D. back,
    - ❑ E. No error

15. Although often invited, we never enjoyed going downtown to the concert hall; parking our car was always so difficult.
    - ❑ A. Although,
    - ❑ B. invited we
    - ❑ C. hall,
    - ❑ D. car,
    - ❑ E. No error

Questions 16 through 26 will test your ability to identify parts of a sentence or phrase that contain errors in mechanics, word choice, or grammar.

16. When <u>you</u> <u>asked</u> for directions at the front desk, <u>with</u> <u>whom</u> did you speak?
    - ❑ A. you
    - ❑ B. asked
    - ❑ C. whom
    - ❑ D. with
    - ❑ E. No error

17. <u>Your</u> really <u>going</u> to enjoy the new play; the actors are <u>quite</u> <u>amazing</u> in their roles.
    - ❑ A. Your
    - ❑ B. going
    - ❑ C. quite
    - ❑ D. amazing
    - ❑ E. No error

18. "The poems," said our English teacher, are due on Friday, June 4."
    - ❑ A. "The poems,"
    - ❑ B. English
    - ❑ C. , are
    - ❑ D. Friday,
    - ❑ E. No error

19. After we played five hockey games between Saturday and Sunday, I go straight home to sleep instead of attending the wind-up.
    - ❑ A. played
    - ❑ B. go
    - ❑ C. sleep
    - ❑ D. attending
    - ❑ E. No error

20. Were going to have to fix the leak in the roof before spring comes; it's always the rainy season for us.
    - ❑ A. Were
    - ❑ B. to have to
    - ❑ C. comes;
    - ❑ D. it's
    - ❑ E. No error

For questions 21 through 26, select the most appropriate replacement for the underlined portion of each sentence.

21. We planned on going for dinner at the new local restaurant than going to see a late movie.
    - ❑ A. than, going to
    - ❑ B. then, going to
    - ❑ C. than going to,
    - ❑ D. then going to

22. The underlying theme of the story had a profound effect on me; it brought tears to my eyes.
    - ❑ A. effect on me:
    - ❑ B. affect on me;
    - ❑ C. effect on me,
    - ❑ D. affect on me,
    - ❑ E. No error

23. While I was driving around the city, I lost my <u>sense of direction and can't</u> find my way back to my hotel.
    - ❑ A. since of direction, and can't
    - ❑ B. sense of direction and can not
    - ❑ C. sense of direction; and can't
    - ❑ D. sense of direction and couldn't

24. The menu for the <u>summer party included hamburgers, hotdogs and potato chips</u> so I had to make a trip to the grocery store.
    - ❑ A. summer's party included hamburgers, hotdogs and potato chips
    - ❑ B. summer party included hamburgers, hotdogs, and potato chips
    - ❑ C. summer party included Hamburgers, hotdogs and Potato Chips
    - ❑ D. summer party included hamburgers, hotdogs, and potato chips;

25. My brother received a scholarship to go to <u>university so he was trying to find themself</u> an apartment that would be within walking distance of the school.
    - ❑ A. university; so he was trying to find themself
    - ❑ B. university so they were trying to find themselves
    - ❑ C. university, so he was trying to find himself
    - ❑ D. university so he was trying to find themself,

26. Our relatives, <u>which live in Southern California,</u> drove all the way to Minnesota for the family reunion.
    - ❑ A. that live in Southern California
    - ❑ B. who are living in Southern California
    - ❑ C. which live in Southern California
    - ❑ D. who live in Southern California

Exam Prep Answers

1. Answer D is correct. A pronoun takes the place of a noun. The word *we* is taking the place of "my cousins and I," making the correct answer a pronoun. Therefore, answers A, B, and C are incorrect.

2. Answer C is correct. Adverbs are used to modify verbs, adjectives, and other adverbs. They are usually identified by an *ly* extension. Because the word *quietly* modifies the verb, it is an adverb. Therefore, answers A, B, and D are incorrect.

3. Answer B is correct. The verb is the action or event occurring in a sentence. The words *was calculated* describe the action being performed. Therefore, answers A, C, and D are incorrect.

4. Answer C is correct. The word *dropped* indicates the action that is taking place. Therefore, answers A, B, and D are incorrect.

5. Answer A is correct. The word *decided* indicates the action that is being performed by the subject of the sentence. Therefore, answers B, C, and D are incorrect.

6. Answer B is correct. The word *threw* indicates the action that was performed by the subject of the sentence. Therefore, answers A, C, and D are incorrect.

7. Answer C is correct. The words *had gone* describe the action or event that was performed. Therefore, answers A, B, and D are incorrect.

8. Answer D is correct. A comma is not required in the sentence. The sentence is correct as it appears. Therefore, answers A and B are incorrect. Answer C is incorrect because the dependent clause precedes the independent clause. If the sentence were written as "Unless there were enough
parent volunteers, the grade one class was not going on the field trip," a comma would be necessary because the dependent clause would precede the independent clause.

9. Answer C is correct. In the preceding sentence, a comma is required before the second set of quotation marks. A comma is not required between the words *man* and *in* or *blue* and *jacket*. Therefore, answers A and B are incorrect. Answer D is incorrect because a comma is required before the quotation marks.

10. Answer B is correct. A comma is required if a sentence includes a list of three or more items. A comma is not required after the word *in*. Therefore, answer C is incorrect. Answer A is incorrect because a comma must be placed between the dependent and independent clauses.

11. Answer B is correct. A comma is required between the city and the state. Answer C is incorrect because a comma is not required between the month and the actual number date. Answer A is incorrect because this comma is required to separate the unessential adjective clause.

12. Answer D is correct. The preceding sentence does not require any commas. Therefore, answers A and B are incorrect. Answer C is incorrect because a comma is only required if there is a list of three or more items.

13. Answer B is correct. A semicolon is used to join two independent clauses. A colon is used to introduce a list. The word *items* should be followed by a colon. Therefore, answers A, C, D, and E are incorrect.

14. Answer B is correct. If a sentence contains an unessential adjective clause, a comma is required before and after the clause. A comma is required before and after the adjective clause *who is a chiropractor*. Therefore, answers A, C, D, and E are incorrect.

15. Answer E is correct. As the sentence is written, it does not contain any errors.

16. Answer E is correct. As the sentence is written, it does not contain any errors.

17. Answer A is correct. The first word of the sentence is intended to mean *you are*. Therefore, the correct word should be *you're*.

18. Answer C is correct. Quotation marks are required at the beginning and end of any direct quotes. Therefore, open quotation marks are required before the word *are*.

19. Answer B is correct. The verb tense within a sentence must remain consistent. Because the sentence begins using a verb in the past tense, the verb *go* must be in the past tense as well. The sentence should read *I went* instead of *I go*.

20. Answer A is correct. The first word of the sentence is intended to mean *we are*. Therefore, it should read *we're* instead of *were*.

21. Answer D is correct. The phrase should read *then going to*. The word *than* is used for comparison.

22. Answer E is correct. The phrase should read *effect on me;*. A semicolon is required because the sentence contains two independent clauses.

23. Answer D is correct. The verb tense within a sentence must remain the same. The verb *can't* should read *couldn't* in order to remain in the past tense.

24. Answer B is correct. If a sentence contains a list of three or more nouns, commas are required to separate them. Therefore, a comma must also be placed after the word *hotdogs*.

25. Answer C is correct. The pronoun must agree with the subject it is referring to. Therefore, the word *themself* should be changed to *himself* because the subject is a singular male.

26. Answer D is correct. Because the adjective clause is referring to specific people, the word *who* should replace the word *which*. The word *which* should only be used when referring to objects.

Need to Know More?

Visit www.ets.org to find specific information about the exam, exam objectives, and sample exam questions.

Stilman, Ann. *Grammatically Correct: The Writer's Essential Guide to Punctuation, Spelling, Style, Usage, and Grammar.* Writer's Digest Books, 1997. ISBN: 0898797764.

Woods, Geraldine. *English Grammar for Dummies.* For Dummies, 2001. ISBN: 0764553224.

Merriam-Webster's Collegiate Dictionary, 11th Edition. Merriam-Webster, 2003. ISBN: 0877798087.

PRAXIS I Essay

Terms you'll need to understand:

✓ Brainstorming
✓ Body paragraph
✓ Conclusion paragraph
✓ Introductory paragraph
✓ Thesis statement
✓ Clustering
✓ Free-writing
✓ Outlining
✓ Topic sentence

Techniques you'll need to master:

✓ Organize ideas for a given topic using outlining
✓ Use different techniques for generating ideas
✓ Understand the structure of an essay
✓ Develop a topic sentence or thesis statement for your essay
✓ Create an introductory paragraph that will capture the attention of a reader
✓ Develop an essay geared toward a specific audience
✓ Understand the purpose of a topic sentence, introductory paragraph, and conclusion
✓ Create an essay that remains focused on the given topic
✓ Summarize the main ideas of an essay in a concluding paragraph
✓ Develop and write an essay within a given amount of time

As you learned in the preceding chapter, the PRAXIS I writing test is divided into two separate sections: the multiple-choice questions and the essay question. Chapter 3 is intended to prepare you for the multiple-choice questions. The purpose of this chapter is to prepare you to write an effective essay within a short period of time.

The essay portion of the test will present you with a topic about which to write. You will have 30 minutes to brainstorm ideas, organize your thoughts, and put them into essay format. Rest assured that you are only being tested on your ability to develop an essay that effectively conveys meaning to the reader. You do not have to be an expert on any particular topic or subject (other than essay writing, of course!).

The essay topics will be issues or arguments. You will be required to discuss a topic and the extent to which you disagree or agree with it. Remember to provide clear examples to support your ideas using personal experiences, observations, and readings.

The essay you create is graded by an experienced teacher. It is given a single overall score based on certain criteria. The essay is graded using a scale similar to the one outlined in Table 4.1.

Table 4.1	Possible Grades That Can Be Assigned to Your Essay
Grade	Description
1	This score is the equivalent of an F. An essay assigned a grade of 1 contains serious errors in mechanics, usage, organization, and so on that are consistent throughout.
2	This score is the equivalent of a D. An essay assigned a score of 2 shows minimal writing skill. The essay contains errors in mechanics and usage. It may not address the essay topic or provide supporting ideas.
3	This score is the equivalent of a C. An essay assigned a score of 3 does demonstrate some writing ability but includes some obvious errors. However, the errors do not occur throughout the essay.
4	This score is the equivalent of a B. An essay assigned a grade of 4 is fairly well written but does contain some problems with organization as well as random errors in mechanics and usage.
5	This score is the equivalent of a B+. An essay assigned a score of 5 meets most of the criteria but contains a few errors in mechanics and language usage. Overall, the essay is well-written.
6	This score is the equivalent of an A+. An essay assigned a score of 6 has met all the required criteria.

The following list outlines some of the criteria used to grade an essay. You should read them over carefully and keep them in mind when it comes time to write your essay.

➤ Does the essay focus on the given topic?

➤ Are there clear, concise examples and details that support the ideas in the essay?

➤ Are the ideas logically organized?

➤ Does the essay make use of a variety of sentence structures?

➤ Is the essay generally free of grammatical errors?

Now that you have a little background information about this portion of the exam, let's take a look at the art of essay writing. This chapter will look at different ways of brainstorming and organizing your ideas, putting your ideas into essay format, and tips on how to write a better essay. A sample essay is also included to demonstrate the concepts and ideas discussed throughout the chapter. The practice questions at the end of the chapter will then allow you to put your essay-writing skills to the test.

Brainstorming

So, you are in the beginning stages of writing an essay. You have been given a topic to write about. This is sometimes the most difficult part of the whole process. You may suddenly feel overwhelmed and not know where to start.

The starting point for creating any essay is usually brainstorming. Brainstorming is an effective way to generate ideas about the essay topic. All you are doing at this point is coming up with as many ideas and thoughts related to the topic as possible. Table 4.2 describes some of the different types of essays that you may encounter.

Table 4.2	Types of Essays
Essay Type	**Description**
Personal essay	This type of essay describes your personal opinion, experiences, or feelings about a given topic.
Argumentative essay	This type of essay argues or debates a specific topic. For example, should students be required to wear uniforms to school?

(continued)

Table 4.2 Types of Essays *(continued)*	
Essay Type	**Description**
Compare-and-contrast essay	This type of essay compares and contrasts different points related to a given topic.
Evaluative essay	This type of essay essentially provides a review of some kind.
Cause-and-effect essay	This type of essay explores the causes of a given topic and/or the effects, for example, the effects of competitive sports in schools.

Taking a few minutes to write down your ideas can make the whole essay-writing experience go much more smoothly. Having all your ideas down before starting will reduce the likelihood of running out of ideas halfway through the essay or even forgetting an important idea or point you wanted to include.

This is a timed exam. You have only 30 minutes to complete the essay. Although the brainstorming step is important in creating a well-written essay, do not spend all your time on this step. Plan to spend about 5 minutes getting your ideas down. Remember, you still have to write the actual essay and review your work at the end.

Now this is no time to be careful about what you write down. In fact, what you should do is write down every idea that comes to mind, regardless of whether you think it may sound silly. You can decide later whether the idea is relevant or not.

Forms of Brainstorming

You can brainstorm your ideas in several different ways. Of course, you can just generate the ideas in your head and not write them down. However, the problem with that is that you have nothing to refer to, and you will more than likely end up leaving important points out of your essay that you wanted to include.

Clustering

Clustering, also referred to as *mapping*, involves placing a circle that contains a specific topic in the middle of the paper. As you come up with ideas, you can create a web, with all your ideas branching off the main topic, as shown in Figure 4.1. As you get going on your cluster, ideas can begin to branch off from subtopics.

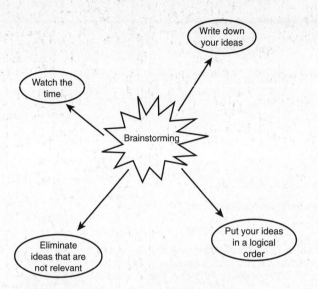

Figure 4.1 Clustering is one form of brainstorming.

Free-writing

Another method of brainstorming is called *free-writing*. This involves writing down as many ideas that come to mind as possible. In other words, you are writing down everything you know about the given topic. Ideas are not organized in any way, so this may make it a little more difficult when it comes to organizing them. Let's take a look at an example of free-writing. If given the topic of "summer," you would take a few minutes (let's say two minutes) to write down everything that came to your mind about the topic. Your result will look something like Figure 4.2.

 Diversity is a positive thing. When you're brainstorming ideas, try to view the topic from many different perspectives. In other words, tackle the topic from a number of different angles. In the end, it will make for a more interesting essay.

When you are done, you should be able to go through your ideas and find something worthy of an essay topic. Remember, the point of free-writing is not to write a coherent essay. It's to get your brain thinking about a specific topic. Therefore, what you write down will not be coherent or make much sense. Your next step in the essay-writing process will be to take those ideas and organize them.

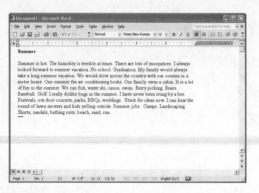

Figure 4.2 Free-writing is another method of brainstorming ideas for a topic.

Many people prefer using the clustering method of brainstorming as opposed to just putting ideas down anywhere on paper. When all your ideas are down, it is usually a little easier with clustering to keep track of them all and to begin organizing them.

Organizing Ideas

The next step in the process should be to make logical connections between the ideas that you've generated. At this point, some ideas may appear to be irrelevant and can be discarded. Making connections between ideas will definitely help you to organize your ideas so that they flow in a logical manner within your essay.

The way in which you organize the ideas within an essay will depend on the type of essay that you are writing. For example, some essays will require you to organize ideas based on chronological order, whereas others will be organized based on their importance (with the most important ideas discussed first). Table 4.3 describes some of the common ways of organizing ideas in an essay.

Table 4.3 Methods of Organization	
Organizational Method	**Description**
Chronological	Ideas are organized as they occurred in time.
Importance	Ideas are organized based on their importance. The most important ideas are usually discussed first.
Topical	Ideas are organized around topics as they would logically be discussed. For example, if you were discussing an operating system, you would more than likely talk about installation first and then configuration followed by customization.

Outlining

Another important part of the writing process is called *outlining*. At this point, you are taking the ideas you generated during the brainstorming process and putting them into logical order. Of course, it is possible to write your essay without creating an outline. However, this does increase the likelihood that the essay will be somewhat disorganized.

Creating a basic outline of your essay before jumping into the actual writing can produce some very positive results. Of course, it will help keep you focused, organized, and on track when you are writing. An outline will allow you to see how your ideas are connected, how transitions occur between ideas, important details that may have been left out, and if there is a good balance. Also keep in mind that your outline is not written in stone, and you may find that when you are doing the actual writing, you need to make changes to it.

A basic outline is going to represent the main ideas that you plan to discuss in your essay. Essentially, it should list the main points in chronological order. You can then add subpoints under your main ideas. These subpoints will be supporting ideas, arguments, and examples relating back to the main idea.

There are different ways in which you can create an outline. A basic outline may follow the following format:

1. Main Idea

  a. Subtopic relating to main idea 1

    i. Subtopic relating to subtopic a

  b. Subtopic relating to main idea 1

2. Main Idea

  a. Subtopic relating to main idea 2

  b. Subtopic relating to main idea 2

There is no rule as to the number of ideas and subtopics required. However, a good rule to follow is if you have a main idea 1, there should be a main idea 2. The same holds true for the subtopics.

Let's take a look at a sample outline that follows this basic format. If you've been given the topic of "Internet Explorer," you might create a cluster similar to the one shown in Figure 4.3. Based on this information generated during a brainstorming session, an outline can be created using the basic format shown after the figure.

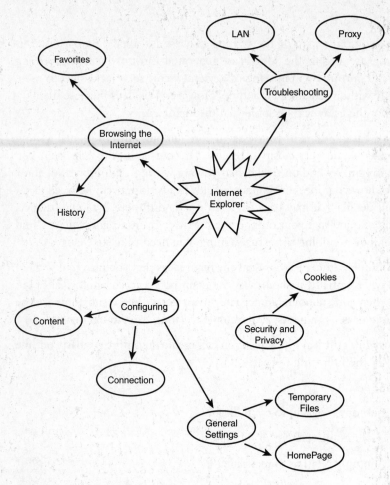

Figure 4.3 Brainstorming ideas related to the topic of Internet Explorer.

1. Configuring Internet Explorer

   a. General Settings

   i. Home Page

   ii. Temporary Internet Files

   b. Content Settings

   c. Security and Privacy

   i. Cookies

   ii. Security Zones

d. Connection Settings

   i. LAN

   ii. Proxy

2. Browsing with Internet Explorer

  a. Getting Connected

    i. Dial-up

  b. Viewing Web Pages

    i. History

    ii. Favorites

3. Troubleshooting Internet Explorer

  a. Connection Problems

    i. Dial-up errors

    ii. LAN errors

  b. Access Problems

  c. Restricted Web Sites

    i. Permissions

As you can probably see, after an outline is created, it would be much simpler to begin writing the essay.

If your written essay is properly organized, a reader should be able to easily develop his own outline from it.

Structuring Your Essay

So, you've taken a few minutes to brainstorm your ideas and have created a basic outline of what you want to include in your essay. Now where do you go? The next step will be for you to actually write the essay. However, before you do, you should know the general structure of an essay.

An essay should include the following components, each of which are discussed in the following section.

➤ Topic sentence

➤ Introductory paragraph

➤ Body

➤ Concluding paragraph

Topic Sentence and Introductory Paragraph

The introductory paragraph is used for two main purposes. First of all, it captures the attention of the reader. Secondly, it serves to let the reader know what the essay is about. So, let's take a look at how you can make the most of an introductory paragraph.

Capturing the Readers' Attention

Chances are the first paragraph that will be read in an essay is the introduction. When writing the introductory paragraph, you need to ask yourself how you can capture the attention of your readers. The first paragraph will pretty much determine a reader's interest (kind of like a first impression). Therefore, make it interesting, attention grabbing, and so on, so that the reader will want to read more.

You can use many techniques to spice up the introductory paragraph, for example, telling an anecdotal story; most readers enjoy reading "real-life" stories. Therefore, you can capture the attention of your readers by telling a short but powerful story in your opening paragraph that relates to the topic covered in the essay. Another technique you can use is to include a shocking or surprising sentence in the introductory paragraph. In either case, just make sure that it relates to the topic covered in the essay.

Anecdotal stories and surprising sentences are just two ways of spicing up the introductory paragraph. Make it interesting, but don't completely overdo it.

Topic Sentence

A topic sentence is often referred to as a *thesis statement*. The topic sentence simply informs the reader what your essay is going to be about. It basically sets the focus for the essay.

Including a topic sentence within your essay is also a good way for you to stay on track in the body of the essay. (Developing the body of the essay is discussed in the next section.) Any ideas or arguments that you discuss in the body of the essay must relate to the topic sentence. If they don't, your essay will more than likely be off topic. Also keep in mind that the topic sentence for an essay does not necessarily need to be the first sentence of the introductory paragraph. For example, if you include an anecdotal story in the introductory sentence, the thesis statement may end up being the last sentence of the introductory paragraph.

The Body of the Essay

The body of the essay consists of the examples, arguments, and so on that you provide to support your ideas. Each paragraph in the body of your essay should contain an argument, statement, or idea related to the essay topic. The first sentence of each paragraph should describe an idea, example, or argument. The rest of the paragraph should provide examples to support the topic sentence.

 Here is a quick tip to use when writing your paragraphs: A lot of people think bigger is always better. You can include big words in your essay, but do not overdo it. Include them where appropriate, but remember that sometimes simple is better.

Here is a good strategy to follow when writing each body paragraph:

1. Begin by putting down one of the main ideas you came up with during the brainstorming process or from your outline.

2. Write down some supporting points for that main idea.

3. Elaborate on each of the supporting points.

So, let's take a look at an example of how you can use this strategy to develop a body paragraph. If your essay topic is "Should students be required to wear uniforms to school?", one of your ideas generated through brainstorming may be "low-income families." Therefore, one of your main ideas for a body paragraph may be "Mandatory uniforms may negatively influence low-income families." Your next step is to write down two or three supporting points for this argument such as:

➤ Secondhand clothing

➤ Cost of a uniform

➤ Multiple uniforms

➤ Replacement

➤ Multiple school-age children

You can then go on and elaborate on your points to establish a body paragraph. For example:

Mandatory school uniforms may negatively impact low-income families. This is due to the cost of a uniform. As a child growing up, I went to a private school that required uniforms. Each uniform was at a cost of nearly 100 dollars. I always had three, so I did not have to wear the same one to school each day. You can also factor in the cost of replacing uniforms. Wearing them day in and day out means they wear out rather quickly, so you can plan on buying a few throughout the school year. So the cost of a school uniform might be too much for a low-income family, especially if they have multiple school-age children. Many of these families rely on secondhand clothing for their children because they cannot afford the cost of purchasing new ones. Therefore, requiring children to wear mandatory school uniforms may not be possible for those families living on a fixed income.

Because you are limited to writing your essay in only 30 minutes, you will need to limit the length of your essay. However, an essay that is too short may not convey the correct message or discuss the topic in enough detail. A good rule of thumb is to have between three to four paragraphs. Your essay should consist of between 300 and 500 words.

Concluding the Essay

You should never end an essay with the last idea. This kind of writing leaves your reader hanging. Every essay should include a concluding paragraph. This is your chance to restate the topic or argument and summarize the main or important points that were discussed. The concluding paragraph should indicate to the reader that the essay is indeed over.

The concluding paragraph can tie into any statements made in the introductory paragraph. What it must do is to summarize the main points discussed in the body of the essay. Try to keep this fairly short; a sentence or two should suffice.

All your conclusion requires is three or four strong sentences that summarize the points you have just written about. There is no specific format that you need to follow for this paragraph. All it should do is bring closure to the essay for the reader.

When you are summarizing the main points discussed within your essay, be careful that you do not restate them exactly as they appear in the body. Reword them as much as possible.

Let's take a look at a sample essay that includes an introductory paragraph, body, and concluding paragraph. The topic of the essay is "study tips." The introductory paragraph introduces the topic of the essay and gives the reader an indication of what to expect. In the following example, the topic sentence for the essay is included at the end of the introductory paragraph. The introductory paragraph also catches the reader's attention using the first sentence. Most people are interested in learning about different ways of improving their chances of passing an exam.

The introductory paragraph is followed by the body of the essay, which includes three paragraphs. Each paragraph begins with a main idea followed by examples or evidence to support each idea. Finally, the essay ends with a concluding paragraph that summarizes the main points of the essay.

It's every candidate's goal to succeed on an exam the first time around. Being well prepared and ensuring you're familiar with all the exam subject matter obviously increase your chances of success. Good study habits get you one step closer to achieving this goal. Reading a book related to the subject matter is certainly recommended, but there are a number of other study tips you can follow as well and incorporate into your study diet.

Classroom training is always recommended when preparing for any type of certification exam. Although it can cost several hundred dollars, instructor-led training is a valuable exam-preparation tool. How can you go wrong having an expert explain test-related subject matter to you in detail? Alternatives to classroom instructor-led training are computer-based training and web-based training. The nice things about computer-based and web-based training are the affordability and flexibility they offer.

Several publishers publish exam-specific study guides. Some of the guides are geared toward a higher level of knowledge, teaching you everything you need to know about a subject. Others provide you with the information you absolutely need to know to pass an exam. If you are studying for an exam on your own, you should begin with a complete study guide, work through it from start to end, and then finish with a book that points out the need-to-know information for the exam. Que's Exam Cram 2 series does an excellent job of distilling all the information that you must know for exam success.

Practice exams are a wonderful way to test your knowledge after you've studied all the required material. A lot of study guides include practice exams designed to mimic the questions you're likely to encounter on the actual exams. There are also an abundance of Web sites that offer practice exams, some of which are free and others that must be purchased. In any case, when you are taking the practice exams, pay close attention to the answers as well. For any questions you answer incorrectly, use the explanations to understand where you went wrong and why the correct answer is indeed correct. Be sure to review study material pertaining to the questions you answered incorrectly before taking the real exams. I recommend that you aim to achieve at least 80% on a practice exam before challenging the real one. If your score is less than this mark, look at the areas in which you are still having difficulty and keep studying additional material.

There are a number of options available when studying for an exam. You can incorporate classroom training, books, and practice tests to ensure a well-balanced study diet. Using a variety of study techniques will certainly increase your chances of passing an exam the first time around.

 Flow is crucial when it comes to essay writing, which means that transitions must be used between paragraphs. This does not mean you should always use transitional phrases such as "as a result," "in addition to," and "while." Be creative. Try using other transitional techniques to move between paragraphs, such as building on a previous idea or repeating keywords used in the previous paragraph.

Here is another example of an essay written on the topic of "Should parents take an active role in their children's school life?"

I think parents should be involved in their children's school. Some kids have parents who aren't very good. I don't mean they are mean or anything. They don't help their kids in school at all. If kids have homework at night, their parents should help them. Kids would definitely know their homework better if they did.

I seen kids in my school have this. One of my friends had parents that didn't help him with his homework. They wouldn't even try and be quiet while my friend tried to get his homework done. Some parents don't think they should help because they don't know how to do the work. With things like algebra and stuff, some parents don't know it. They should still try and help with the homework though.

After you have read over the essay, you can more than likely see that it contains some serious problems. First of all, it does not address the actual question being asked in the essay topic. There are problems with organization. There is only a single example given, which again, does not address the topic. The essay also contains errors in sentence structure and grammar. Now, let's take a look at a sample essay that would be considered to be very well-written.

My parents were great! They, like many others, have always felt it was their duty to support their children and local schools. However, there are a lot of parents who do not feel this way at all. To these parents, school life and home life are completely separate and have nothing to do with each other. In my opinion, its very important for parents to take an active role in their child's school life.

During teacher training seminars, one of my professors indicated that bad habits in children are more often picked up at home than they are at school. Looking back on my childhood, I strongly believe this to be true. Since family life is such an important part of a student's life, it makes much more sense that the school and the parents were working together to achieve the same goal.

How can parents be involved in the child's school life? One way is to communicate with the teachers to stay informed with what is going on. I have seen the numerous benefits that can be had when parents and teachers communicate, especially with younger school-aged children. Of course, the communication must go both ways. The teachers can actively keep the parents involved by sending home progress reports and newsletters. Parents should put in an effort as well by making a point of visiting the school as often as possible. This way the responsibility of educating children is that of both teachers and parents.

There is concrete evidence that suggests students whose parents maintain open lines of communication with teachers are more likely to excel in academics. All parents need to take an active role in education and realize that they are also responsible for educating their children.

This sample essay is considered to be well-written. Ideas are adequately organized and concrete examples are provided to support them. There is an obvious introductory paragraph as well as a conclusion. However, as you will see, there are a few small problems with grammar. Hopefully, these small errors would be corrected during the review and editing process!

Tips for Writing Essays

Now that you are familiar with the essay-writing process and the components that should be included in an essay, let's take a look at some of the ways in which you can improve your essay. You should pay close attention to the topics discussed in the following section because they are based on the criteria that will be used to grade the essay you write for the PRAXIS exam. Also keep in mind when you are writing your essay that there is no right or wrong answer.

Since this is a timed exam, you have to use your time wisely. Here is a general guideline to follow for writing the essay so that you make the most of the 30 minutes. Spend 5 minutes each on brainstorming and outlining, 15 minutes on writing the actual essay, and 5 minutes on reviewing and correcting your work.

Using a Variety of Sentence Structures

There is no doubt that you will want to create an essay that is interesting to the reader. One of the techniques that you can use to make an essay more appealing is to use a variety of sentence structures. Chapter 3 included a discussion of the different types of sentence structures including simple, compound, and complex sentences. When you are writing your essay, try to include as many different types of sentences as possible.

One of the things you really want to pay attention to when writing an essay is to avoid the use of run-on sentences. These are the sentences that seem to go on forever. A run-on sentence contains two or more clauses that are not connected by the correct conjunction or punctuation. The following example would be considered a run-on sentence: "I'm not using my new computer to its full potential it did not come with a manual so I don't really know how to use it correctly."

Here are a few other tips you can try to add some variety to your sentences.

➤ Try adding a question into a paragraph. The sample essay at the end of the chapter demonstrates how this can be done.

➤ Depending on the tone of your essay, you can inject a command into it.

➤ If possible, begin a sentence using a coordinating conjunction such as the word *but*.

➤ Occasionally break away from the standard sentence type where the subject is always followed by the verb.

Using some of the tips discussed here will ensure that your essay does not sound monotonous to the reader. If you have ever listened to someone speak in a monotone fashion, it is usually rather sleep-inducing. You do not want to end up with an essay that is going to put your reader to sleep.

Writing to the Audience

One of the things you can do to improve upon your essay is to think about your audience. For whom are you writing? It makes it easier to convey a message if you identify your intended audience.

The topic of "tone" is also important when writing your essay. The language you use in an essay will essentially set the tone. For example, using slang words or even contractions can make an essay sound rather informal. For the PRAXIS exam, it is recommended that you go with a more formal tone and avoid using slang terms within your essay.

Maintaining Focus

For the essay portion of the exam, you'll be given a specific topic about which to write. One of the criteria upon which your essay will be graded is focus. Does your essay stay focused on the essay topic? When you are writing or reviewing your essay, eliminate any sentences or ideas that do not relate to the topic.

If you have ever read an essay that contains ideas that are unrelated to the main topic, they probably stuck out more than anything else you read. You may have been thinking "What is the writer talking about?" or even "This sentence does not belong." During the review process, listen to how the sentences sound. If a sentence or idea is not related to the essay topic, it will stand out. Delete it, or if necessary, move it to another section of the essay for which it is better suited.

Review Your Work

So, you have finished writing your essay. Now it's time to review what you've written. You may think this is a waste of time, but it is one of the most important aspects of the writing process. Now is your chance to go through your work to identify and correct any errors.

Here are some of the things you should look for when reviewing your essay:

➤ Does your essay include an obvious topic sentence or thesis statement?

➤ Does your introductory paragraph adequately describe to the reader what the essay is about?

➤ Does the tense shift throughout your essay?

➤ Are there clear transitions between paragraphs?

➤ Does your essay flow? Are the ideas well organized?

➤ Are the ideas in each paragraph clearly developed and supported?

➤ Do your ideas maintain focus on the topic of the essay?

➤ Are there any errors in grammar? These may include spelling errors, run-on sentences, punctuation errors, and so on.

➤ Does your essay maintain objectivity? For example, is it written in first person or third person? This should remain consistent throughout the essay.

One of the most common errors that people make in writing is misuse of the following words: *your* and *you're*; *they're*, *their*, and *there*; and *its* and *it's*. Read over your essay carefully and watch out for these errors.

While you are reviewing your work, also keep the following list of essay-writing "dos and don'ts" in mind.

➤ Do answer the question in the essay topic with which you are presented.

➤ Do use personal experiences to support ideas.

➤ Do have a clear introduction and conclusion.

➤ Do recognize the difference between the misuse and the correct use of different words.

➤ Do review your work; check spelling and punctuation carefully.

➤ Do argue a point using your own opinion.

➤ Do use commas properly; include semicolons where appropriate.

➤ Do not wander off the given topic.

➤ Do not use contractions.

➤ Do not use slang terms.

➤ Do not use "I think."

➤ Do not include any ideas for which you do not have supporting evidence.

Tips for the Computer-Based Test

As with all the other PRAXIS components, there are both paper-based and computer-based versions of the writing test. If you opt to take the computer-based version, you'll be required to use the computer for the essay component as well. This means typing your essay in a word processing program.

 If you do not have sufficient typing skills, you should consider taking the paper-based version of the exam instead. Since you only have 30 minutes to compose the essay, you do not want to waste precious time due to poor typing skills.

There is nothing different between the paper-based exam and the computer-based version. The essay topic is the same, as is the amount of time you have to compose the essay.

If you have opted to take the computer-based version, you should still compose your essay using the techniques outlined in the previous sections. Along with that information, here are some additional tips to assist with the computer-based exam format.

➤ Be sure to save your work frequently. For example, this can easily be done in Microsoft Word by clicking the icon that resembles a floppy disk.

➤ Take advantage of different keyboard shortcuts. Use Ctrl+A to select all text in a document. Ctrl+X cuts the selected text from the document. Ctrl+C copies all the selected text. Use Ctrl+V to paste text.

➤ Word processing programs usually have a spell checker and a grammar checker. However, it's still important to leave time at the end to review your work.

Sample Essay

Now that you've gone through the entire essay-writing process, let's put it all together. The following section will show you a sample essay, beginning as a single topic and going through the brainstorming and outlining processes, the writing of the actual essay, and finally the revisions.

 You may also want to attempt writing your own sample essay based on the given topic before reading the entire section. The more practice, the better. I also recommend timing yourself so that you get used to writing an essay in 30 minutes.

The essay topic for the following example is "Mandatory school uniforms in public schools."

Brainstorming Session

The first thing you want to do is generate some ideas pertaining to the topic. This is done during your brainstorming sessions. Remember to pick an idea that you could essentially write pages about. This guarantees that you will not run out of things to write about. The central idea used for brainstorming was "mandatory school uniforms." The ideas generated relate to this topic. The results of the free-writing session are listed here:

➤ Cost

➤ Multiple children/multiple uniforms

➤ Low-income families

➤ Fashion/style

➤ Standardized dress

➤ Government coercion

➤ Loss of individuality

➤ Less violence

➤ Gangs

Creating the Outline

Based on the information generated during the brainstorming session, the next step is to establish an outline. This involves taking your ideas and putting them into some kind of logical order. Here is a sample outline based on the preceding list of points:

1. Introductory paragraph

2. Cost

    a. cost of uniforms

    b. multiple uniforms

    c. low-income families

    d. multiple children

3. Individuality

    a. loss of individuality

    b. fashion/style

4. Violence

    a. gangs

    b. reduced violence in schools

5. Conclusion

Based on the preceding outline, you can begin writing the essay. Remember at this point that you should plan to spend only about 15–20 minutes on the actual writing so that you leave enough time to review your work at the end.

Writing the Essay

The following essay is based on the outline just created for the topic of mandatory school uniforms. Notice that the essay does not follow the outline exactly. This is the point of an outline. It gives you a starting point, but as you are writing, you may find that changes must be made.

The following essay begins with an introductory paragraph that includes a topic sentence informing readers what to expect from the essay. There are also three body paragraphs that use the points listed in the outline and a concluding paragraph.

During my childhood, I spent some time in a private school and some in a public school. I was able to experience both worlds; that of mandatory school uniforms and being able to wear the latest fashions to school. This is a debate that is going on in many schools today. Should students be required to wear mandatory school uniforms in public schools? As with any argument, there are pros and cons.

Mandatory school uniforms may negatively impact low-income families. This is due to the cost of a uniform. Each uniform was at a cost of nearly 100 dollars. I always had three, so I did not have to wear the same one to school each day. You can also factor in the cost of replacing uniforms. Wearing them day in and day out means they wear out rather quickly so that you can plan on buying a few throughout the school year. So the cost of a school uniform might be too much for a low-income family, especially if they have multiple school-age children. Many of these families rely on secondhand clothing for their children because they cannot afford the cost of purchasing new ones. Therefore, requiring children to wear mandatory school uniforms may not be possible for those families living on a fixed income.

As parents we are always trying to teach our children to be themselves. This goes hand in hand with individuality and being able to freely express yourself. Clothing is definitely one form of expression. By requiring all students to wear the same uniform to school, are we not condemning individuality, possibly giving children the idea that expressing yourself, being unique from everyone else, and wearing what you want is not acceptable? If we want our children to grow up feeling comfortable in expressing their uniqueness and individuality, we should be allowing them to wear the clothes that best express who they are to school.

Conversely, there are some pros to implementing mandatory school uniforms. One of the arguments put forth is that implementing this will reduce the number of gangs and the amount of violence in schools. Gang members can usually be identified by some unique piece of clothing. If schools implement a standard dress code among students, gang members will no longer be able to wear their group clothing to school. There is also the issue of violence breaking out over clothing. I recall an incident in our local public school where a teenager was beaten up over a shirt. This obviously would not have occurred had there been a standardized dress code.

This issue of mandatory school uniforms will always be in debate. There are those who support the idea with the intention of reducing gangs and violence in public schools. Then there are those on the other side of the fence who oppose it for the reasons of cost and the right to self-expression. Even though I experience both worlds, I'm still undecided and sitting on the middle of the fence.

Editing and Reviewing

Finally, when the essay is complete, you'll need to take a few minutes to edit and review your work. Refer to the section entitled "Review Your Work" earlier in the chapter for specific things that you should be looking for at this time.

One problem that clearly stands out with this essay is that the writer does not take a clear stance on the issue. When you are presented with a topic on the PRAXIS exam, you will be expected to take a clear stance on the issue. You will need to support your stance using your own personal experiences, observations, and readings.

Exam Prep Questions

Use a brainstorming technique to generate ideas for each topic listed in questions 1 through 3. Try to generate at least five different ideas for each essay topic. Answers will vary.

1. Businesses should provide mandatory drug tests for all their employees and potential employees.

2. All potential school teachers should be required to complete mandatory computer training.

3. Smoking should be banned on all public property, including restaurants, lounges, and clubs.

For questions 4 through 6, create a sample outline for each of the ideas generated through brainstorming sessions based on the previous questions.

4. Businesses should have mandatory drug tests for all their employees and potential employees.

5. All potential school teachers should be required to complete mandatory computer training.

6. Smoking should be banned in all restaurants, lounges, and clubs.

For questions 7 through 9, create a thesis statement for each outline you created in questions 4 through 6.

7. Businesses should provide mandatory drug tests for all their employees and potential employees.

8. All potential school teachers should be required to complete mandatory computer training.

9. Smoking should be banned on all public property, including restaurants, lounges, and clubs.

For questions 10 through 12, write an introductory paragraph based on the outlines you created in questions 4 through 6. Include the thesis statements you just created in your introductory paragraphs.

10. Businesses should provide mandatory drug tests for all their employees and potential employees.

11. All potential school teachers should be required to complete mandatory computer training.

12. Smoking should be banned on all public property, including restaurants, lounges, and clubs.

Write a single body paragraph based on the outlines created in questions 4 through 6. Use personal experiences, observations, and readings to support the ideas in each of your paragraphs. Remember to use the outlines you created earlier to organize the paragraphs.

13. Businesses should have mandatory drug tests for all their employees and potential employees.

14. All potential school teachers should be required to complete mandatory computer training.

15. Smoking should be banned on all public property, including restaurants, lounges, and clubs.

The concluding paragraph for the sample essay in question 16 has been removed. Write a concluding paragraph for the essay based on the existing introduction and body paragraphs.

16. My parents were great! They, like many others, have always felt it was their duty to support their children and local schools. However, there are a lot of parents who do not feel this way at all. To these parents, school life and home life are completely separate and have nothing to do with each other. In my opinion, it's very important for parents to take an active role in their child's school life.

During teacher training seminars, one of my professors indicated that bad habits in children are more often picked up at home than they are at school. Looking back on my childhood, I strongly believe this to be true. Since family life is such an important part of a student's life, it makes much more sense for the school and the parents to be working together to achieve the same goal.

How can parents be involved in the child's school life? One way is to communicate with the teachers to stay informed with what is going on. I have seen the numerous benefits that can be had when parents and teachers communicate, especially with younger school-aged children. Of course, the communication must go both ways. The teachers can actively keep the parents involved by sending home progress reports and newsletters. Parents should put in the effort as well by making a point of visiting the school as often as possible. This way, the responsibility of educating children is that of both teachers and parents.

For questions 17 and 18, write a short essay (between 300 and 500 words) based on the given topics. Use the writing process discussed in the chapter. Be sure that your essay includes an introductory paragraph, a body, and a conclusion. Also, try timing yourself to see if you can complete each one within 30 minutes.

17. Computers do not provide any benefits. The only thing they do is make life more complicated.

18. Competitive sports should not be allowed in schools.

Exam Prep Answers

1. Answers will vary. Ideas may include some of the following: discrimination, criminal record checks, business environment, public image, cost and expense, potential revenue loss, safety, positive workplace.

2. Answers will vary. Ideas may include some of the following: potential learning experiences, Internet, job market and marketability, email, technology is advancing not disappearing, sharing information, parents, other teachers.

3. Answers will vary. Ideas may include some of the following: second-hand smoke, litter, children, addiction, cancer, lungs, quitting.

4. Answers will vary. Your outline should include introductory and concluding paragraphs. The body of the essay should include two to three paragraphs with examples, evidence, and so on supporting your ideas. A possible outline follows.

   1. Introductory paragraph

   2. Criminal record checks

   3. Business environment

      a. Positive workplace

      b. Safety

      c. Public image

   4. Potential revenue loss

      a. Loss of clients

      b. Sick days/time off work

   5. Concluding paragraph

5. Answers will vary. Your outline should include introductory and concluding paragraphs. The body of the essay should include two to three paragraphs with examples, evidence, and so on supporting your ideas. A possible outline follows.

   1. Introductory paragraph

   2. Potential learning experiences

      a. Internet

      b. Software programs

   3. Preparing students for the real world

      a. Marketability

      b. Job skills

   4. Sharing information

      a. Parents

      b. Other teachers

   5. Concluding paragraph

6. Answers will vary. Your outline should include introductory and concluding paragraphs. The body of the essay should include two to three paragraphs with examples, evidence, and so on supporting your ideas. A possible outline follows.

   1. Introductory paragraph

   2. Secondhand smoke

      a. Dangers

      b. Cancer

      c. Children

   3. Addiction

      a. Smokers

      b. Quitting

      c. Positive influences

   4. Physical environment

      a. Litter

      b. Odor/smell

   5. Concluding paragraph

7. Answers will vary. Your thesis statement must clearly tell the reader what the essay is about. It must set the focus for the rest of the essay. A possible thesis statement is shown in the following paragraph. As you can see, the topic sentence indicates to the reader that the topic of the essay will be the benefits of mandatory drug testing.

   "There are a number of benefits to implementing mandatory drug testing within a business environment."

8. Answers will vary. Your thesis statement must clearly tell the reader what the essay is about. It must set the focus for the rest of the essay. A possible thesis statement is shown in the following paragraph.

The statement indicates to the reader that the rest of the essay is going to argue that mandatory computer-based training should be implemented.

"Mandatory computer training can be beneficial to both potential teachers and their students."

9. Answers will vary. Your thesis statement must clearly tell the reader what the essay is about. It must set the focus for the rest of the essay. A possible thesis statement is shown in the following paragraph. It indicates to the reader that the remaining essay will argue that smoking should be banned.

"There is nothing positive about allowing people to smoke anywhere."

10. Answers will vary. Your introductory paragraph should capture the readers' attention. It must also include a thesis statement informing the readers what the essay is about. For example:

As a business owner, part of my responsibility is to create an environment for my employees that is safe, positive, and conducive to performing work-related tasks. What kind of a work environment would there be if there were a chance that one or more of my employees were involved in drugs? There are a number of benefits to implementing mandatory drug testing within a business environment.

11. Answers will vary. Your introductory paragraph should capture the readers' attention. It must also include a thesis statement informing the readers what the essay is about. For example:

Technology is not going to disappear. It only changes and advances with the times. Most jobs require employees to have some skill with a computer. If you do not, chances are that the next person does. So, why should teachers be exempt from mandatory computer training? Mandatory computer training can not only provide benefits for teachers but for their students as well.

12. Answers will vary. Your introductory paragraph should capture the readers' attention. It must also include a thesis statement informing the readers what the essay is about. A sample introduction based on the essay topic is shown in the following paragraph.

There is nothing I dislike more than going out for a nice evening and coming home smelling like cigarette smoke. Not only does my clothing stink, but there is also the thought of how much secondhand smoke I managed to inhale during the evening. Thankfully, smoking was banned in my city over a year ago. But when I travel to other places where it is still allowed, I wonder what is taking them so long. As far as I am concerned, there is nothing positive about allowing people to smoke anywhere.

13. Answers will vary. Your body paragraph should include a topic sentence and evidence to support it. A sample paragraph is shown following. It begins with a topic sentence and expands on it through the use of personal experiences, observations, and readings.

All employers are responsible for creating a positive environment for their business. Looking back on my various work experiences, it is much easier to perform job tasks in a workplace that is safe and positive. An environment that may contain drugs or drug users would produce the opposite results. First of all, people may not feel safe being around an individual who abuses drugs. This in turn can affect their job performance and attitudes. Furthermore, it may also have a negative impact on business clients. How comfortable would your clients be knowing that the person helping them is a drug user? I would undoubtedly be uncomfortable and would take my business elsewhere.

14. Answers will vary. Your body paragraph should include a topic sentence and evidence to support it. A sample paragraph follows. It begins with a topic sentence and expands on it through the use of personal experiences, observations, and readings.

One of the jobs of the education system is to teach students skills that can be used in the real world. Since computers have become such a common tool used in homes and businesses, shouldn't computer skills be considered a necessity? How can teachers provide their students with these skills if they do not have any basic computer skills themselves? The school in my community promotes technology in the classroom, and all students who leave the school have some computer skills. This gives them one more set of skills that they can use in the real world. These students also have an advantage over those students who have none. Therefore, I strongly believe that all potential teachers should be required to take some basic computer training so that they can then transfer these skills to their students.

15. Answers will vary. Your body paragraph should include a topic sentence and evidence to support it. A sample paragraph follows. It begins with a topic sentence and expands on it through the use of personal experiences, observations, and readings.

Wherever there is a smoker, there is secondhand smoke. There are so many studies that have been done proving the dangers of secondhand smoke to us non-smokers. I am opposed to smoking, and I am aware that smoking causes cancer. Why should I have to be exposed to secondhand smoke then? Why would I want to expose my children to the dangers of secondhand smoke when it is my job to protect them? Therefore, any establishment that serves people who do not smoke should definitely ban smoking.

16. Answers will vary. The concluding paragraph should summarize the ideas discussed in the essay and provide closure to the essay.

17. Answers will vary.

18. Answers will vary.

Need to Know More?

 Visit www.ets.org to find specific information about the exam, exam objectives, and sample essay topics.

 Stilman, Ann. *Grammatically Correct: The Writer's Essential Guide to Punctuation, Spelling, Style, Usage, and Grammar.* Writer's Digest Books, 1997. ISBN: 0898797764.

 Donald, R.C. *Writing Clear Essays, 3rd Edition.* Pearson Education, 1995. ISBN: 013455478.

PART II
PLT

5

PRAXIS II Principles of Learning and Teaching

. . . .

Terms You'll Need to Understand:

✓ Zone of Proximal Development
✓ Motivation
✓ Summative Evaluation
✓ Formative Evaluation
✓ Diagnostic
✓ Norm-referenced
✓ Criterion-referenced
✓ Theorists

Techniques You'll Need to Master:

✓ Understand the various behavioral theories
✓ Understand how to use the various theories to influence your teaching
✓ Recognize student diversity in a classroom
✓ Plan lessons that meet the needs of all students, including exceptional learners
✓ Use a variety of assessment techniques
✓ Understand how gender and cultural differences impact communication
✓ Answer short-answer questions based on a given case history

Principles of Learning and Teaching

All teachers are required to take one of the Principles of Learning and Teaching (PLT) tests, depending on the grade level they intend to teach. The purpose of the PLT exam is to assess a beginning teacher's knowledge of various teaching-related principles. These principles include things such as evaluation and assessment techniques, human development, classroom management, and so on.

There are four different PLT tests:

➤ PLT: Early Childhood

➤ PLT: Grades K–6

➤ PLT: Grades 5–9

➤ PLT: Grades 7–12

Each test is two hours in length and presents four different case histories, each of which is followed by three short-answer questions. There also are two additional sections that each contain 12 multiple-choice questions.

The case studies presented are based on different teaching situations. The three short-answer questions that follow each case history relate back to the specific teaching situation. The multiple-choice questions cover a variety of different topics, but they do not relate to the case histories.

The exam contains two different types of case studies:

➤ *Document-based*—This type of case study presents you with various classroom notes, such as lesson plans, observations, and so on.

➤ *Narrative*—This type of case study provides you with an account of what is happening in a classroom.

When you are taking a PLT exam, pay close attention to the time because you only have two hours to complete the test. Ideally, you should plan to spend approximately 25 minutes on each of the case studies. This includes reading the case study and answering the three short-answer questions. Plan to spend about 10 minutes answering each of the multiple-choice sections. As with any timed exam, do not spend too much time on any one section, or you may not have enough time remaining to answer the rest of the questions.

PLT Exam Topics

All of the PLT exams cover the same exam objectives, which are outlined in the following list. The difference between the exams is that you will encounter different types of questions. For example, you may have to evaluate a case history based on a group of students between the ages of 14 and 16 on the PLT: Grades 7–12 exam, whereas the PLT: Grades K–6 exam may present you with a case history based on a group of 6-year-old students.

The main objectives that are covered on the PLT are

➤ Students as Learners

➤ Instruction and Assessment

➤ Communication Techniques

➤ Teacher Professionalism

Students as Learners

This test category covers topics such as human development, different learning styles, human motivation, and so on. You can find a list of all the objectives covered under this content category on the ETS website. The subobjectives for this content area are also outlined in the following list:

➤ Student Development and the Learning Process

➤ Students as Diverse Learners

➤ Student Motivation and the Learning Environment

Student Development

One of the most important things you need for this portion of the test is an understanding of the different behavioral theorists and how their work applies to student development. The theorists and theories you should be familiar with are summarized in Table 5.1.

 Make sure you are familiar with the different theorists including Kohlberg, Erickson, Piaget, Gilligan, and Vygotsky.

Table 5.1	Behavioral Theorists
Theorist	**Theory**
Kohlberg	Kohlberg's theory focuses on moral development. According to Kohlberg, children go through three levels of moral development. During stage 1, the focus is on self-interest. In stage 2, the focus changes to family and community. Finally, in stage 3, the focus is on ethical principles.
Erickson	Erickson's theory focuses on personal and social development. As children go through different levels of development, they will encounter and resolve crises. Erickson's stages of development include Initiative vs. guilt (3–6 years) Industry vs. inferiority (6–12 years) Identity vs. identity confusion (12–18 years)
Piaget	The focus of Piaget's theory is on cognitive development. The stages of development include Sensorimotor (birth–2 years) Preoperational (2–7 years) Concrete Operational (7–11 years) Formal Operational (11 and older)
Skinner	Skinner's theory focuses on operant conditioning. According to the theory, behaviors are strengthened through positive and negative re-inforcements.
Vygotsky	Vygotsky's theory focuses on cognitive development. This theory states that children learn from others when they are working within their zone of proximal development.
Bandura	Bandura's theory focuses on social learning. According to Bandura's theory, children learn throughobservation.

Student Diversity

This subobjective covers different aspects of student diversity in a classroom. You need to know about different learning styles, multiple intelligences, and performance modes (such as concrete operational thinkers, visual learners, and aural learners).

According to Gardner, another theorist, a person can have up to eight separate intelligences including interpersonal, intrapersonal, spatial, and so on. Therefore, when it comes to teaching, you must use a variety of techniques and provide a variety of activities so that students can develop all of their intelligences.

The exceptional learners category also falls under the topic of student diversity. Exceptionalities can include behavioral disorders, physical challenges, perceptual challenges, learning disabilities, and so on. In terms of teaching and the PLT exam, remember that you must meet the needs of all students, including those with exceptionalities, when planning your lessons.

Another consideration when discussing classroom diversity is the topic of second languages. Be prepared to encounter some test questions that may deal with how students acquire English as a second language.

Finally, you need to consider the influence of various experiences on students' learning. This also falls under the topic of diversity because students bring to the classroom a variety of different experiences, talents, and prior knowledge.

Motivation

Motivation is a very important factor when discussing student learning. You need to look at strategies for motivating students that you can implement in the classroom.

Maslow's theory states that people usually want to satisfy their deficiency needs, such as the need for esteem, before satisfying their growth needs.

There are several different ways in which you can motivate your students. For example, being knowledgeable and excited about the content areas you are teaching is important in terms of motivating students. In addition, creating lessons and activities that are interesting and challenging (within the zone of proximal development) is important. Another great way of motivating students is through building early success. If students believe they can succeed with the tasks you present them in the classroom, you have a solid start toward motivating positive behaviors.

Instruction and Assessment

This content area covers the topics of planning for instruction, different teaching strategies, and different assessment strategies.

The specific subobjectives covered in this content area as outlined on the ETS website include

➤ Instructional Strategies

➤ Planning Instruction

➤ Assessment Strategies

One important thing you need to keep in mind when it comes to instructional strategies is that it's crucial to activate students' prior knowledge and also connect current information with future lessons. This, in turn, makes it easier for students to understand why they are learning something.

 You need to be familiar with the different instructional methods such as direct instruction, discovery learning, group learning, cooperative learning, and so on.

When it comes to planning for instruction, you must plan lessons and activities that will meet the needs of all students in your classroom, as mentioned earlier in the section "Student Diversity."

In terms of assessment, there are a number of different strategies you can use. The type of evaluation you use will depend on what you want to assess. Table 5.2 outlines the different types of evaluations.

Table 5.2 Types of Evaluations	
Evaluation	**Description**
Formative	A formative evaluation is usually given during a unit of instruction. Formative evaluations are performed on a regular basis to determine whether students are learning the content.
Summative	A summative evaluation is performed at the end of a unit. For example, you may perform a summative evaluation at the end of a social studies unit.
Diagnostic	A diagnostic evaluation will identify strengths and weaknesses.
Norm-referenced	This type of evaluation compares one student to other students.
Criterion-referenced	This type of evaluation compares a student to a set of criteria, such as curriculum objectives.

Communication Techniques

This content area involves effective communication techniques teachers use to reach students. As a beginning teacher, you need to be aware of the gender differences and cultural differences that impact communication within the classroom. The specific topics that fall under the category of communication include the following:

➤ Basic, effective verbal and nonverbal communication techniques

➤ The effect of cultural and gender differences on communication in the classroom

➤ Types of communication and interaction that can stimulate discussion in different ways for particular purposes

One of the more important topics you are likely to encounter involves questioning techniques. Questioning is yet another way of teaching your students—that is, if you use good questioning techniques. Some important points to remember when using questioning techniques (and for the PRAXIS exams) appear in the following list:

➤ Incorporate questioning into your planning. Plan ahead and think about the types of questions you want to ask students before a lesson.

➤ Make sure your questions are clear and concise so that students can understand them.

➤ Use a random selection process when choosing a student to answer the question.

➤ Give students a suitable amount of time to formulate an answer.

➤ Provide positive, supportive feedback to students. Negative feedback may embarrass a student in front of classmates.

➤ Encourage students to think through an answer instead of simply giving it to them.

➤ Keep the line of questioning on track. Do not allow students to stray off topic in their answers.

Teacher Professionalism

The final objective covered on the PLT is teacher professionalism. This includes *reflecting* on your own teaching as a means of making improvements, involving parents and other caregivers in children's education, and knowing the literature associated with students' rights and teacher responsibilities.

The main topics covered under this category include

➤ The Reflective Practitioner

➤ The Larger Community

Sample PLT Questions

Now that you are familiar with the type of content you will find on the PLT exams (remember, the objectives are the same across all of the PLT exams), let's take a look at some sample case studies so that you can get an idea of what to expect when you encounter the exam. This text won't cover samples for every grade level; however, the examples that follow will give you an idea of the types of questions you will face, no matter what level you teach.

Case History K–6

Scenario

Mary is a first-year grade two teacher. There are a total of 20 students in her class. The community in which Mary teaches is middle to upper class. One student in particular, Kyle, is often distracted and inattentive during class. He and his mother recently moved into the community. He often comes to school poorly groomed, tired, and without breakfast. Mary has asked her mentor to observe a language arts class and suggest ways in which she can help Kyle stay more on task.

Observation: Mary Smith's Class, March 20

Mentor Classroom Observation:

At 8:45 a.m., 19 students enter the classroom. They all proceed to hang their bags on designated hooks. Students get their home reading out and place it in a container beside Ms. Smith's desk. Students continue to perform various tasks and eventually settle into their seats.

9:04—Students begin writing in journals without direction. Several students follow Ms. Smith, seeking help with their writing. There is minimal conversation as students share ideas with one another.

9:15—Ms. Smith begins circulating the classroom and helping individual students. Several students are conferring with each other. Ms. Smith looks at Kyle's journal and asks him to pay attention to his printing, telling him that he can print much better than he is currently doing.

9:20—Students begin pairing up to edit their work. Ms. Smith notices that Kyle is not editing. She asks if he is done, and he responds with a "No." Ms. Smith continues assisting other students.

9:25—Ms. Smith reminds students of the time. They have five minutes left to hand in their journals. At this time, Kyle gets out of his seat with his journal. He approaches four different students, asking them to edit his work. All of them refuse. Ms. Smith notices this and asks Kyle to bring her his journal. She edits his work for him.

9:30—All journals are handed in. Students move to the classroom library where they all select a book. Some students get books from their school bags. Students get into groups of two for paired reading.

9:35—Kyle has not yet chosen a book. Ms. Smith asks him to quickly pick a book and find a partner.

9:40—Kyle is sitting at his desk reading his book without a partner. Ms. Smith asks another group of boys if Kyle can join them. Kyle joins the group of boys.

9:45—As the other boys take turns reading their books, Kyle looks around the classroom. Ms. Smith is circulating the classroom and listening to the students read.

9:55—The students are asked to put their books back and to get out their spelling books. Ms. Smith cautions several boys to use inside voices while in the classroom. Ms. Smith continues to dictate the spelling words.

10:00—Ms. Smith circulates while giving the spelling test. She looks over Kyle's shoulder to see his work. She once again cautions him to pay attention to his printing. Many of the students look toward Kyle. Kyle looks hurt and embarrassed and begins erasing some of his spelling words.

Post-Observation Interview Notes:

Ms. Smith informs her mentor that Kyle's academic work is in the top of the class. He excels above most other students in mathematics. He is very bright. However, Ms. Smith feels that Kyle is too distracted and does not pay enough attention to his work. The mentor feels that there may be other explanations for his behavior.

Question 1

Ms. Smith is concerned about the fact that Kyle often comes to school tired, without breakfast, poorly groomed, and inattentive. Provide two ways in which Ms. Smith can connect Kyle's school life with his home life for the benefit of his learning. For each option, explain how it will help Kyle's learning. Base your response on the principles of fostering positive relationships with family to support learning and well-being.

Question 2

Ms. Smith is concerned that Kyle does not seem interested in his work.

Explain two ways in which Ms. Smith might motivate Kyle to become more interested in his work.

For each option, explain how Ms. Smith could modify her instruction to better meet Kyle's needs. Base your response on the principles of motivation and learning theory.

Case History 5–9

Mr. Dueck is a first-year teacher in a middle school. The following is a lesson plan from his unit on matter for his grade five students.

Lesson Plan—What Is Matter?

Statement of Children's Conceptions/Views

Going into this lesson, the students realize that all objects are not the same. They are aware that objects fit into particular groups but are not sure what the correct groupings are.

Lesson Objectives

After using concrete objects and participating in a discussion, the students will

➤ Be able to state what matter is

➤ Understand that there are three states of matter (solids, liquids, and gases)

➤ Be able to state the characteristics of each state of matter

➤ Be able to place particular examples of matter into the appropriate group

Materials

➤ Containers of water

➤ Balloons filled with air

➤ Rocks

Lesson Procedure:

1. Provide each student with a list of the items they gave as examples of matter during the exploration activity.

2. Ask the students to choose partners and categorize the examples of matter into solids, liquids, and gases.

3. Discuss their categorizations and explain to them through direct teaching that matter takes up space and has mass. Students should record this information in their notebooks for future use.

4. Give each group a solid, a liquid, and a gas (refer to the list of required materials).

5. Have each group examine the items and record the similarities and differences.

6. On the board, note the students' findings:

   ➤ A solid has a definite shape and size.

   ➤ A liquid has a definite size and takes the shape of the container.

   ➤ A gas has no definite size and takes the shape of the container.

7. Have a group discussion.

8. Do an assessment.

Question 1

A lesson plan should demonstrate several aspects of effective teaching. Identify one strength and one weakness of Mr. Dueck's lesson plan. Explain how each one demonstrates and does not demonstrate aspects of effective planning. Your response should be based on the principles of effective planning.

Question 2

Identify two ways in which Mr. Dueck could strengthen his assessment so that students have more opportunity to demonstrate their learning and knowledge. Explain how each could provide students with the opportunity to demonstrate their accomplishments. Base your assessment on the different forms of evaluation.

Grading the Short-Answer Questions

The grading for the short-answer questions is based on numerical values. A short answer can be assigned a grade between 0 and 2, where 2 is the highest possible score and 0 is the lowest. Table 5.3 summarizes how the short answers are graded.

Table 5.3 PLT Short-Answer Scores	
Score	Description
0	A response rated 0 does not respond to the question appropriately. It does not contain any supported evidence. It demonstrates little knowledge and understanding of concepts, theories, and so on.
1	A response rated 1 shows some understanding of the aspects related to the question. It responds appropriately to the question but does not provide a strong explanation. It demonstrates some knowledge and understanding of concepts, theories, and so on.
2	A response rated 2 shows a thorough understanding of the aspects related to the question. It responds appropriately to the question and provides a strong explanation along with relevant evidence. It demonstrates thorough knowledge and understanding of concepts, theories, and so on.

Test-Taking Strategies for the PLT Exams

As mentioned earlier, the PLT exam consists of both multiple-choice and short-answer questions. The short-answer questions are likely to pose the most difficulty because they require you to construct a concise, accurate response based on a lengthy case study. The following section will provide you with some exam-taking tips that you can use when completing the PLT exam.

Managing Your Time

Remember that the PLT exam is timed, and you only have two hours to complete it. Therefore, you will want to make sure that you manage your time wisely. Two hours is not a lot of time when you have to read four lengthy case studies, construct two concise, accurate responses for each one, and then answer an additional 24 multiple-choice questions. Here are a few tips you can use when it comes to managing your time:

➤ Start managing your time right from the start. Before you begin the exam, do a quick time check. This way, you'll know exactly when you started the exam.

➤ Do a time check at specific intervals, such as every 15 or 30 minutes.

➤ Because there are four case studies and 120 minutes in which to answer all the questions, a good guideline to follow is to spend 30 minutes on each case study. Check your progress after the first 30 minutes. At this point, you should be at least a quarter of the way through the exam.

➤ After you've answered a few questions, you should be ready to re-evaluate your strategy and determine how you can answer the questions more efficiently.

Strategies for Short-Answer Questions

The short-answer questions with which you are presented will be based on the case studies in the exam, just as you saw in our examples earlier in the chapter. The most difficult aspect of answering these questions will be to formulate an appropriate response in a short amount of time. The answer does not necessarily have to be lengthy, but it does have to be concise and accurate. It must answer the question that is asked.

The following examples show the type of short-answer questions you are likely to encounter on the exam.

Question 1

Mrs. Danchura briefly mentions some of the modifications that have been made for a few of her students. Review the comments put forth by Mrs. Danchura for Sally and David. For each student, describe one way in which Mrs. Danchura might have modified the lesson differently in order to provide a better learning experience. Your response should be based on the principles of varied instructions for different kinds of learners.

Question 2

Mrs. Buckingham has developed a Project Plan. Identify two strengths of her Project Plan. Describe how each strength demonstrates an aspect of effective planning. Your response should be based on the principles of planning instruction.

Here are some tips you can use when tackling the short-answer questions:

➤ Read the questions before you read over the case studies. That way, you can begin thinking about your answers as you read.

➤ Make notes throughout the case study, highlighting the information that is pertinent to your answer. You can refer back to your notes and highlights when answering the questions.

➤ After you have read the case study, make a quick outline of your answer. The statements you make in your answer should be supported by examples and explanations.

➤ Refer to the case study while answering the questions.

➤ If the question asks for a specific number of items (for example, describe two ways in which the lesson plan could have been modified), make sure your response contains the required number of items.

➤ Reread your answer. You can keep it brief, but make sure it answers the question being asked.

When you are formulating your answers, it is very important that you back up your statements through examples and explanations. Anyone can create a list of information, but a good answer will support the statements that are made. Also, make sure your answer applies to the specific case study.

PRAXIS II Subject Assessments

The PRAXIS II Subject Assessments section is designed to measure your knowledge in the subject area you plan to teach and also how well you teach in that area. More than 140 subject tests are available. The subject assessments you are required to take will depend on your teaching specialty and also the state requirements for the state(s) in which you potentially want to teach. The following sections will discuss some of the Subject Assessment tests. To get a comprehensive look at all of the subject matter exams, be sure to visit the Praxis II section on the ETS website (www.ets.org).

See Appendix A for a complete list of exams and exam codes that are available.

When preparing for any of the subject assessments, be sure to visit the ETS website at www.ets.org. Sample questions are available for each of the different exams. Use them to test your knowledge and become familiar with the type of questions you are likely to encounter.

Art

There are three different PRAXIS II exams that cover different areas of art, as outlined in Table 5.4. These exams are geared toward those who are completing a teacher education program and plan to teach art.

Table 5.4 PRAXIS II Subject Assessment: Art Exams	
Exam	**Description**
Art: Content Knowledge	This exam tests your knowledge about concepts related to the subject matter of art.
Art: Content, Traditions, Criticism, and Aesthetics	This exam tests your ability to analyze and discuss various works of art.
Art Making	This exam tests your knowledge and skills associated with the elements and principles of design.

Art: Content Knowledge

The Art: Content Knowledge exam is designed to measure your knowledge about concepts that are deemed important to the subject matter of art. Candidates who are taking this exam normally have a degree in art or art education. The exam consists of 120 multiple-choice questions from three different content areas, which you must answer in 120 minutes.

For the Art: Content Knowledge exam, you need to be familiar with all Discipline-Based Art Education (DBAE) areas, such as art production, art criticism/aesthetics, and art history. You should also study multicultural art; know various artists such as Romare Bearden and so on; and know the historical context of various art forms, including the Holocaust, the Harlem Renaissance, WPA murals, the feminist movement, and so on.

The following content areas are covered on the Art: Content Knowledge exam:

➤ Traditions in Art, Architecture, Design, and the Making of Artifacts

➤ Art Criticism and Aesthetics

➤ The Making of Art

If you are looking for a book that covers much of the information you need to know for the Art: Content Knowledge exam, try *World of Art* by Henry Sayre.

Art: Content, Traditions, Criticism, and Aesthetics

The Art: Content, Traditions, Criticism, and Aesthetics exam is designed for those persons who plan to teach art education. The exam consists of three 20-minute essays in which you must analyze and discuss various works of art.

Be prepared to answer questions pertaining to the content, meaning, and historical importance of different works of art.

This exam covers the following content areas:

➤ The Content of Works of Art

➤ Global Traditions in Art, Architecture, and Design

➤ Criticisms and Aesthetics

Biology

The PRAXIS II exams include five different biology exams outlined in Table 5.5. These exams are designed for those individuals who plan to teach biology. They assess whether an examinee has the necessary knowledge and understanding required for a beginning teacher of biology.

Table 5.5 PRAXIS II Subject Assessment: Biology Exams	
Exam	**Description**
Biology and General Science	This exam tests your knowledge of secondary biology and general science.
Biology: Content Essays	This exam tests your knowledge and ability to analyze biological concepts. The exam consists of three questions, one from each of the following categories: cell and molecular biology, genetic evolution, and organismal biology.
Biology: Content Knowledge Part 1	This exam tests your knowledge of biological sciences; basic principles of science; and issues and applications concerning science, technology, and society.
Biology: Content Knowledge Part 2	This exam tests your knowledge of molecular and cellular biology; classical genetics and evolution; diversity of life, plants, and animals; and ecology.
Biology: Content Knowledge	This exam tests your knowledge of the basic principles of biology.

Biology: Content Knowledge

The Biology: Content Knowledge exam is designed to assess whether a beginning teacher has the required knowledge to teach biology in a secondary school setting. The exam consists of 150 multiple-choice questions, which you have two hours to answer.

 Most of the questions on the Biology: Content Knowledge exam are based on topics that would be covered in an introductory college-level biology course. Therefore, if you have taken any biology courses during your teacher education, you should do fine. You should also be prepared to answer several questions pertaining to molecular biology and botany.

The following content areas are covered on the Biology: Content Knowledge exam:

➤ Basic Principles of Science

➤ Molecular and Cellular Biology

➤ Classical Genetics and Evolution

➤ Diversity of Life, Plants, and Animals

➤ Ecology

Mathematics

The PRAXIS II mathematics tests are geared toward those inidviduals who plan to teach middle school or secondary school mathematics. The mathematics exams are outlined in Table 5.6.

Table 5.6 PRAXIS II Subject Assessment: Mathematics Exams	
Exam	**Description**
Mathematics: Content Knowledge	This exam tests your knowledge of secondary school mathematics including problem solving, communication, reasoning, and mathematical connections.
Mathematics: Pedagogy	This exam is designed to test your knowledge of the pedagogical aspects of teaching mathematics.

(continued)

Table 5.6 PRAXIS II Subject Assessment: Mathematics Exams *(continued)*	
Exam	Description
Mathematics: Proofs, Models, and Problems Part 1	This exam tests your knowledge of the following six areas: arithmetic and basic algebra, geometry, analytical geometry, functions and their graphs, probability and statistics, and discrete mathematics.
Middle School Mathematics	This exam tests your knowledge of middle school mathematics. Exam topics include geometry, algebra, data, and problem solving.

A great website to use in preparing for the PRAXIS II math tests is www.praxismathexam.com. You'll find free practice tests that you can use to access your knowledge.

Mathematics: Content Knowledge

The Mathematics: Content Knowledge exam consists of 50 multiple-choice questions that must be answered within 120 minutes. Also note that a graphing calculator is required. This content knowledge test is specifically geared toward those individuals who plan on teaching secondary school mathematics. It tests a beginning teacher's knowledge of problem solving, communication, reasoning, and mathematical connections.

The Mathematics: Content Knowledge test covers the following content areas:

➤ Arithmetic and Basic Algebra, Geometry, Trigonometry, and Analytical Geometry

➤ Functions and Their Graphs, and Calculus

➤ Probability and Statistics, Discrete Mathematics, Linear Algebra, Computer Science, and Mathematical Reasoning and Modeling

Some of the exams permit you to use calculators, so you should spend some time getting familiar with the calculator you intend to use before taking the test.

Mathematics: Pedagogy

The Mathematics: Pedagogy exam differs in format from the other mathematics exams in that it consists of three essay questions, which you have one hour to complete. This exam deals with math instruction. The specific content categories covered by this exam include

➤ Planning Instruction

➤ Implementing Instruction

➤ Assessing Instruction

The three essay questions deal with the competencies and knowledge required of a beginning teacher in order to teach secondary mathematics.

English

The PRAXIS II English exams are designed for those examinees who plan to teach English in a secondary school. The exams assess whether a test-taker has the necessary knowledge to be a beginning teacher of English in a secondary school.

The PRAXIS II English exams are outlined in Table 5.7.

Table 5.7 PRAXIS II Subject Assessment: English Exams	
Exam	**Description**
English Language, Literature, and Composition: Content Knowledge	This exam is designed to test your knowledge of and competencies in literature and reading, the English language, and composition and rhetoric.
English Language, Literature, and Composition: Essays	This exam focuses on your ability to analyze literary texts as well as to understand and articulate arguments pertaining to key issues in the study of English.
English Language, Literature, and Composition: Pedagogy	This exam is designed to test your ability to teach literature and respond to student writing.
English to Speakers of Other Languages	This exam tests your knowledge of teaching English to Speakers of Other Languages (ESOL).

English Language, Literature, and Composition: Content Knowledge

The English Language, Literature, and Composition: Content Knowledge exam is made up of 120 multiple-choice questions that you must answer within 120 minutes. The test is designed to assess whether a beginning teacher has the skills, understanding, and competencies to teach English in a secondary school setting. The exam covers the following three content categories:

➤ Reading and Understanding Text

➤ Language and Linguistics

➤ Composition and Rhetoric

 The questions you are likely to encounter on the exam are based on content that you would find in a college-level English program. Therefore, when you are studying, you should plan to study from a college-level textbook.

English Language, Literature, and Composition: Essays

The English Language, Literature, and Composition: Essays exam consists of four essay questions you must complete in two hours. The purpose of this exam is to assess the examinee's ability to analyze literary texts and to formulate and articulate arguments pertaining to the study of English. The format for the essay questions is as follows:

➤ One essay question will ask you to interpret a piece of poetry.

➤ One essay question will ask you to interpret a piece of prose.

➤ One essay question will ask you to evaluate the argument and rhetorical features of a given passage dealing with the study of English.

➤ One question will ask you to defend your position on an issue related to the study of English.

The specific content categories that are covered on this particular exam include

➤ Interpreting Literature: Poetry

➤ Interpreting Literature: Prose

➤ Issues in English: Understanding Literary Issues

➤ Issues in English: Literary Issues and Literary Texts

 Plan to spend about 30 minutes on each essay question when you take the exam.

French

The PRAXIS II French exams are designed to assess a beginning teacher's knowledge and competencies in French. Two different French exams are available. They are outlined in Table 5.8.

Table 5.8 PRAXIS II Subject Assessment: French Exams	
Exam	Description
French: Content Knowledge	This exam measures your knowledge of various language skills and of the cultures of France and other French-speaking regions.
French: Productive Language Skills	This exam tests your ability to speak and write French.

French: Content Knowledge

The French: Content Knowledge exam contains 120 questions organized into four different sections. You have a total of two hours to answer all the questions. The suggested pacing when taking the exam is as follows: Plan to spend 30 minutes on Section I, 35 minutes on Section II, 35 minutes on Section III, and 20 minutes on Section IV.

A good study resource for the PRAXIS II French exams is Barron's *How to Prepare for the SAT II French Guide*.

➤ Interpretive Listening (in French)

➤ Structure of the Language (Grammatical Accuracy)

➤ Interpretive Reading (in French)

➤ Cultural Perspectives (in French and in English)

General Science

The general science exams included in the PRAXIS II Subject Assessments are designed to measure an examinee's knowledge and skill in secondary-level general science. The general science exams are outlined in Table 5.9.

Table 5.9 PRAXIS II Subject Assessment: General Science Exams	
Exam	**Description**
General Science: Content Essays	This exam tests your knowledge in three different areas: physical science, life science, and earth and space science.
General Science: Content Knowledge Part 1	This exam is designed to test your knowledge of secondary general science such as scientific concepts, principles, phenomena, and interrelationships. The exam covers the following: life science; earth/space science; science, technology, and society; and methodology, measurement, and safety.
General Science: Content Knowledge Part 2	This exam is designed to test your knowledge of secondary general science such as scientific concepts, principles, phenomena, and interrelationships. The exam covers the following: physics; chemistry; life science; earth/space science; and science, technology, and society.
General Science: Content Knowledge	This exam tests your knowledge of secondary general science. Exam topics include scientific concepts, principles, phenomena, and interrelationships.

General Science: Content Knowledge

The General Science: Content Knowledge exam will assess the knowledge and competencies of a beginning teacher who plans to teach general science at the secondary school level. The exam includes 120 multiple-choice questions that must be answered in 120 minutes. The test covers the following content categories:

➤ Scientific Methodology, Techniques, and History

➤ The Physical Sciences

➤ The Life Sciences

➤ The Earth Sciences

➤ Science, Technology, and Society

One of the most difficult challenges with this exam is that it covers such a wide range of material. You basically have one minute to answer each question in order to complete the entire exam. Reflecting upon and recalling information in such a short amount of time can be difficult.

Be prepared to encounter some more advanced-level general science questions that you would normally find in a college-level course such as physics, chemistry, life science, or earth science.

General Science: Content Essays

The General Science: Content Essays exam requires the examinee to answer three different essay questions, one for each of the content categories shown in the following list. You have one hour to complete all three essays. The exam is designed to measure the knowledge and skills required for a beginning teacher of secondary-level general science. You are expected to be proficient in general science topics that would be covered at the freshman college level.

You can expect to encounter questions that are more advanced than those topics you would actually be teaching in a secondary school. This is due to the fact that teachers are expected to have a higher level of understanding than the students they are teaching.

The content categories covered on this exam include

➤ Fundamental Concepts in Physical Science

➤ Fundamental Concepts in Life Science

➤ Fundamental Concepts in Earth and Space Science

Social Studies

There are several different PRAXIS II Social Studies exams that are designed to measure the knowledge and skills of a beginning teacher who is wanting to teach social studies in secondary schools.

The social studies exams are summarized in Table 5.10.

Table 5.10 PRAXIS II Subject Assessment: Social Studies Exams	
Exam	**Description**
Social Studies: Analytical Essays	This exam tests your knowledge of the United States and world subject matter as well as historical and contemporary issues.

(continued)

Table 5.10 PRAXIS II Subject Assessment: Social Studies Exams *(continued)*	
Exam	**Description**
Social Studies: Content Knowledge	This exam tests your knowledge of United States history; world history; government/civics/political science; geography; economics; and the behavioral science fields of sociology, anthropology, and psychology.
Social Studies: Interpretation and Analysis	The questions on this exam test your knowledge, skills, and abilities in the following topic areas: United States history; world history; government/civics/political science; geography; economics; and the behavioral science fields of sociology, anthropology, and psychology.
Social Studies: Interpretation of Materials	This exam tests your knowledge in the following areas: United States history, world history, government/civics/political science, geography, and economics.
Social Studies: Pedagogy	This exam measures your knowledge and ability of planning and teaching social studies to secondary-level students.

Let's look at two of these exams in more depth.

Social Studies: Content Knowledge

The Social Studies: Content Knowledge exam is designed to assess whether a beginning teacher has the knowledge and skills necessary to teach social studies at the secondary level. The exam is two hours long with a total of 130 multiple-choice questions.

Be prepared to answer multiple-choice questions that are very specific. You can find sample test questions for this exam using the Test at a Glance provided by ETS.

The following content categories are covered on the Social Studies: Content Knowledge exam:

➤ United States History

➤ World History

➤ Government/Civics/Political Science

➤ Geography

➤ Economics

➤ Behavioral Sciences

Social Studies: Analytical Essays

The Social Studies: Analytical Essays exam consists of two essay questions, which must be completed in one hour. Both of the exam questions include topics from the following disciplines: world history, United States history, government/civics/political science, geography, and economics.

This particular exam covers the following content categories:

➤ United States: History or Contemporary Issues

➤ World: History or Contemporary Issues

Music

The PRAXIS II Music exams are designed to measure the knowledge and ability of those individuals who plan to teach music. The PRAXIS II Music exams are outlined in Table 5.11.

Table 5.11 PRAXIS II Subject Assessment: Music Exams	
Exam	**Description**
Music: Analysis	This exam tests your ability to identify performance errors and analyze musical scores.
Music: Concepts and Processes	This exam tests your understanding of performance techniques and your ability to design an instructional sequence.
Music: Content Knowledge	This exam is designed to measure your knowledge of the core concepts of music education.
Music Education	This exam is geared toward those who plan to teach music in kindergarten through grade 12. The exam measures your knowledge of the core concepts of music education.

Let's investigate two of these music exams in more depth.

Music: Analysis

The Music: Analysis exam consists of three short-answer questions, which you have one hour to answer. The questions are based on the following content categories:

➤ Listening for Performance Errors

➤ Analytical Musical Scores

The questions are based on two brief musical scores—an instrumental chamber ensemble and a choral ensemble. Each score contains errors that you are required to identify and describe. You are also expected to state exactly where the errors occur in a score.

Music: Content Knowledge

The Music: Content Knowledge exam is designed to assess the knowledge and skills of individuals who plan to teach music in kindergarten through grade 12. The test covers music-related content that you would likely find in undergraduate music and music education courses. This particular test tends to cover content that is common across all grades. Approximately half of the questions on this test are based on recorded excerpts.

There are 135 multiple-choice questions on this test, and they are divided into two different sections. You have a total of 120 minutes to answer all the questions. The first section contains 40 questions that are each based on a musical excerpt. The second section contains 95 multiple-choice questions that are not based on listening to excerpts. Be prepared to encounter questions in this section that are accompanied by printed musical excerpts or diagrams.

The Music: Content Knowledge test covers the following content categories:

➤ Music History and Literature

➤ Music Theory

➤ Performance

➤ Music Learning, K–12

➤ Professional Practices

Be prepared to answer questions pertaining to Edwin Gorden and The Music Learning Theory.

Physical Education

The PRAXIS II Physical Education exams are designed to measure the knowledge and skills of those individuals who plan to teach physical education in kindergarten through grade 12. The physical education exams are outlined in Table 5.12.

Table 5.12 PRAXIS II Subject Assessment: Physical Education Exams	
Exam	**Description**
Physical Education: Content Knowledge	This exam covers topics from the following categories: fitness, fundamental movements, and sports that comprise the content of physical education classes; knowledge of areas in the natural and social sciences that provide the foundation for teaching these activities; and knowledge of crucial topics in health and safety.
Physical Education: Movement-Forms Analysis and Design	This exam covers the following topics: fitness, fundamental movements, and sports that comprise the content of physical education classes; knowledge of areas in the natural and social sciences that provide the foundation for teaching these activities; and knowledge of crucial topics in health and safety. It is designed to measure how well you can select activities for a specific purpose, meet student needs, and provide support for your decisions.
Physical Education: Movement-Forms Video Evaluation	This exam assesses the following: your ability to identify unsafe aspects of movement and performance, your ability to communicate to performers, and your ability to identify critical features in movement forms and exercises.

Physical Education: Content Knowledge

The Physical Education: Content Knowledge exam is designed to assess an examinee's knowledge and understanding of K–12 physical education. There are 120 multiple-choice questions that must be answered in 120 minutes.

The content categories covered in this exam include

➤ Fundamental Movement, Motor Development, and Motor Learning

➤ Movement Forms

➤ Fitness and Exercise Science

➤ Social Science Foundations

➤ Biomechanics

➤ Health and Safety

This exam covers both elementary and secondary physical education. However, elementary physical education is more prominent on the test. The exam also emphasizes the seven most common activities: soccer, tennis, track and field, basketball, volleyball, swimming, and softball.

Middle School Education

There are five different PRAXIS II exams geared toward middle school education. These exams are designed to test the knowledge and understanding of individuals planning to teach in a middle school. The middle school PRAXIS II exams are outlined in Table 5.13.

Table 5.13 PRAXIS II Subject Assessment: Middle School Education Exams	
Exam	**Description**
Middle School: Content Knowledge	This exam is designed for those planning to teach the middle years. The questions are based on topics from the following subject areas: literature and language studies, mathematics, history/social studies, and science.
Middle School English Language Arts	This exam consists of questions from the following three categories: knowledge of concepts relevant to reading and literature study, knowledge of the development and use of the English language, and knowledge of concepts relevant to the study of composition and rhetoric.
Middle School Mathematics	This exam tests your knowledge of middle school mathematics. The exam questions measure your knowledge of the following topics: arithmetic and basic algebra, geometry, functions and graphs, data, probability, discrete mathematics, and problem solving.
Middle School Science	This exam tests your knowledge of scientific principles, facts, methodology, philosophy, and scientific concepts. Questions on the exam are based on the following topics: scientific methodology, techniques, and history; basic principles; physical sciences; life sciences; science, technology, and society; and short content essays.
Middle School Social Studies	This exam tests your knowledge of United States history, world history, government/civics, geography, economics, sociology, and anthropology.

Middle School: Content Knowledge

The Middle School: Content Knowledge exam consists of 120 multiple-choice questions from the four main subject areas of literature and language arts, mathematics, history/social studies, and science. You have a total of 120 minutes to complete all the questions.

Middle School Mathematics

The Middle School Mathematics exam covers the following content categories:

➤ Arithmetic and Basic Algebra

➤ Geometry and Measurement; Coordinate Geometry, Functions and Graphs

➤ Data, Probability, Statistical Concepts; Discrete Mathematics, and Computer Science

➤ Problem-Solving Exercises (including Content-Specific Pedagogy)

 If you are not familiar with the different mathematical formulas, spend some time brushing up on them. You will encounter questions that require you to recall such formulas.

Middle School English Language Arts

The Middle School English Language Arts exam is made up of 90 multiple-choice questions and two short-answer questions. You have 120 minutes to answer all 92 questions.

The exam covers the following objectives:

➤ Reading and Literature

➤ Language and Linguistics

➤ Composition and Rhetoric

➤ Short Essays—Literary Analysis and Rhetorical Analysis

Like the other middle school exams, this exam is designed to test whether an examinee has the knowledge and competencies required for a beginning teacher to teach language arts at the middle school level.

As already mentioned, this exam consists of two short-answer questions along with multiple-choice questions. One of the short-answer questions asks you to interpret a piece of literary or nonfiction text. The question asks you to discuss the rhetorical elements of a piece of writing. Plan to spend approximately 30 minutes answering the short-answer questions and 90 minutes answering the multiple-choice questions.

 When preparing for the Middle School English Language Arts exam, I would recommend picking up a middle school literature textbook and paying close attention to the literature and grammar handbooks that are usually at the back of such a textbook. You will find that a lot of this information is on the PRAXIS II exam.

Elementary Education

There are several different PRAXIS II exams pertaining to elementary education. These exams are geared toward those individuals planning to teach in the primary through upper elementary grades.

The elementary education exams are outlined in Table 5.14.

Table 5.14 PRAXIS II Subject Assessment: Elementary Education Exams	
Exam	**Description**
Elementary Education: Content Area Exercises	This exam tests your knowledge and understanding of elementary education.
Elementary Education: Content Knowledge	This exam is designed for those individuals who plan to teach primary through upper elementary grades. The questions cover topics in the following four subject areas: language arts/reading, mathematics, social studies, and science.
Elementary Education: Curriculum, Instruction and Assessment	This exam tests your knowledge of curriculum planning, instruction design, and assessment of student learning.
Elementary Education: Curriculum, Instruction, and Assessment K-5	This exam tests your knowledge of curriculum planning, instruction design, and assessment of student learning with a focus on kindergarten through grade 5.

Let's examine two of these exams further.

Elementary Education: Content Knowledge

The Elementary Education: Content Knowledge exam consists of 120 multiple-choice questions, which must be answered in 120 minutes. The questions focus on the four main subject areas. Each subject area makes up 25% of the test questions.

The Elementary Education: Content Knowledge exam covers the following objectives:

➤ Language Arts

➤ Mathematics

➤ Social Studies

➤ Science

Elementary Education: Curriculum, Instruction, and Assessment

The Elementary Education: Curriculum, Instruction, and Assessment exam is made up of 110 multiple-choice questions. Again, you have a total of 120 minutes to answer all the questions.

The exam covers the following content categories:

➤ Reading and Language Arts, Curriculum, Instruction, and Assessment

➤ Mathematics Curriculum, Instruction, and Assessment

➤ Science Curriculum, Instruction, and Assessment

➤ Social Studies Curriculum, Instruction, and Assessment

➤ Arts and Physical Education Curriculum, Instruction, and Assessment

➤ General Information About Curriculum, Instruction, and Assessment

This exam is typically geared toward those individuals who plan to teach in the elementary grades. Test-takers have usually completed some type of teacher education program. The exam assesses an examinee's understanding of curriculum planning, instructional design, and student assessment. Most of the questions are in the context of a specific subject area.

Exam Prep Questions

In other chapters, you have found practice questions at this point. Because this chapter is a survey of many types of exams, we really can't present practice questions as such. However, here is a review list of important items to keep in mind for exam day:

➤ Be prepared for the type of questions you will encounter on the exam. Some exams consist of multiple-choice, short-answer, and/or essay questions.

➤ Know how much time you have to complete the entire exam.

➤ During the exam, keep an eye on the time. Have some idea in mind as to how much time you plan to spend on each question.

➤ For essay and short-answer questions, make sure you are providing the information that is being requested. Stay on track and answer the questions.

➤ For essay and short-answer questions, make sure you provide evidence to support your ideas and statements.

PRAXIS III Classroom Performance Assessment

Terms you'll need to understand:

- ✓ Learning outcomes
- ✓ Teacher professionalism
- ✓ Learning activities
- ✓ Prior knowledge

Techniques you'll need to master:

- ✓ Understand the four domains that make up the PRAXIS III exam
- ✓ Understand and meet the 19 criteria that span the four domains
- ✓ Use lesson plans to organize content for student learning
- ✓ Identify the importance of the classroom environment in student learning
- ✓ Establish a safe classroom environment that is conducive to learning
- ✓ Present content in a variety of ways to meet student diversity
- ✓ Maintain teacher professionalism

The PRAXIS III Classroom Performance Assessment is required before you can apply for teacher licensure. It is very different from the PRAXIS I and PRAXIS II components in that there is no exam for PRAXIS III. This is a direct classroom assessment designed to assess your skills in a classroom setting.

The PRAXIS III Classroom Performance Assessment uses three different means to assess a beginning teacher. The results of the assessment are based on direct observation of a beginning teacher's classroom practice, a review of the documentation prepared by the teacher, and a semistructured interview.

The PRAXIS III Classroom Performance Assessment takes into account 19 different assessment criteria from the following four domains:

➤ *Domain A*—Organizing content knowledge for student learning

➤ *Domain B*—Creating an environment for student learning (the classroom environment)

➤ *Domain C*—Teaching for student learning (instruction)

➤ *Domain D*—Teacher professionalism (professional responsibilities)

 Review the 19 criteria outlined in this chapter. When you feel that you are meeting all the criteria, you are ready to take the exam.

Organizing Content Knowledge for Student Learning

Domain A is "organizing content knowledge for student learning." The criteria found in this domain will basically assess your ability when it comes to planning to teach. In other words, how much do you think about the content before it is taught? Do you think creatively about the content? This will be evident in how you organize your lessons and content for the students you are teaching.

 This domain also focuses on the actual lesson plan. A well-developed lesson plan will cover all the criteria outlined in Domain A.

Domain A Criteria

Domain A covers five different criteria that relate to planning, as follows:

➤ *Becoming familiar with relevant aspects of students' background knowledge and experiences.* Prior knowledge is essential for learning. This criterion assesses your ability to gain information about students' prior knowledge and skills on a particular topic. You should be familiar with various techniques for learning students' backgrounds and previous experiences. Do you understand the importance of prior knowledge? Do you know how to gain background information about students' prior knowledge?

➤ *Articulating clear learning goals that are appropriate to the students for the lesson.* The learning goals are the outcomes you hope to achieve from the lesson. In other words, what do you want the students to learn? Be sure to clearly articulate the learning outcomes for a lesson and not mix them up with the activities that students will be doing. Are your learning outcomes clearly stated? Are they appropriate?

➤ *Demonstrating an understanding of the connections between the content that was learned previously, the current content, and the content that remains to be learned in the future.* This criterion deals with sequencing content and identifying the relationships between lessons. Is there a connection between the past and future lessons?

➤ *Creating or selecting teaching methods, learning activities, and instructional materials or other resources that are appropriate to the students and are aligned with the goals of the lesson.* This criterion deals with a teacher's ability to use teaching methods, activities, materials, and so on that relate to each other as well as to the learning outcomes of the lesson. This includes having an awareness of the differences between students in the classroom and using a variety of methods, activities, and materials to meet these differences. Are your teaching methods, materials, and resources aligned with the learning outcomes? Are they appropriate for the students you are teaching?

➤ *Creating or selecting evaluation strategies that are appropriate for the students and are aligned with the goals of the lesson.* Evaluation strategies are used to determine whether students have met the learning outcomes for a lesson. The evaluation strategies must relate to the learning outcomes of the lesson. Because students have a diverse set of needs, a variety of learning outcomes should be used to accommodate them. Are your evaluation methods systematic? Are they appropriate for the learning outcomes and students?

Most states have performance and curriculum standards to which teachers must adhere, and both short-term and long-term lesson planning must take these standards into account. This is a fairly important point for new teachers to know because teacher interviewers will most likely question you about your plans for incorporating state standards into your full curriculum and daily plans and activities.

Domain A Self-Evaluation

In preparing yourself for the PRAXIS III exam, you can use the following questions when planning your lessons as a means of self-evaluation to ensure that you are meeting the criteria in Domain A.

➤ Describe the skills and backgrounds of the students in your classroom.

➤ What learning outcomes do you want to achieve from the lesson and why?

➤ How does the lesson relate to previous lessons and lessons that will be taught in the future?

➤ Devise a lesson plan that organizes the lesson. Include teaching methods you will use, materials, and learning activities.

➤ How do you plan to evaluate your students' understanding of the lesson content?

Creating an Environment for Student Learning

The criterion in Domain B deals with the classroom environment. One of the goals of a teacher is to establish an environment that facilitates learning. Therefore, your classroom environment is one of the things upon which you will be evaluated.

A good learning environment provides both physical and emotional safety for students. This is done by establishing a level of fairness in the classroom, standards for behavior in the classroom, and a level of respect. The classroom environment must promote self-esteem among all students. There should be a sense of community in the classroom where both students and teacher display respect for one another as individuals.

Domain B Criteria

There are five different criteria in Domain B upon which you will be evaluated. The specific criteria for this domain are discussed in the following list.

➤ *Creating a climate that promotes fairness*—This criterion deals with a teacher's ability to create a classroom environment that promotes and facilitates fairness among all students regardless of race or gender. Is your behavior towards all students fair? Does your classroom environment promote fairness?

➤ *Establishing and maintaining rapport with students*—This criterion deals with a teacher's ability to positively interact with students as people. Rapport comes in many different forms, and it can be achieved in a number of different ways, but it must be appropriate for the students in the classroom. Have you successfully established rapport with students? Do you use a variety of techniques to establish rapport?

➤ *Communicating challenging learning expectations to each student*—This criterion deals with a teacher's ability to present students with challenging learning outcomes and communicating a belief that all students can achieve success. Having high standards for students and creating an environment that encourages them to strive for success can in turn make them produce high-quality work and take pride in what they accomplish. Do you encourage all students in the classroom to meet high learning outcomes?

➤ *Establishing and maintaining consistent standards of classroom behavior*—This criterion deals with a teacher's ability to develop standards for behavior in the classroom and consistently maintain those standards. Do you respond appropriately to misbehavior? Do you demonstrate respect for all students?

➤ *Making the physical environment as safe and conducive to learning as possible*—The focus of this criterion is on the physical setting where student learning is to take place. Is the learning environment safe? Is it conducive to learning?

Teaching for Student Learning

Domain C focuses on the actual teaching and on helping students to understand the content and move beyond their current understanding and knowledge of a topic. The assessment for this domain is based on classroom observation.

Domain C Criteria

Domain C consists of five different criteria designed to evaluate your teaching abilities, as follows:

➤ *Making learning goals and instructional procedures clear to students*—The focus of this criterion is on a teacher's ability to clearly communicate learning outcomes and instructional procedures for learning activities to students. Are your goals and procedures accurate, and can all students perform them?

➤ *Making content comprehensible to students*—This criterion focuses on a teacher's ability to make the lesson content understandable to students. This involves presenting the content in such a way that it is meaningful to the students. Remember, one of the best ways to do this is to call on the prior knowledge and experiences of students. Is the lesson content accurate and clear to students? Is the lesson logical and coherent?

➤ *Encouraging students to extend their thinking*—The focus of this criterion is on a teacher's ability to use a variety of instructional techniques to get students thinking independently, creatively, and/or critically.

➤ *Monitoring students' understanding of content through a variety of means, providing feedback to students to assist learning, and adjusting learning activities as the situation demands*—The focus of this criterion is on monitoring student comprehension, providing students with feedback, and making the necessary adjustments in instruction. Are you actively monitoring students' understanding of the content? Are you providing students with feedback? Are you able to adjust your instruction as necessary?

➤ *Using instructional time effectively*—This criterion evaluates how effectively a teacher uses his or her time. This includes setting an appropriate pace for instruction and having a balance between instructional and non-instructional time. Do you perform non-instructional procedures efficiently? Is the pace of your instruction appropriate?

Teacher Professionalism

The focus of Domain D is on teacher professionalism. In order to improve your skills in any type of job, you need to take the time to reflect on your current practices and skills. As a teacher, you need to reflect on your current teaching practices in order to make improvements over time. Teacher professionalism also means sharing information with other individuals including co-workers, professionals, and parents.

Domain D Criteria

Domain D consists of four different criteria designed to evaluate your teacher professionalism, as follows:

➤ *Reflecting on the extent to which the learning goals are met*—As a teacher, you need to reflect on classroom events to determine whether learning outcomes are being met. Do you reflect on lessons as a means of improving future instruction?

➤ *Demonstrating a sense of efficacy*—This criterion focuses on the ways in which a teacher demonstrates a sense of efficacy by looking for new ways to help students learn. The teacher realizes that he or she is in control of the learning environment and demonstrates this by providing students with a variety of learning experiences. Do you look for new, specific, and practical ways of helping students in your classroom succeed?

➤ *Building professional relationships with colleagues to share teaching insights and to coordinate learning activities for students*—This criterion focuses on a teacher's relationships with other professionals and how to work together for the benefit of the students. Are you aware of the resources available to you? Do you use them efficiently? Do you interact with other professionals to provide better learning and instruction for your students?

➤ *Communicating with parents or guardians about student learning*—This criterion focuses on a teacher's communication with parents and guardians. Are you aware of the different forms of communication available? Do you communicate with parents about classroom events?

 Make sure you are familiar with the 19 criteria you will be evaluated on. These are the things your assessor will be looking for during your classroom assessment.

PRAXIS III Tips

If you are preparing to take the PRAXIS III exam, you have obviously gone through formal teacher training. This component of the exam can be extremely nerve-wracking because it is based on a direct evaluation of your teaching practices. An assessor will come into your classroom and observe you. If you are confident that you have met all 19 criteria, it should be safe to say that you can relax, and the assessment will more than likely go smoothly.

There is no right or wrong way of teaching, so the PRAXIS III exam can be difficult to prepare for. You will need to rely on what you have been taught during your formal instruction and what you have learned through your classroom experiences. The best advice is to relax and just do what you have been trained to do. Keep a positive attitude toward the assessment and use it as a tool for improving your current teaching practices.

Practice Exam #1

PRAXIS Reading

For questions 1 and 2, determine the correct definition for the word given.

1. Technological advances that signify progress in a modern society don't come without consequences. These advances can sometimes have adverse affects on the environment and subsequently the means to supply future wants and needs. Therefore, it is to the benefit of current society, and the benefit of future generations, that we make it a priority to develop the stewardship necessary to use resources in a way that sustains our environment.

   The word *sustains* means
   - ❏ A. Ends
   - ❏ B. Experiences
   - ❏ C. Suffers
   - ❏ D. Maintains
   - ❏ E. Quits

2. After the long journey home, the old man was very gaunt and pale-looking.

   What is the meaning of the word *gaunt*?
   - ❏ A. Healthy
   - ❏ B. Plump
   - ❏ C. Thin
   - ❏ D. Tired
   - ❏ E. Active

3. The security guard's expression deterred rowdiness at the game.

The word *deterred* means

❑ A. Encouraged
❑ B. Prevented
❑ C. Heartened
❑ D. Resulted in
❑ E. Inspired

Questions 4 and 5 require you to read the entire passage, and then select the best answers to the questions following the passage.

From a military standpoint, during Roman Emperor Justinian's reign, recoveries were made in Africa and Italy, and a foothold was established in Spain. These actions, however, exhausted the eastern Roman Empire in Italy and gave the Persians in the east a chance to gather strength.

During Justinian's wars, raids also devastated the Balkans; the aqueducts around Rome suffered damage, returning parts of the countryside to marshes; and, probably most significantly, the Italian economy suffered greatly as well.

The impact of the prolonged wars on the treasury of the empire was a result of several factors. Armies had to be fed and paid. The money to do so was taken from the people in the form of property taxes in Constantinople in the eastern part of the empire, the area then under threat from the Persians. Only about a third of the taxes due the empire were actually being collected.

Additionally, the bubonic plague, which began in Constantinople in 542 and worked its way through the empire until 558, ended the period of economic growth and intensified the problems caused by already overstrained resources. Although Justinian and John the Economist devised ways to collect money, Justinian also had a need for allowances for army supplies and military pay. Raising money during an expanding economy hadn't been the problem it now proved to be.

4. What is the main idea of the passage?
❑ A. The war had prolonged effects.
❑ B. Justinian needed to raise money for his army.
❑ C. Justinian and John the Economist devised a number of different ways to increase revenue.
❑ D. People were being overtaxed.

5. What is the best summary of the third paragraph?
❑ A. Justinian was looking for new ways to raise money.
❑ B. Money was taken from the people.
❑ C. The war cost the empire a lot of money.
❑ D. The people were being overtaxed.

Questions 6 through 20 require you to read the passages provided and then select the best answers to the questions following the passages.

Justinian appeared to have difficulty establishing priorities. Goals like the one of reconquering the west were put into action without the means in place to provide his commander with enough troops to do the job effectively. Not only were there not enough troops to accomplish the goal, but supplies and pay for those troops were inadequate as well.

Beyond that, Justinian did not seem to have a clear plan of action before he began a conquest, and many decisions were made without consideration of the consequences. One commander, Belisarius, was assigned to different areas of the country. First, he was given the job of winning the west, only to be recalled to take command against the Persians. Belisarius was recalled to Italy in 544 A.D. and then later ordered to fight the Vandals in North Africa.

Rather than making the money and energy commitment necessary to win back the west and become emperor of the Roman Empire, Justinian instead split his forces, didn't supply those forces adequately, and spent large amounts of the tax dollars on the reconstruction of Constantinople.

The Nika riot in January of 532 A.D. resulted from further lack of Justinian's leadership. Rival chariot race supporters took part in rowdy street demonstrations that escalated into riots. When city authorities attempted to take custody of some rioters with the intention of executing them, the riots intensified. Justinian dismissed two of those authorities in an effort to appease the rioters, but the riots continued for several days. As Justinian lost his ability to deal with or make decisions about the situation, members of his staff threatened to leave the palace. The situation was diffused when Justinian's wife Theodora took part in a formal debate in which she emphasized that the emperor should remain in place, even despite the threat of death. Her speech so rallied his troops that Justinian was able to maintain his authority as emperor. However, her actions also resulted in Theodora gaining more authority in the affairs of the empire.

6. When was Belisarius recalled to Italy?

   ❑ A. 532 A.D.
   ❑ B. 544 A.D.
   ❑ C. 542 A.D.
   ❑ D. 534 A.D.

7. Who took command against the Persians?

   ❏   A. Nika
   ❏   B. Theodora
   ❏   C. Justinian
   ❏   D. Belisarius

8. Why was Justinian's conquest unsuccessful?

   ❏   A. Justinian fractured his forces.
   ❏   B. Justinian did not have a clear plan in mind.
   ❏   C. Justinian did not provide his commander with enough troops.
   ❏   D. Justinian did not supply his troops with adequate pay.
   ❏   E. All of the above.

9. What is the main idea of the fourth paragraph?

   ❏   A. Justinian's actions indicated that he could no longer deal with his staff.
   ❏   B. Theodora's leadership skills rallied the troops.
   ❏   C. Justinian attempted to appease the rioters.
   ❏   D. Justinian's actions proved that he lacked leadership skills.

Windows XP has a utility to back up customized settings called the Save My Settings wizard. However, when undertaking the task of rebuilding a user's system, beware of power users with a programming background or power users who currently use files that contain macros. The utility, which is great for default user settings, custom templates, and custom toolbars, may not be adequate for add-ins.

For example, an application developer might write an Excel macro to control the most important component of Microsoft Word, its automation server. As a result, Excel acts as the client application and Word as the server application. VB applications can also be written that control Excel. This process of one application controlling another was once known as OLE Automation; it is now referred to as Automation.

Automation allows a user to develop complex macros that can control objects from other applications. Because such macros allow the user to interact with multiple applications and not even realize the interaction is occurring, they become powerful tools when creating application files. Automation provides a seamless interface for the end user.

Automation most often occurs in complex documents. Automation can assist the end user, but it complicates the IT technician's job. One example would be when a developer uses Automation so that behind the scenes the Access database populates an Excel application; the end user could be unaware of this interaction with the Access database. Therefore, if Access is not reinstalled on the system, the Excel file will not run properly. Without Access installed, when the macro is executed, it will cease executing when it tries to locate the library file for the Access application and will generate an error message.

Add-ins are also often used for automated mail. Redemption, for example, allows Outlook VBA projects to bypass Microsoft's built-in safety features. During most programmed automated mail tasks, prompts appear that warn when the address book is being interrogated or when another program is trying to send out mail. When Redemption is installed and used to program such events, it eliminates these warning messages.

Before the system was rebuilt, it worked. When it comes to making it work again, it is the programmer/developer's job to ensure that add-ins and reference library files work seamlessly. Serious errors will occur if these add-ins or reference library files are missing from a system; any file that uses the library files will no longer function properly.

If library files don't function properly, one can rectify that problem by determining which files are missing, and then reinstalling and reactivating the user in the application. After the appropriate library files are installed, follow these steps:

1. Open the file that contained the error message about the missing reference library file.

2. Open the Visual Basic Editor (VBE) window. Click the Tools menu, select Macro, and then click the Visual Basic Editor submenu option.

3. Select the References option from the Tools menu.

4. Scroll through the available references and find the required object library file.

5. Check the box beside the reference.

6. Click OK to close the References dialog box.

After completing these steps, execute the macro that had the reference library error message. This should eliminate the problem without modifying the original code. If further problems persist, consult the programmer/developer of the application to verify whether or not the reference library priority is in the correct position in the References dialog box.

10. The step-by-step directions explain how to
   - ❏ A. Reinstall Windows XP
   - ❏ B. Reinstall a library file
   - ❏ C. Use the Save My Settings wizard
   - ❏ D. Install Redemption
   - ❏ E. Create a macro

11. What is the purpose of Automation?

❏ A. Automation is used to eliminate reference library errors.

❏ B. The process of one application controlling another is referred to as Automation.

❏ C. It allows you to develop complex macros that have the ability to control objects from a variety of applications.

❏ D. It allows you to automatically transfer your settings from one computer to another.

12. What is the main idea of the fourth paragraph?

❏ A. Automation can cause numerous problems when not properly used.

❏ B. Automation allows you to develop complex macros that have the ability to control objects from a variety of applications.

❏ C. Although Automation can make it easier for the end users, it can make things more difficult for IT staff.

❏ D. An Excel file may not run if Access is not installed on the computer.

13. What is the meaning of the word *daunting*?

❏ A. Overwhelming

❏ B. Comfortable

❏ C. Simple

❏ D. Demoralizing

During Justinian's reign, the Ostrogoths under the leadership of King Theodoric ruled Italy. King Theodoric attempted to maintain the remnants of the Roman civilization by fostering agriculture and commerce, repairing public buildings and roads, supporting education, and preserving a policy of religious toleration. However, because King Theodoric was an Arian Christian and the local bishops and religious leaders were Catholics, despite Rome flourishing under his rule, many did not welcome Theodoric's rule. Justinian and other leaders in the east also viewed King Theodoric with hostility because they wanted to reconquer Rome for the empire.

Conquering the Ostrogoths was part of Justinian's goal of restoring the Roman Empire. Justinian, who was from a western province and spoke Latin, viewed himself as the rightful heir to the throne in Rome.

14. In the passage, the word *fostering* means

❏ A. Discouraging

❏ B. Allowing

❏ C. Granting

❏ D. Promoting

15. What is the main idea of this passage?

❏ A. King Theodoric ruled Italy.

❏ B. King Theodoric was an Arian Christian.

❏ C. Justinian planned to reconquer the west to restore the Roman Empire.

❏ D. Justinian was neglecting the eastern empire.

16. Which of the following statements is true regarding the rule of Italy during the time of Justinian?

❏ A. King Theodoric forced all people to become Arian Christians.

❏ B. Italy was conquered and revived.

❏ C. The Ostrogoths were conquered.

❏ D. Italy flourished under the rule of King Theodoric.

17. What was Justinian's underlying goal?

❏ A. Justinian's goal was not to restore the Roman Empire.

❏ B. Justinian's goal was to rule the Roman Empire.

❏ C. Justinian's goal was to conquer the Ostrogoths.

❏ D. Justinian's goal was to reconquer Italy.

Many critics of U.S. higher education complain about the disproportionate emphasis on competitive athletics and other nonacademic activities at the expense of the intellect. These critics argue that this has resulted in the decline of scholarship and has caused other weaknesses, such as superficial content in the college curriculum.

On the other hand, American colleges and universities do provide opportunities for the improvement of educational competence through junior and community colleges, general education, and other means.

Because of the Fulbright Act and consequent legislation, in 1967 the United States attracted more than 100,000 students from some 170 countries to its higher education facilities. Despite criticism of the quality of education in this country, the U.S. continues to attract large numbers of foreign students.

Major universities like Oxford and Cambridge are also international centers of higher learning. European and other countries attract large numbers of foreign students, too. One in particular, the Patrice Lumumba University in Moscow, was established in October of 1960 by the Soviet Union to train students from developing countries in Latin America, Asia, and Africa. In the case of the latter, however, because the university was infamous for training the terrorist Carlos the Jackal and other guerillas and revolutionaries from those countries, after the fall of the Soviet Union, it was renamed Russian People's Friendship University. One fourth of that university's budget now comes from foreign students.

18. Where was the Patrice Lumumba University established?

❏ A. October of 1960

❏ B. Moscow

❏ C. Asia

❏ D. Germany

❏ E. 1920

19. According to the passage, which of the following factors has contributed to the decline of scholarship within the U.S.?

  ❑ A. Emphasis on sports

  ❑ B. Unqualified faculty members

  ❑ C. Higher educational facilities in other countries

  ❑ D. The lack of finances

20. What contributed to the increase in foreign students attending higher education facilities in the U.S?

  ❑ A. The support provided through state aid

  ❑ B. The large number of junior and community colleges

  ❑ C. The creation of the Fulbright Act

  ❑ D. The elevation of state colleges to university status

PRAXIS Writing

For questions 21 through 23, choose the answer that shows the part of the sentence that is not punctuated correctly.

21. If students appear bored, and uninterested, adjustments must be made to make the lessons more exciting for the students.

  ❑ A. If students appear bored,

  ❑ B. and uninterested,

  ❑ C. adjustments must be made

  ❑ D. exciting for the students

  ❑ E. No error

22. When deploying teaching strategies, teachers need to take into consideration preoperational, concrete operational, and formal operational stages of thinking.

  ❑ A. When deploying teaching strategies,

  ❑ B. into consideration preoperational,

  ❑ C. concrete operational,

  ❑ D. formal operational stages of thinking

  ❑ E. No error

23. A simple way of evaluating how much your students have learned would be to check student's marks; adjustments should be made to lessons if marks are fairly low.

  ❑ A. how much your students have learned

  ❑ B. check student's marks

  ❑ C. adjustments should be made

  ❑ D. marks are fairly low

  ❑ E. No error

For question 24, choose the correct replacement for the portion of the sentence that appears underlined.

24. Our children, <u>who are in grades 1 and 4,</u> attend elementary school in the local school division.

    ❑ A. that are in grades 1 and 4,

    ❑ B. that are in grades 1, and 4,

    ❑ C. which are in grades 1 and 4,

    ❑ D. who are in grades 1 and 4

    ❑ E. No error

For questions 25 through 32, choose the underlined item in the sentence that is incorrect.

25. "<u>Your</u> next writing <u>assignment,</u>" said our English <u>teacher,</u> "is due on Friday, <u>June 13.</u>

    ❑ A. Your

    ❑ B. assignment,"

    ❑ C. teacher,

    ❑ D. June 13.

    ❑ E. No error

26. Our <u>parents</u> plan to move to <u>there</u> summer house at the lake <u>where</u> we spent most of our <u>summers</u> as children.

    ❑ A. parents

    ❑ B. there

    ❑ C. where

    ❑ D. summers

    ❑ E. No error

27. She informed <u>her</u> <u>confident</u> of the <u>situation;</u> she was certain the information <u>would not</u> be made public.

    ❑ A. her

    ❑ B. confident

    ❑ C. situation;

    ❑ D. would not

    ❑ E. No error

28. The school where my brother used to <u>go,</u> <u>that</u> is across the street from my <u>father's</u> <u>house,</u> is closing next year.

    ❑ A. go,

    ❑ B. that

    ❑ C. father's

    ❑ D. house,

    ❑ E. No error

29. It was a <u>hot, damp</u> <u>summer; consequently,</u> there were more mosquitoes <u>than</u> normal.
    - ❑ A. hot, damp
    - ❑ B. summer;
    - ❑ C. consequently,
    - ❑ D. than
    - ❑ E. No error

30. We needed the following items for our <u>dads</u> retirement <u>party: paper plates,</u> napkins, <u>forks,</u> and knives.
    - ❑ A. dads
    - ❑ B. party:
    - ❑ C. paper plates,
    - ❑ D. forks,
    - ❑ E. No error

31. The only time <u>they</u> had time to <u>themself</u> during the day was <u>after</u> they put <u>their</u> children to bed.
    - ❑ A. they
    - ❑ B. themself
    - ❑ C. after
    - ❑ D. their
    - ❑ E. No error

32. After going <u>threw</u> all the security at the <u>airports,</u> we decided to take the train home <u>instead</u> of using <u>our</u> plane tickets.
    - ❑ A. threw
    - ❑ B. airports,
    - ❑ C. instead
    - ❑ D. our
    - ❑ E. No error

For questions 33 through 36, choose the answer that correctly replaces punctuation in the sentence that is not correct.

33. The hockey team will fold next year unless the number of fans attending the games increases.
    - ❑ A. team,
    - ❑ B. year,
    - ❑ C. unless,
    - ❑ D. games,
    - ❑ E. No error

34. Unless the student count increases over the next year the school will be closed and students will be bused to another one.
    - ❑ A. Unless,
    - ❑ B. increases,
    - ❑ C. year,
    - ❑ D. closed,
    - ❑ E. No error

35. During the past semester, our math teacher has been teaching us about addition, subtraction, division and multiplication.
    - ❑ A. semester
    - ❑ B. addition
    - ❑ C. subtraction
    - ❑ D. division,
    - ❑ E. No error

36. My great-aunt on my father's side of the family was born in Calgary Alberta on June 23, 1941.
    - ❑ A. great-aunt,
    - ❑ B. family,
    - ❑ C. in,
    - ❑ D. Calgary,
    - ❑ E. No error

For question 37, determine the correct definition for the word given.

37. The child was very slipshod when doing his homework for school the next morning.

The word *slipshod* means
    - ❑ A. Careless
    - ❑ B. Without regard
    - ❑ C. Thorough
    - ❑ D. Tired

For questions 38 through 40, choose the correct replacement for the portion of the sentence that is underlined.

38. The menu for the <u>summer party included hamburgers, hot dogs and potato chips,</u> so I had to make a trip to the grocery store.
    - ❑ A. summer's party included hamburgers, hot dogs and potato chips,
    - ❑ B. summer party included hamburgers, hot dogs, and potato chips,
    - ❑ C. summer party, included hamburgers, hotdogs and potato chips,
    - ❑ D. summer party included, hamburgers, hot dogs, and potato chips,
    - ❑ E. No error

39. The underlying theme of the story had a profound <u>effect on me;</u> it
    brought tears to my eyes.
    - ❑ A. effect on me:
    - ❑ B. affect on me;
    - ❑ C. effect on me,
    - ❑ D. affect on me,
    - ❑ E. No error

40. Our relatives, <u>that live in Southern California,</u> drove all the way to
    Minnesota for the family reunion.
    - ❑ A. they live in Southern California
    - ❑ B. who are living in Southern California
    - ❑ C. which live in southern California
    - ❑ D. who live in Southern California
    - ❑ E. No error

PRAXIS Mathematics

Questions 41 through 60 deal with mathematics. Read each question and
choose the best answer. Be sure to have extra paper nearby so you can perform calculations on it.

41. Which of the following correctly represents $\frac{1}{4}$ of 2,000,000?
    - ❑ A. 250,000
    - ❑ B. 3 / 2,000,000
    - ❑ C. 1 / 2,000,000
    - ❑ D. 500,000

42. A store is having a sale. All items are 20% off the original price.
    Employees also get an additional 20% off the lowest price. How much
    will an employee pay for an item with a regular price of $575.00?
    - ❑ A. $368.00
    - ❑ B. $352.00
    - ❑ C. $460.00
    - ❑ D. $345.00

43. The sale price for a refrigerator is $1,280.30. This is 30% off the origi-
    nal price. What is the original price of the item?
    - ❑ A. $1,500
    - ❑ B. $1,829
    - ❑ C. $1,889
    - ❑ D. $1,575

44. On Monday, John spent $5.45 on dinner. On Tuesday and Thursday, he spent a total of $8.75. On Wednesday, he spent $7.50. On Friday, he spent the same amount that he spent on Tuesday and Thursday. What was the average amount spent?

   ❏ A. $5.50
   ❏ B. $6.09
   ❏ C. $7.29
   ❏ D. $7.84

45. Round the number 1,284.846723 to the nearest tenth.

   ❏ A. 1,284
   ❏ B. 1,284.8
   ❏ C. 1,284.9
   ❏ D. 1,284.95

46. What is the mean for the following list of numbers: 12, 16, 21, 27, 31, and 33?

   ❏ A. 12
   ❏ B. 27
   ❏ C. 23.3
   ❏ D. 24
   ❏ E. 33

47. What is the correct answer for the following mathematical equation?

   $-32 + -57 = ?$

   ❏ A. 89
   ❏ B. 78
   ❏ C. –98
   ❏ D. –89

48. What is the correct answer for the following mathematical equation rounded to the nearest tenth?

   $0.0001 + 23.573 + 0.98 + 47 + 12.7995 = ?$

   ❏ A. 85
   ❏ B. 84.4
   ❏ C. 83.2
   ❏ D. 82.35

49. What is the correct answer for the following mathematical equation?

   $5.79 \times 10^6 = ?$

   ❏ A. 5,790,000
   ❏ B. .00000579
   ❏ C. 57,900,000
   ❏ D. 1,000,000

50. What is the correct mathematical equation for the following number?

    476,000 = ?

    ❏ A. 476×10^2
    ❏ B. 47.6×10^3
    ❏ C. 4.76×10^4
    ❏ D. 4.76×10^5

51. Of the following, which answer is not a fractional equivalent to $\frac{2}{3}$?

    ❏ A. $\frac{10}{15}$
    ❏ B. $\frac{12}{18}$
    ❏ C. $\frac{20}{30}$
    ❏ D. $\frac{8}{9}$

52. What is the correct answer for the following mathematical equation?

    0.25 + 0.35 = ?

    ❏ A. $\frac{7}{10}$
    ❏ B. $\frac{3}{5}$
    ❏ C. $\frac{2}{4}$
    ❏ D. $\frac{1}{3}$

53. If $x > \frac{3}{5}$, which of the following could be a value of x?

    ❏ A. $\frac{3}{6}$
    ❏ B. $\frac{4}{7}$
    ❏ C. $\frac{5}{7}$
    ❏ D. $\frac{18}{57}$

A. Company, Inc.

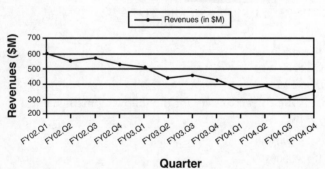

Figure 7.1 Graph of A. Company, Inc.'s revenues.

54. If the graph shown in Figure 7.1 represents *A. Company, Inc.*'s actual revenue as of the end of fiscal year 2004, which of the following statements is most accurate?

❑ A. Revenues are trending upward.

❑ B. Revenues are flat.

❑ C. Revenues are on a declining trend.

❑ D. Not enough information given.

55. What is the next number in the series: 1, 2, 4, 5, 25...?

❑ A. 6

❑ B. 26

❑ C. 36

❑ D. 625

56. 5.2 miles is equal to how many yards?

❑ A. 1,760

❑ B. 5,280

❑ C. 9,152

❑ D. 27,456

57. $\sqrt{237}$ is approximately equal to?

❑ A. 14

❑ B. 15

❑ C. 16

❑ D. 17

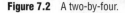

Figure 7.2 A two-by-four.

58. Determine the length of a two-by-four, which is represented by the black arrow drawn on the tape measure shown in Figure 7.2.

❑ A. 4 in.

❑ B. $8\frac{5}{8}$ in.

❑ C. $56\frac{9}{16}$ in.

❑ D. $56\frac{5}{8}$ in.

59. Laurel is landscaping her back yard. If her back yard measures 35 feet wide by 60 feet long and she wants to apply an even layer of soil across the whole back yard, what other measurement does Laurel need to determine the number of cubic yards of topsoil to order?

   ❑ A. None. She already has enough information.
   ❑ B. The cost per cubic yard of the topsoil.
   ❑ C. The amount of topsoil she used on her front yard.
   ❑ D. The desired depth of the layer of topsoil.

60. Which of the following graphs most accurately represents the data in Table 7.1?

Table 7.1	Monthly Energy Cost by Season
Season	**Monthly Energy Cost (in dollars)**
Spring	100
Summer	175
Fall	125
Winter	190

   ❑ A.

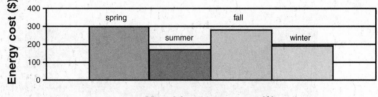

   ❑ B.

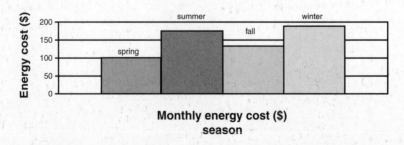

❑ C.

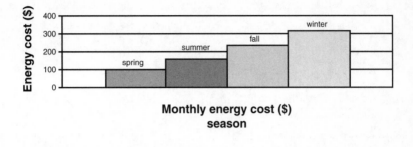

❑ D.

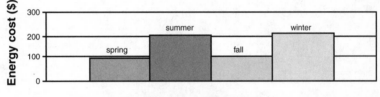

PRAXIS Essay

For questions 61 through 63, develop an essay for each of the given essay topics.

61. "Alcoholic beverages should be banned from colleges and universities, regardless of whether students are of legal drinking age."

62. "Extracurricular activities take away from the more important courses in school, such as English and math."

63. "Competitive sports should not be allowed in schools."

Answer Key for Practice Exam #1

1. D	19. A	37. A
2. C	20. C	38. B
3. B	21. A	39. E
4. A	22. E	40. D
5. C	23. B	41. D
6. B	24. E	42. A
7. D	25. D	43. B
8. E	26. B	44. B
9. D	27. B	45. B
10. B	28. B	46. C
11. C	29. E	47. D
12. C	30. A	48. B
13. A	31. B	49. A
14. D	32. A	50. D
15. C	33. E	51. D
16. D	34. C	52. B
17. B	35. D	53. C
18. B	36. D	54. C

55. B	**58.** D	**61.** Answers will vary.
56. C	**59.** D	**62.** Answers will vary.
57. B	**60.** B	**63.** Answers will vary.

PRAXIS Reading

Question 1

Answer D is correct. In the sentence, the word *sustains* means maintains. Answers A and E are incorrect because they are antonyms for the word *sustains*. Answers B and C are incorrect because they are incorrect definitions for the word *sustains*.

Question 2

Answer C is correct. In the sentence, the word *gaunt* means thin or skinny. Answer B is incorrect because plump is an antonym for the word *gaunt*. Answers A, D, and E are incorrect because they do not correctly define the word.

Question 3

Answer B is correct. In the given sentence, the word *deterred* means prevented. Answers A, C, D, and E are incorrect definitions for the word *deterred*. In fact, the word *encouraged* is an antonym for the word *deterred*.

Question 4

Answer A is correct. The main idea behind the given passage is that the war had many prolonged effects. Answers B, C, and D are incorrect because they are all supporting ideas within the passage.

Question 5

Answer C is correct. The best summary of the third paragraph is that the war had a great effect on the economy and cost the empire a lot of money. Therefore, answers A, B, and D are incorrect.

Question 6

Answer B is correct. The passage clearly states that Belisarius returned to Italy in 544 A.D. Therefore, answers A, C, and D are incorrect.

Question 7

Answer D is correct. The passage clearly states that Belisarius took command against the Persians. Therefore, answers A, B, and C are incorrect.

Question 8

Answer E is correct. Justinian was unsuccessful in his conquest because of all the listed factors. Therefore, all the answers A, B, C, and D are correct.

Question 9

Answer D is correct. The main idea of the fourth paragraph is that Justinian lacked leadership skills. Therefore, answers A, B, and C are incorrect. The incorrect answers are all supporting ideas within the fourth paragraph.

Question 10

Answer B is correct. The directions within the passage explain how to reinstall a library file. Therefore, answers A, C, D, and E are incorrect.

Question 11

Answer C is correct. The passage states that Automation allows you to develop complex macros that have the ability to control objects from a variety of applications. Therefore, answers A, B, and D are incorrect.

Question 12

Answer C is correct. The main idea of the fourth paragraph is that Automation can be useful for end users but can make an IT person's job more difficult. Therefore, answers A, B, and D are incorrect.

Question 13

Answer A is correct. The word *daunting* also means overwhelming. Therefore, answers B, C, and D are incorrect. The word *comfortable* is an antonym for the word *daunting*. Although the word *demoralizing* is a synonym for the word *daunting*, it is incorrect for the given context.

Question 14

Answer D is correct. In the passage, the word *fostering* also means promoting. Therefore, answers A, B, and C are incorrect. The word *discouraging* is an antonym for the word *fostering*.

Question 15

Answer C is correct. The main idea behind the passage is that Justinian planned to reconquer the west in order to restore the Roman Empire. Therefore, answers A, B, and D are incorrect.

Question 16

Answer D is correct. The first paragraph of the passage indicates that Italy flourished during the reign of Justinian under the rule of King Theodoric. Therefore, answers A, B, and C are incorrect.

Question 17

Answer B is correct. The underlying goal of Justinian was to become ruler of the entire Roman Empire. Therefore, answers A, C, and D are incorrect.

Question 18

Answer B is correct. The Patrice Lumumba University was established in Moscow. Therefore, answers A, C, D, and E are incorrect. The question asks *where* the university was established, not *when*.

Question 19

Answer A is correct. The first paragraph clearly states that the emphasis on competitive athletics has contributed to the decline of scholarship in the U.S. Therefore, answers B, C, and D are incorrect.

Question 20

Answer C is correct. The third paragraph of the passage states that the Fulbright Act contributed to the attracting of more than 100,000 students from some 170 countries to its higher educational facilities.

PRAXIS Writing

Question 21

Answer A is correct. A comma is not required because only two adjectives are being used. If there was a series of three or more adjectives, a comma would be required. The rest of the sentence does not contain any errors. Therefore, answers C and D are incorrect. Answer B is incorrect because a comma is required after a dependent clause at the beginning of a sentence.

Question 22

Answer E is correct. The sentence does not contain any errors as it is written. Answer A is incorrect because a comma is required after the dependent clause. Answers B and C are incorrect because commas are required if there is a list of three or more objects in a sentence.

Question 23

Answer B is correct. Because the word *students* is plural, the correct form should be *students'* instead of *student's*. Answers A, C, and D are incorrect. These parts of the sentence do not contain any errors.

Question 24

Answer E is correct. The underlined part of the sentence does not contain any errors as it is written. Therefore, answers A, B, C, and D are incorrect.

Question 25

Answer D is correct. This part of the sentence is incorrect because it requires closing quotation marks at the end of the quote. Answers A, B, and C are incorrect because these parts of the sentence do not contain any errors.

Question 26

Answer B is correct. The proper form of the word that must be used is *their* instead of *there* because it is being used to show ownership. Therefore, answers A, C, and D are incorrect because they do not represent errors within the sentence.

Question 27

Answer B is correct. The word *confident* should be replaced with the word *confidant*. Answers A, C, and D are incorrect because they do not represent errors within the given sentence.

Question 28

Answer B is correct. The word *that* should be replaced with the word *which*. Answers A, C, and D are incorrect because they do not represent errors within the given sentence.

Question 29

Answer E is correct. The sentence contains no error as it is written. Therefore, answers A, B, C, and D are incorrect.

Question 30

Answer A is correct. An apostrophe and an *s* are required at the end of the word *dad* because it is referring to ownership. Answers B, C, and D are incorrect because they do not represent errors within the given sentence.

Question 31

Answer B is correct. The correct form of the plural pronoun should be *themselves*. Answers A, C, and D are incorrect because they do not represent errors within the given sentence.

Question 32

Answer A is correct. The word *threw* is incorrect. The correct word that should be used is *through*. Answers B, C, and D are incorrect because they do not represent errors within the given sentence.

Question 33

Answer E is correct. The sentence does not contain any errors as it is written. Therefore, answers A, B, C, and D are incorrect.

Question 34

Answer C is correct. A comma is required after the dependent clause. Therefore, a comma must be placed after the word *year*. Answers A, B, and D are incorrect because they do not represent errors within the sentence.

Question 35

Answer D is correct. A comma must be placed after the word *division*. Therefore, answers A, B, and C are incorrect.

Question 36

Answer D is correct. A comma must be used to separate the proper names of places. In this instance, a comma is required between Calgary and Alberta. Therefore, answers A, B, and C are incorrect.

Question 37

Answer A is correct. In the given sentence, the word *slipshod* also means careless. Therefore, answers B, C, and D are incorrect. The word *thorough* is an antonym for slipshod.

Question 38

Answer B is correct. If a sentence contains a series of three or more nouns, commas are required to separate them. Therefore, a comma must also be placed after the word *hot dogs*. Answers A, C, and D are therefore incorrect.

Question 39

Answer E is correct. The phrase "effect on me;" is correct; a semicolon is required because the sentence contains two independent clauses. Therefore, answers A, B, C, and D are incorrect.

Question 40

Answer D is correct. Because the sentence is referring to people, the correct word that should be used is *who*. Therefore, answers A, B, and C are incorrect.

PRAXIS Mathematics

Question 41

Answer D is correct. 500,000 is $\frac{1}{4}$ of 2,000,000. You can find the answer by multiplying 2,000,000 by 0.25 (the decimal value of $\frac{1}{4}$). Therefore, answers A, B, and C are incorrect.

Question 42

Answer A is correct. An employee would pay $368.00 for the item. Therefore, answers B, C, and D are incorrect.

Question 43

Answer B is correct. The original price of the item is $1,829. Therefore, answers A, C, and D are incorrect.

Question 44

Answer B is correct. John spent an average of $6.09 each day. To find the answer, add together the amounts spent each day and divide the answer by the number of days in the week.

Question 45

Answer B is correct. The given number rounded to the nearest tenth equals 1,284.8. Therefore, answers A, C, and D are incorrect.

Question 46

Answer C is correct. The mean is the average of all values. To find the mean, simply add all the values together, and then divide the answer by the number of values you added together. The mean for the given numbers is 23.3. Therefore, answers A, B, and D are incorrect.

Question 47

Answer D is correct. A negative number plus a negative number will result in a negative answer. The correct answer is -89. Therefore, answers A, B, and C are incorrect.

Question 48

Answer B is correct. The question asks for the correct answer rounded to the nearest tenth. The correct answer to the equation is 84.4. Therefore, answers A, C, and D are incorrect.

Question 49

Answer A is correct. The correct answer for the equation is 5,790,000. 10^6 equals 1,000,000 and 1,000,000 multiplied by 5.79 equals 5,790,000. Therefore, answers B, C, and D are incorrect.

Question 50

Answer D is correct. The number 476,000 is equal to 4.76×10^5. 10^5 equals 100,000. When this number is multiplied by 4.76, the answer is 476,000. Therefore, answers A, B, and C are incorrect.

Question 51

Answer D is correct. The question asks which of the answers is not a fractional equivalent to $\frac{2}{3}$. $\frac{8}{9}$ is not a fractional equivalent to $\frac{2}{3}$. Therefore, answers A, B, and C are incorrect.

Question 52

Answer B is correct. $0.25 + 0.35 = 0.60$. This value can be converted to a fraction of $\frac{6}{10}$. When the fraction is reduced, it equals $\frac{3}{5}$. Therefore, answers A, C, and D are incorrect.

Question 53

Answer C is correct. To solve this problem, you can convert the fractions in each answer choice into decimals, which are easier to compare with each other. $\frac{3}{5} = .6$, so you know that the correct answer must be greater than .6. Answer A is incorrect because $\frac{3}{6} = .5$ and .5 is less than .6. Answer B is incorrect because $\frac{4}{7} = .571...$ and .571... is less than .6. Answer C is correct because $\frac{5}{7} = .71$ and .71 is greater than .6. Answer D is incorrect because $\frac{18}{57} = .315...$ and .315... is less than .6.

Question 54

Answer C is correct. Although the very last data point (FY04, Q4) ticked up a bit, to find the trend in the data you must consider several points on the graph. Overall, the company's revenue trend is declining. Answer A is incorrect because one point alone does not constitute a trend. Answer B is incorrect because although there is some up and down fluctuation in the data, the overall slope of the graph is negative. Answer D is incorrect because you are provided with 12 data points overall, which are more than enough to establish a trend. Remember that to establish a trend, you must be able to look back at a pattern of historical data; you do not have to know what the next few data points in the future will be.

Question 55

Answer B is correct. To arrive at the right answer to this problem, you must recognize the pattern of operations being performed on the numbers in the series. Look at the relationship between adjacent numbers to determine what operation is being performed.

Number	Next Number	Operation Performed to Get There
1	2	+ 1
2	4	2^2
4	5	+ 1
5	25	5^2
25	?	?

Now that we've picked up on that pattern, filling in the next blank is easy. Continuing your table...

Number	Next Number	Operation Performed to Get There
4	5	+ 1
5	25	5^2
25	2 6	+ 1

Answers A, C, and D are incorrect because they deviate from the pattern we discovered.

Question 56

Answer C is correct. To solve this problem you must know that 1 mile = 1,760 yards. Therefore, 5.2 miles = 5.2 × 1,760 = 9,152 yards. Answer A is incorrect because 1,760 is the number of yards in 1 mile. Answer B is incorrect because 5,280 is the number of feet (3 feet = 1 yard) in 1 mile. Answer D is incorrect because 27,456 equals the number of feet in 5.2 miles.

Question 57

Answer B is correct. To solve this problem, you must understand how to calculate the square root of a number and how to estimate. First of all, remember that squaring and taking the square root of a number are inverse operations:

Another way of expressing this is $\sqrt{x^2} = x$

Plug the answer choices into the equation to find the answer:

$$\text{For answer A, } x = 14, \text{ so } \sqrt{x^2} = \sqrt{14^2} = \sqrt{196}$$
$$\text{For answer B, } x = 15, \text{ so } \sqrt{x^2} = \sqrt{15^2} = \sqrt{225}$$
$$\text{For answer C, } x = 16, \text{ so } \sqrt{x^2} = \sqrt{16^2} = \sqrt{256}$$
$$\text{For answer D, } x = 17, \text{ so } \sqrt{x^2} = \sqrt{17^2} = \sqrt{289}$$

Look at each of the answers and determine which one is closest to $\sqrt{237}$.

Answer B is correct because the difference between 237 and 225 equals 12, which is smaller than the difference between 196 and 237 (answer A), between 256 and 237 (answer C) and between 289 and 237 (answer D).

Question 58

Answer D is correct. This problem calls for you to read a calibrated scale. Length, measured in inches, is given by the black numbers on the bottom of the tape measure. The black arrow drawn to represent the length of the two-by-four appears between the numbers 56 and 57. Therefore, answers A and B are incorrect. To determine which of the remaining answers is correct, count the number of black line gradations between 56 and 57. There are 16 such lines. The arrow drawn on the tape measure is pointing at the tenth line. In other words, it falls $\frac{10}{16}$ or $\frac{5}{8}$ of the way between 56 and 57 inches. Therefore, answer C is incorrect and answer D, $56\frac{5}{8}$ inches, is correct.

Question 59

Answer D is correct. This is essentially a question that requires you to know how to calculate volume. Because Laurel's back yard is rectangular and you are given the length and width in the problem, the only information you need is the desired height (or depth) of the layer of topsoil to be applied in order to calculate the volume of topsoil she'll have to order. Answer A is incorrect because the depth or height of topsoil is needed for the volume calculation. Answer B is incorrect because the cost per cubic yard (a unit of volume) is not related to the amount of soil needed to do the job. Answer C is incorrect because this problem deals only with Laurel's back yard, not her front yard.

Question 60

Answer B is correct. To solve this problem you must match the data in the table provided to the graphs that appear in the answer choices. Remember, there can be only one correct answer. Answer B is correct because the data table and graph match exactly. Answer A is incorrect because its values for spring and fall do not match those in the data table. Answer C is incorrect because, although the value for spring matches, the values for all three other seasons do not. Answer D is incorrect because, although the values are close, they do not match those in the data table. Answer D is what is called a "distracter" answer because although it is incorrect, its values are close to the correct answer and share its pattern of rises and falls in the bars of its graph.

PRAXIS Essay

Question 61

Answers will vary.

Question 62

Answers will vary.

Question 63

Answers will vary.

Practice Exam #2

Reading Comprehension

Questions 1 through 17 consist of passages of text followed by questions about what you have read.

Soils formed under relatively humid climates tend to be acidic and lack soluble mineral salts. This is because of the leaching action of the water. Most of the soils found in the eastern half of the U.S. mainland, as well as along the northwest coast, have developed under such conditions. Soils that are found in forested regions are generally better suited for forestry, pasturage, and nonfarm uses. However, soils that have developed under the vegetation of deciduous forests are still good for farm uses such as cropland. This type of soil is gray-brown in color and is generally richer.

Gray-brown soils produce some of the most productive farmland and can be found in various regions of the U.S. In the eastern part of the country, this soil type exists in an area extending from southern New England to northern Virginia and west around the lower part of Lake Michigan. In the western part of the U.S, gray-brown soils occur in parts of Washington, Oregon, Idaho, and northern California. The gray-brown soils found in the Willamette River valley of Washington and Oregon, the area around Lake Michigan, and the belt of land extending from northeast Virginia through Maryland, Delaware, and New Jersey have made for some of the most productive farmland in the U.S. Farms in these areas are known for their vegetables, dairy products, fruit, eggs, and poultry.

Gray-brown soils are not the only types of forest-developed soils. Gray-hued podzols are best suited for woodlands and pasturage, as opposed to croplands, although there are areas in Maine that produce successful potato crops in gray-hued podzols with the help of fertilizers. This soil type can be found in northern New England, in the upper reaches of the Great Lakes, and in some higher parts of the Appalachians. There are also red and yellow types of forest soils. These soil types are commonly found in the southeastern to eastern parts of Oklahoma and Texas and in scattered patches in the mountain ranges of the west coast. The red and yellow soils in the southeast are suitable for cash crops, such as cotton and tobacco. The best types of red and yellow soils are found in the Nashville basin of Tennessee and in the bluegrass region of Kentucky. The soils in this region are derived from limestone.

Prairie soils tend to be rich and deep. They are neither acid nor alkaline to any marked degree. Soils of this type are good for grass crops, such as corn, oats, sorghum, barley, and wheat. Some of the best prairie soils and general farming conditions in the entire country are found in the eastern part of the interior Great Plains in a strip of land extending from southern Minnesota through Iowa and parts of Illinois, Missouri, Kansas, Oklahoma, and Texas. The rainfall in this region has been sufficient to support a lush growth of tall, deep-rooted grasses, yet not so heavy as to cause excessive depletion of mineral salts from the ground.

1. What is the main idea of the passage?
   - ❑ A. There are different soil conditions throughout the U.S.
   - ❑ B. Rich and deep soils are good for crops of the grass family.
   - ❑ C. Soil affects farming conditions.
   - ❑ D. Humid climates produce acidic soils.

2. What is the main idea in the second paragraph?
   - ❑ A. Some of the best soils and farmland are found in the interior Great Plains.
   - ❑ B. Many areas that have forest-developed soils are ill suited for cultivation and are better utilized for forestry, pasturage, and nonfarm uses.
   - ❑ C. Some of the gray-brown soils found in parts of the U.S. are particularly productive for farmland.
   - ❑ D. The gray-brown soils are found in a region extending from southern New England to northern Virginia and west around the lower part of Lake Michigan.

3. What is the meaning of the word *depletion?*
   - ❑ A. Abundance
   - ❑ B. Reduction
   - ❑ C. Weakening
   - ❑ D. Restoration

4. What type of soil is found in the Nashville basin of Tennessee?
   - ❑ A. Gray-brown soils
   - ❑ B. Gray-hued podzols
   - ❑ C. Deep-rooted soils
   - ❑ D. Yellow and red soils

5. In what part of the country will you find gray-brown soil?

❏ A. Nashville basin
❏ B. Southern New England
❏ C. Appalachians
❏ D. Northern New England

Near the northwest extremity of the Gulf of Tunis was an ancient city named Utica. It was approximately 20 miles from the modern-day city of Tunis. It is believed that this ancient city was founded around 1100 B.C. as a Phoenician colony. Utica was a thriving port and played an important role in the Punic Wars that occurred between Rome and Carthage. However, it was eventually eclipsed by the power of Carthage.

During the Third Punic War, between 149 and 146 B.C., the city of Utica submitted to Rome. As a result, the city was named the capital of the Roman province of Africa. It was also rewarded with a large portion of Carthaginian territory.

Utica also became famous after the Battle of Pharsalus in 48 B.C. It became a famous rallying point of the adherents of Pompey during the civil war between the two Roman leaders, Gaius Julius Caesar and Gnaeus Pompeius Magnus. Emperor Augustus awarded municipal rights to the city. Emperor Hadrian awarded the city the honorary title of a Roman colony.

Utica was eventually captured by the Vandals in 439 A.D. under Genseric. In 534 A.D., the Byzantines went on to regain Utica. Finally, near the end of the seventh century, Utica was destroyed by the Arabs. Ruins of Utica are still visible just west of the Medgerda River. They include an amphitheater with a capacity of 20,000, a theater, baths, reservoirs, and quays.

6. Who gave Utica a share of Carthaginian territory?

❏ A. Rome
❏ B. Arabs
❏ C. 149–146 B.C.
❏ D. Caesar

7. Under which emperor was Utica declared a Roman colony?

❏ A. Gaius Julius Caesar
❏ B. Hadrian
❏ C. Genseric
❏ D. Gnaeus Pompeius Magnus

8. What is the main idea of the third paragraph?

  ❑ A. Utica was eventually destroyed by the Arabs.

  ❑ B. Utica became a flourishing seaport.

  ❑ C. Due to changes in the coastline, Utica is now five miles from the coastline.

  ❑ D. Utica became a famous rallying point and eventually a Roman colony.

9. What is the meaning of the word *eclipsed*?

  ❑ A. Overshadowed

  ❑ B. Hidden

  ❑ C. Covered

  ❑ D. Energized

In 1935, the Social Security Act was passed. This legislation was passed to give financial protection to wage earners and their families through old-age, survivor, and disability insurance. It also laid out various requirements for federal-state unemployment insurance; for federal public assistance; and for family, maternal, child-health and disability grants to states to help with funding. Since 1966, it has also defrayed some of the medical care costs for the elderly through health insurance.

The Department of Health, Education, and Welfare was created in 1953. The responsibility of this department is to administer the social security programs of the federal government; the Public Health Service, which grants funds to hospitals and medical research; the Food and Drug Administration; and the Office of Education.

By 1971, the expenditures for the federal social-welfare programs per year had almost tripled from 10 years earlier, reaching $92 billion. Some of the funds went to welfare programs such as veterans' benefits, educational programs, housing programs, and health and medical programs. The majority of the funds, almost 75% of the $92 billion, were spent on social insurance programs and public aid. By the late 1960s, the federal government maintained some 440 hospitals, implemented a school lunch program in 71,000 different schools throughout the country, and donated nearly 855 million pounds of extra food in a single year.

10. When was the Department of Health, Education, and Welfare established?

  ❑ A. 1960

  ❑ B. 1966

  ❑ C. 1971

  ❑ D. 1953

11. How many hospitals did the federal government support in the late 1960s?

   ❑ A. 400
   ❑ B. 440
   ❑ C. 4,000
   ❑ D. 4,400

Steam is defined as water that is in a hot vapor state. Steam engineering is the technology used to generate power from steam for heating purposes. Both of these are important components in engineering technology.

Heat can raise the vapor pressure of any liquid. This is due to the fact that high temperatures increase the speed at which individual molecules in the liquid move. Liquid turns into a vapor state when it reaches the boiling point. At this temperature, molecular activity is great enough to cancel out the forces of attraction between molecules. The boiling point of water at sea-level atmospheric pressure (14.7psi, or pounds per square inch) is 100°C (212°F). At this critical temperature, the addition of each 970.3 British thermal units (BTUs) of heat will convert 1 pound of water to 1 pound of steam at the same temperature. According to Boyle's Law, for water under pressure, the boiling point rises with the increase of pressure up to a pressure of 3208.2psi. At this pressure, water boils at a temperature of 374.15°C (705.47°F), which is its critical point.

Sometimes when water is boiling, a white vapor is visible. This is due to the fact that a quantity of small water droplets have been taken up with steam. However, this is not pure steam because pure steam is dry and invisible. This white vapor also appears when dry steam is exhausted into the atmosphere, which has a comparatively cool temperature. When some of the steam cools and condenses, the white vapor is formed. This is often referred to as wet steam.

Saturated steam is formed when steam is heated to the exact boiling point corresponding to the pressure that exists. Superheated steam is produced when steam is heated beyond the exact boiling point. Superheating can also be achieved by compressing saturated steam and using a process known as throttling. Throttling passes steam from a high-pressure vessel to a low-pressure one.

12. Steam that is heated to the exact boiling point corresponding to the pressure that exists is called

   ❑ A. Steam
   ❑ B. Vapor
   ❑ C. Saturated steam
   ❑ D. Superheated steam

Harold Clayton Urey was a famous American chemist. He was origi-nally from Walkerton, Indiana. He attended the universities of Montana and California. He went on to have an active career as a chemist. In 1917, he went to work for the Barrett Chemical Company in Philadelphia, Pennsylvania. In 1919 he went on to teach at various universities. Between 1919 and 1957 he taught successively at the fol-lowing: the University of Montana, Johns Hopkins University, Columbia University, the University of Chicago, and the University of Columbia. He went on to be designated the professor-at-large of chemistry of the University of California in 1958.

Harold Clayton Urey was awarded the Nobel Prize in chemistry in 1934. This was for his discovery of heavy hydrogen, also known as deuterium, and for his isolation of heavy water. After winning the Nobel prize, he went on to work at Columbia University as director of war research in the atom-bomb project. His other accomplishments include contributions to the development of the hydrogen bomb.

Harold Clayton Urey also performed research in the fields of geo-physics and geological paleontology. He co-authored *Atoms, Molecules, and Quanta* with American physicist Arthur Edward Ruark. He also authored *The Planets*.

13. Where did Urey first teach chemistry?
    - ❑ A. Columbia University
    - ❑ B. The University of Montana
    - ❑ C. Johns Hopkins University
    - ❑ D. The University of Chicago

14. What happened in 1958?
    - ❑ A. Harold Clayton Urey was born.
    - ❑ B. Harold Clayton Urey was awarded the Nobel Prize in chemistry.
    - ❑ C. Harold Clayton Urey discovered heavy hydrogen.
    - ❑ D. Harold Clayton Urey was named professor-at-large of chemistry.

15. What was Harold Clayton Urey awarded the Nobel Prize for?
    - ❑ A. For writing *Atoms, Molecules, and Quanta*.
    - ❑ B. For contributing to the development of the hydrogen bomb.
    - ❑ C. For discovering heavy hydrogen and isolating heavy water.
    - ❑ D. For being named professor of chemistry.

In 1965, the population of Sweden was 7,766,424. By 1970, the population had risen to approximately 8,046,000. In 1969, it was determined that the population density of Sweden was 46 people per square mile. The majority of the population, almost 90%, was concentrated in southern Sweden, whereas the northern mountain regions were sparsely populated. It has also been determined that 77% of the population has chosen urban living over rural living.

Sweden consists of 24 different provinces. Each province has its own governor, who is chosen by the central government, as well as its own council that is elected by the people. The 24 provinces include: Alvsborg, Blekinge, Gavleborg, Goteborg and Bohus, Gotland, Halland, Jamtland, Jonkoping, Kalmar, Kopparberg, Kristianstad, Kronoberg, Malmohus, Norrbotten, Orebro, Ostergotland, Skaraborg, Sodermanland, Stockholm, Uppsala, Varmland, Vasterbotten, Vasternorrland, and Vastmanland.

Sweden has three major cities: Stockholm, Goteborg, and Malmo. Stockholm is the country's capital and is the largest city. In 1968, its population was 756,000. Goteborg, an industrial center and seaport, was the second largest city with a population of 444,000. Malmo, a commercial center and seaport, had a population of 256,000.

In terms of religion, the majority of the population (over 95%) is Lutheran, with a small number of people following Roman Catholicism or Judaism. The state church of Sweden is the Evangelical Lutheran Church. All children become members of this church at birth. However, there is no obligation to actively participate. Withdrawal from the church has also been permitted since 1952. There are 13 Lutheran dioceses in Sweden. Each diocese is headed by its own bishop. The other Protestant groups in Sweden include: the Baptists, the Mission Covenant Church, the Pentecostal movement, and the Salvation Army.

16. What is the meaning of the word *sparsely*?
    - ❑ A. Empty
    - ❑ B. Densely
    - ❑ C. Lightly
    - ❑ D. Heavily

17. Withdrawal from the church has been permitted since
    - ❑ A. 1952
    - ❑ B. 1965
    - ❑ C. 1970
    - ❑ D. 1972

Grammar, Punctuation, and Usage

Questions 18 through 24 cover grammar, punctuation, and usage. Follow the instructions given for each group of questions.

For questions 18 through 22, identify from the underlined items which part of the sentence, if any, is incorrect.

18. Spitz is a <u>playful bushy-haired, white</u> dog and has a <u>small head</u> with a <u>pointed snout</u> and <u>small, pointy, upright</u> ears.
    - ❏ A. playful bushy-haired, white
    - ❏ B. small head
    - ❏ C. pointed snout
    - ❏ D. small, pointy, upright
    - ❏ E. No error

19. In an experiment in the early <u>1950s,</u> Dr. <u>Peter N. Witt</u> of the <u>Upstate Medical Center,</u> <u>Syracuse, N.Y.,</u> fed spiders either barbiturates or tranquilizers.
    - ❏ A. 1950s,
    - ❏ B. Peter N. Witt
    - ❏ C. Upstate Medical Center,
    - ❏ D. Syracuse, N.Y.,
    - ❏ E. No error

20. <u>Farming,</u> <u>although</u> somewhat limited because of the necessity of <u>irrigation</u> and livestock <u>raising,</u> is an important industry in Utah.
    - ❏ A. Farming,
    - ❏ B. although
    - ❏ C. irrigation
    - ❏ D. raising,
    - ❏ E. No error

21. In the <u>U.S.,</u> rising civilian dismay with the Vietnamese conflict led to <u>many-sided</u> <u>protests,</u> frequently resulting in direct confrontations between the <u>demonstrators,</u> often college students, and National Guardsmen.
    - ❏ A. U.S.,
    - ❏ B. many-sided
    - ❏ C. protests,
    - ❏ D. demonstrators,
    - ❏ E. No error

22. <u>Oswald Spencer, a German philosopher,</u> was born in <u>Blankenburg</u> and was educated at the universities of Halle, <u>Munich</u> and Berlin.
    - ❑ A. Oswald Spencer,
    - ❑ B. a German philosopher,
    - ❑ C. Blankenburg
    - ❑ D. Munich
    - ❑ E. No error

For questions 23 and 24, choose the answer that corrects the underlined portion of the sentence.

23. The theme of the movie <u>affected me profoundly;</u> it brought tears to my eyes.
    - ❑ A. effected me profoundly:
    - ❑ B. affected me profoundly,
    - ❑ C. effected me profoundly,
    - ❑ D. affected me profoundly:
    - ❑ E. No error

24. The story she wrote about a girl <u>that</u> she called Mary Jane became an American classic.
    - ❑ A. which
    - ❑ B. whom
    - ❑ C. who
    - ❑ D. No error

PRAXIS Mathematics

Questions 25 through 45 present math problems. Choose the mathematically correct answer for each question.

25. If $6x + 7 = 31$, then $3x + 6 = $?
    - ❑ A. 16
    - ❑ B. 18
    - ❑ C. 20
    - ❑ D. 22

26. Jacob has two ten-dollar bills, a twenty-dollar bill, and three five-dollar bills. Jacob buys two items; one item costs $12.84, and the other item costs $22.75. How much money does he have left?
    - ❑ A. $18.00
    - ❑ B. $4.41
    - ❑ C. $32.25
    - ❑ D. $19.41

27. Round 788.847 to the nearest hundredth.
    - ❏ A. 790
    - ❏ B. 780
    - ❏ C. 788.8
    - ❏ D. 788.85

28. $8 + 6 \times 7 - 9 = ?$
    - ❏ A. 41
    - ❏ B. 89
    - ❏ C. 39
    - ❏ D. 47

29. $\{5 + [6 - (2 \times 2 + 1) + 3 \times 4] - 3\} = ?$
    - ❏ A. 12
    - ❏ B. 15
    - ❏ C. 17
    - ❏ D. 21

30. $2^3 \times 2^4 = ?$
    - ❏ A. 128
    - ❏ B. 256
    - ❏ C. 512
    - ❏ D. 4,096

31. Which of the following fractions is equivalent to $\frac{5}{6}$?
    - ❏ A. $\frac{2}{6}$
    - ❏ B. $\frac{25}{30}$
    - ❏ C. $\frac{20}{30}$
    - ❏ D. $\frac{15}{24}$

32. Which number is missing from the following sequence:
    4, 9, 19, __, 79?
    - ❏ A. 27
    - ❏ B. 35
    - ❏ C. 37
    - ❏ D. 39
    - ❏ E. 41

33. Brady makes $140.00 for 9 hours of work. How much will Brady make for 15 hours if he is working at the same pay rate? Round the answer to the nearest dollar.
    - ❏ A. $233.00
    - ❏ B. $220.00
    - ❏ C. $230.00
    - ❏ D. $240.00

34. Felicia ran a marathon. She started at 8:30 a.m. and crossed the finish line at 2:15 p.m. How long did it take Felicia to run the marathon?
    - ❑ A. 4 hours and 15 minutes
    - ❑ B. 4 hours and 20 minutes
    - ❑ C. 5 hours and 35 minutes
    - ❑ D. 5 hours and 45 minutes

35. Which of the following represents $6\frac{3}{8}$ as an improper fraction?
    - ❑ A. $\frac{63}{8}$
    - ❑ B. $\frac{17}{8}$
    - ❑ C. $\frac{51}{8}$
    - ❑ D. $\frac{24}{8}$

36. $2.65 \times 10^5 = ?$
    - ❑ A. 26,500
    - ❑ B. 265,000
    - ❑ C. 2,650,000
    - ❑ D. 26,500,000

37. Diane needs $2\frac{1}{2}$ cups of sugar to make a dessert. How many cups will she need to make four desserts?
    - ❑ A. 8
    - ❑ B. $8\frac{1}{2}$
    - ❑ C. 9
    - ❑ D. 10

38. 40% of what number is 300?
    - ❑ A. 200
    - ❑ B. 250
    - ❑ C. 350
    - ❑ D. 500
    - ❑ E. 750

39. How many years will Felicia need to invest $2,000.00 in order to earn $200.00 if the interest rate is 5%, without taking into account any compound interest?
    - ❑ A. One year
    - ❑ B. Two years
    - ❑ C. Three years
    - ❑ D. Five years

40. Felicia is purchasing a new desk. The regular price is $540.00. She receives a 20% employee discount. How much is the desk?

 ❏ A. $540.00
 ❏ B. $520.00
 ❏ C. $432.00
 ❏ D. $430.00

41. Select the answer choice in which the terms are given in order from least to greatest value:

 ❏ A. $-4.5, \frac{1}{8}, 0, .711$

 ❏ B. $\frac{1}{3}, .375, 2, \frac{14}{5}$

 ❏ C. $\frac{16}{4}, 3.78, 1\frac{3}{8}, \frac{8}{16}$

 ❏ D. $.441, .474, 0, \frac{5}{6}$

Questions 42 and 43 refer to the information in the two pie charts given in Figure 9.1.

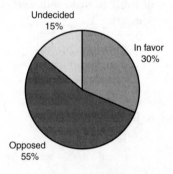

Students' opinion survey

Undecided
15%

In favor
30%

Opposed
55%

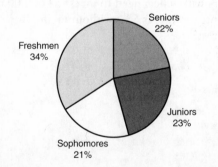

Student body composition (total number of students = 300)

Seniors
22%

Freshmen
34%

Juniors
23%

Sophomores
21%

Figure 9.1 Sample pie charts.

42. If every student responded to the opinion survey, how many more students we are opposed to the dress code than are in favor of it?
    - ❑   A. 45
    - ❑   B. 75
    - ❑   C. 120
    - ❑   D. 165

43. If five-sixths of all seniors are opposed to the dress code, how many underclassmen are either in favor of the dress code or undecided?
    - ❑   A. 124
    - ❑   B. 135
    - ❑   C. 165
    - ❑   D. 234

44. Which of the following equations is false?
    - ❑   A. $x + y = y + x$
    - ❑   B. $lm = ml$
    - ❑   C. $(x - y) - 7 = x - (y - 7)$
    - ❑   D. $5(b + c) = 5b + 5c$

45. Sonya and Ling met for dinner in the city. Upon leaving the restaurant, Sonya drove 6 miles due north to her apartment and Ling drove 8 miles due west to her house. How far apart do Sonya and Ling live "as the crow flies" (that is, in a straight line)?
    - ❑   A. 10 miles
    - ❑   B. 14 miles
    - ❑   C. 28 miles
    - ❑   D. 48 miles

PRAXIS Essay

For questions 46 through 50, develop an essay for each of the given essay topics.

46. Parents should be penalized financially when their child is late for school or is absent without reason.

47. Students with low test scores should not be permitted to participate in extracurricular activities.

48. All schools should require their staff members to participate in random drug testing.

49. Dress codes should be enforced in all schools.

50. Schools place too much emphasis on sports. It takes away from academics.

Answer Key for Practice Exam #2

1. A	**18.** A	**35.** C
2. C	**19.** E	**36.** B
3. B	**20.** E	**37.** D
4. D	**21.** E	**38.** E
5. B	**22.** D	**39.** B
6. A	**23.** E	**40.** C
7. B	**24.** B	**41.** B
8. D	**25.** B	**42.** B
9. A	**26.** D	**43.** A
10. D	**27.** D	**44.** C
11. B	**28.** A	**45.** A
12. C	**29.** B	**46.** Answers will vary.
13. B	**30.** A	**47.** Answers will vary.
14. D	**31.** B	**48.** Answers will vary.
15. C	**32.** D	**49.** Answers will vary.
16. C	**33.** A	**50.** Answers will vary.
17. A	**34.** D	

Reading Comprehension

Question 1

Answer A is correct. The main idea of the passage is that different soil types are found throughout the U.S. Therefore, answers B, C, and D are incorrect. The remaining answers are presented as ideas and supporting topics in the passage.

Question 2

Answer C is correct. The main idea of the second paragraph is that the gray-brown soils found in parts of the U.S. are particularly productive for farmland. Therefore, answers A and B are incorrect. Answer D is a supporting idea within the second paragraph.

Question 3

Answer B is correct. In the sentence, the word *depletion* means reduction. Therefore, answers A, C, and D are incorrect. *Restoration* is an antonym for *depletion*. The word *depletion* also means weakening. However, this answer is incorrect for the sentence context.

Question 4

Answer D is correct. The passage clearly states that yellow and red soils are found in the Nashville basin of Tennessee. Therefore, answers A, B, and C are incorrect.

Question 5

Answer B is correct. The passage states that gray-brown soils can be found in southern New England. Therefore, answers A, C, and D are incorrect.

Question 6

Answer A is correct. When Utica surrendered to Rome, Rome rewarded it with a share of the Carthaginian territory. Therefore, answers B, C, and D are incorrect.

Question 7

Answer B is correct. The passage states that Utica was declared a Roman colony under Emperor Hadrian. Therefore, answers A, C, and D are incorrect.

Question 8

Answer D is correct. The main idea of the third paragraph is that Utica became a famous rallying point and was then declared a Roman colony. Therefore, answers A, B, and C are incorrect.

Question 9

Answer A is correct. The word *eclipsed* also means overshadowed. Therefore, answers B, C, and D are incorrect.

Question 10

Answer D is correct. The Department of Health, Education, and Welfare was established in 1953. Therefore, answers A, B, and C are incorrect.

Question 11

Answer B is correct. The passage states that during one year in the late 1960s, the federal government supported 440 hospitals. Therefore, answers A, C, and D are incorrect.

Question 12

Answer C is correct. Steam that is heated to the exact boiling point corresponding to the pressure that exists is called saturated steam. Therefore, answers A, B, and D are incorrect.

Question 13

Answer B is correct. Harold Clayton Urey first taught chemistry at the University of Montana. He then went on to teach at Johns Hopkins and Columbia universities, as well as the universities of Chicago and Columbia. Therefore, answers A, C, and D are incorrect.

Question 14

Answer D is correct. The passage states that Harold Clayton Urey was named professor-at-large of chemistry in 1958. Therefore, answers A, B, and C are incorrect.

Question 15

Answer C is correct. Harold Clayton Urey was awarded the Nobel Prize in chemistry for his discovery of heavy hydrogen and isolation of heavy water. Therefore, answers A, B, and D are incorrect.

Question 16

Answer C is correct. The word *sparsely* also means lightly. Therefore, answers A, B, and D are incorrect. The words *densely* and *heavily* are antonyms for the word *sparsely*.

Question 17

Answer A is correct. The passage states that withdrawal from the church without further obligation has been permitted since 1952. Therefore, answers B, C, and D are incorrect.

Grammar, Punctuation, and Usage

Question 18

Answer A is correct. A comma is required between the adjectives *playful* and *bushy-haired*. A comma is required between two or more adjectives if they are coordinate rather than cumulative. Therefore, answers B, C, D, and E are incorrect.

Question 19

Answer E is correct. The sentence does not contain any errors as it is written. Therefore, answers A, B, C, and D are incorrect.

Question 20

Answer E is correct. A comma is required after the word *Farming*. A comma is required before and after an unessential adjective clause, and this is the case in the sentence in number 20. The unessential adjective clause is "<u>although</u> somewhat limited because of the necessity of <u>irrigation</u> and livestock <u>raising</u>." Therefore, answers A, B, C, and D are incorrect.

Question 21

Answer E is correct. As the sentence is written, there are no errors. Therefore, answers A, B, C, and D are incorrect.

Question 22

Answer D is correct. A comma is required after Munich. A comma is required when there is a list of three or more objects. Therefore, answers A, B, C, and E are not suitable answers to this question.

Question 23

Answer E is correct. The sentence is correct as it is written.

Question 24

Answer B is correct. Because the sentence is referring to a person, the word *that* should be replaced with the word *whom*. Therefore, answers A, C, and D are incorrect.

PRAXIS Mathematics

Question 25

Answer B is correct. Because x is equal to 4, $3x + 6 = 18$. Therefore, answers A, C, and D are incorrect.

Question 26

Answer D is correct. Jacob has $55.00, and he spends $35.59, so Jacob will have a total of $19.41 left over. Therefore, answers A, B, and C are incorrect.

Question 27

Answer D is correct. 788.847 rounded to the nearest hundredth is 788.85. Therefore, answers A, B, and C are incorrect.

Question 28

Answer A is correct. $8 + 6 \times 7 - 9 = 41$. To complete the equation, you must follow the correct order of operations, which means that multiplication must be performed before addition and subtraction. Therefore, answers B, C, and D are incorrect.

Question 29

Answer B is correct. To complete the equation, you must follow the correct order of operation. Because there are parentheses inside parentheses, you must work from the inside out. Therefore, the correct answer is 15. Answers A, C, and D are incorrect.

Question 30

Answer A is correct: $2^3 \times 2^4 = 128$. You can find the answer by directly adding the exponents. Therefore, answers B, C, and D are incorrect.

Question 31

Answer B is correct. $\frac{25}{30}$ is equivalent to $\frac{5}{6}$ because $5 \times 5 = 25$ and $6 \times 5 = 30$. Therefore, answers A, C, and D are incorrect.

Question 32

Answer D is correct. The missing number in the sequence is 39. Therefore, answers A, B, C, and E are incorrect.

Question 33

Answer A is correct. Brady will make $233.00 for 15 hours of work. The pay rate can be determined by dividing 140 by 9. You can then multiply the answer by 15 to get the total amount made. Therefore, answers B, C, and D are incorrect.

Question 34

Answer D is correct. It took Felicia 5 hours and 45 minutes to complete the marathon. Therefore, answers A, B, and C are incorrect.

Question 35

Answer C is correct. $6\frac{3}{8}$ can be represented as an improper fraction, which would be $\frac{51}{8}$. Therefore, answers A, B, and D are incorrect.

Question 36

Answer B is correct. $2.65 \times 10^5 = 265,000$. $10^5 = 100,000$ and $100,000 \times 2.65 = 265,000$. Therefore, answers A, C, and D are incorrect.

Question 37

Answer D is correct. To make four desserts, Diane will need a total of 10 cups of sugar. You can find the answer by multiplying $2\frac{1}{2}$ by 4.

Question 38

Answer E is correct. 40% of 750 is 300. Therefore, answers A, B, C, and D are incorrect.

Question 39

Answer B is correct. Felicia will need to invest her money for two years in order to make $200.00 if the interest rate is 5%. Therefore, answers A, C, and D are incorrect.

Question 40

Answer C is correct. Felicia would pay $432.00 for the desk after the 20% discount. Therefore, answers A, B, and D are incorrect.

Question 41

Answer B is correct. It is the only answer choice in which all terms are listed in order from least to greatest. Answer A is incorrect because $\frac{1}{8}$ is greater than 0, but appears before 0 in the series. Answer C is incorrect because its terms are listed in order from greatest to least. Answer D is incorrect because its first two terms (.441, .474) are greater than its third term (0).

Question 42

Answer B is correct. To solve this problem, you must first calculate the number of students who are opposed to the dress code and the number of students who are in favor of it. Then, you can calculate the difference between those two values to find the answer:

 NOTE

To find the percentage of students opposed and in favor of the dress code, refer to the pie chart titled "Students' Opinion Survey" in Figure 9.1.

Number of students opposed = 300 students × 55% = 300 × .55 = 165

Number of students in favor = 300 students × 30% = 300 × .30 = 90

Number opposed – number in favor = 75

Answer A is incorrect because it gives the number of students who are undecided (300 × 15% = 45). Answer C is incorrect because it gives the number of students opposed minus the number undecided. Answer D is incorrect because it gives the number of students opposed.

Question 43

Answer A is correct. To solve this problem, first refer to the pie chart titled "Student Body Composition" in Figure 9.1 for information to help you calculate the number of seniors:

300 students × 22% = 300 × .22 = 66 seniors

Therefore, if five-sixths of seniors are opposed, then the number of seniors opposed = $(\frac{5}{6}) \times 66 = (5 \times 66)/6 = 5 \times 11 = 55$.

Now, the total number of students opposed = 300 × 55% = 300 × .55 = 165.

Therefore, the number of underclassmen opposed = number of students opposed − number of seniors opposed:

165 − 55 = 110 underclassmen opposed

The number of underclassmen in favor or undecided is equal to the number of underclassmen minus the number of underclassmen opposed.

Therefore, the number of underclassmen = number of students − number of seniors = 300 − 66 = 234.

Finally, the answer is equal to 234 − 110 = 124 underclassmen in favor or undecided.

Answer B is incorrect because it gives the total number of students in all classes who are in favor or undecided. Answer C is incorrect because it gives the total number of students opposed. Answer D is incorrect because it gives the total number of underclassmen.

Question 44

Answer C is correct. The equation in Answer C is false because subtraction is not associative; operations within the parentheses must be performed before the other operations. Answer A is incorrect because addition is commutative, so the equation is true. Answer B is incorrect because multiplication is also commutative, so the equation is true. Answer D is incorrect because multiplication is distributive over addition, so the equation is true.

Question 45

Answer A is correct. To solve this problem you must use the Pythagorean theorem. The Pythagorean theorem applies to right triangles like the one formed in this drawing between the three points of the restaurant, Sonya's apartment, and Ling's house. Knowing this, you can write the formula to determine the length x (the "straight line" distance between S and L).

$$x^2 = (RS)^2 + (RL)^2$$
$$x = \sqrt{(RS)^2 + (RL)^2}$$
$$x = \sqrt{(6)^2 + (8)^2}$$
$$x = \sqrt{36 + 64}$$
$$x = \sqrt{100}$$
$$x = 10 \text{ miles}$$

Answers B, C, and D are all incorrect because they do not use the Pythagorean theorem to solve for x.

PRAXIS Essay

Question 46

Answers will vary.

Question 47

Answers will vary.

Question 48

Answers will vary.

Question 49

Answers will vary.

Question 50

Answers will vary.

Practice Exam #3

Reading Comprehension

Questions 1 through 10 consist of passages of text followed by questions about what you have read.

The dissension that occurred throughout the Kingdom of Bavaria over the death of Maximilian Joseph, Elector of Bavaria (1727–1777) resulted in the War of the Bavarian Succession. The next elector of Bavaria after Maximilian Joseph was Charles Theodore (1724–1799). Charles Theodore had illegitimate children whom he wanted recognized as princes of the Holy Roman Empire. However, Austria, under the rule of Maria Theresa and her son Joseph II, had an old claim on Lower Bavaria and a section of the Upper Palatinate. Charles Theodore had to recognize this claim in order to persuade Joseph II to recognize his illegitimate children. By 1778, Austrian troops occupied part of Bavaria.

Frederick the Great had planned on uniting Prussia with the margravates of Ansbach and Bayreuth. Therefore, he would not approve of any move that would strengthen Austria's presence in southern Germany. For that reason, Frederick the Great and Charles Augustus Christian, the next in line in the Bavarian succession, protested against Charles Theodore for the elimination of a third of Bavaria. Frederick the Great also enlisted Frederick Augustus III, Elector of Saxony, later Frederick Augustus I, King of Saxony, to protest against Charles Theodore.

Even with all the protests, Austria still refused to withdraw its claims in parts of Bavaria. As a result, war broke out. So in 1778, Frederick the Great and Henry, Prince of Saxony, invaded the Kingdom of Bohemia. Throughout the brief skirmishes between forces, the Austrian forces, under Joseph II, managed to hold the boundary between Silesia and Austrian lands. The dispute was finally settled by Frederick and Maria Theresa with Russia and France acting as mediators.

It was the Treaty of Teschen (1779) that ended the war. The treaty resulted in the following: (1) that Austria return to Bavaria all of the territory it had acquired in the previous year, except a small district on the east side of the Inn River; (2) that Austria agree to the future union of Prussia with Ansbach and Bayreuth; and (3) that the elector of Saxony receive a money indemnity in lieu of his claims to Bavarian territory.

1. Why did Charles Theodore have problems making his children princes of the Holy Roman Empire?
   - ❑   A. His children were not of age.
   - ❑   B. His children were not legitimate.
   - ❑   C. He did not recognize Austrian claims on Bavaria.
   - ❑   D. He did not have any sons.

2. Why did Frederick the Great not support any moves that would strengthen Austria's power?
   - ❑   A. He did not want them to interfere with his plans of uniting with Prussia.
   - ❑   B. He did not want Charles Theodore's children named as princes in the Holy Roman Empire.
   - ❑   C. He wanted to name Charles Augustus Christian as the next in line in the Bavarian succession.
   - ❑   D. He wanted to negotiate the Treaty of Teschen.

Famous scientists of sound in the nineteenth century included British physicists John Tyndall and John William Scott, Third Baron Rayleigh, and the Germans Hermann Ludwig Ferdinand Helmholtz and Karl Rudolf Konig. John Tyndall was a great simplifier and popularizer of the science of sound. Lord Rayleigh was a scientific synthesist, and his book, *The Theory of Sound* (1877–1878), summarized in concise form virtually all that was known about that subject. Hermann Ludwig Ferdinand Helmholtz was both a physician and a physicist, who elaborated the nature of the process of hearing. Karl Rudolf Konig designed and made tuning forks, as well as other acoustic apparatus. He also pioneered the study of ultrasonics.

Three major inventions of the nineteenth century were useful in the study of sound. These were the microphone, the phonograph, and the telephone. During the twentieth century, physicists used various instruments to make further advances in the study of sound. Using electronic oscillators, waves of any type can be produced electronically and then converted into sounds by electromagnetic or piezoelectric means. Alternatively, a microphone can convert sounds into electrical currents that can be amplified electronically without distortion. A cathode-ray oscilloscope can then be used to analyze the electrical currents. By the 1940s, sound could be recorded and reproduced.

During the twentieth century, research was also done in the area of generating and propagating underwater sound. Research in this area stemmed from military needs during World War I. Even more progress in this area was made during World War II.

3. Who designed tuning forks?

 ❑ A. Germans
 ❑ B. Americans
 ❑ C. French
 ❑ D. British

4. After sound is converted into electrical currents, it can be analyzed using?

 ❑ A. A microphone
 ❑ B. A tuning fork
 ❑ C. An electronic oscillator
 ❑ D. A cathode-ray oscilloscope

5. What is the main idea of the second paragraph?

 ❑ A. Scientific advances allowed waves of any type to be produced electronically.
 ❑ B. Several advances in the study of sound were made during the nineteenth and twentieth centuries.
 ❑ C. Most advances in the study of sound occurred after 1940.
 ❑ D. The telephone, microphone, and phonograph greatly assisted in further advancing the study of sound.

Plastic surgery is one of many forms of medicine. It deals with adjusting or changing a part of the body that is damaged or deformed. The need for plastic surgery may stem from congenital malformations, such as a cleft palate or a harelip. Plastic surgery may also be necessary after sustaining injury or from deforming surgery required to treat a disease such as breast cancer. Plastic surgery is mainly geared toward correcting birth defects, restoring function to body parts, and improving appearance.

Plastic surgery dates back as early as 2000 B.C. and was one of the earliest forms of surgery. In ancient India, amputation of the nose was a habitual form of punishment. As a result, nose reconstructive surgeries were performed where the nose was rebuilt using a portion of the forehead. It was not until the sixteenth century that real advances were made in the field of plastic surgery. The Italian physicist Gasparo Tagliacozzi played an important role in the study of plastic surgery during that time. The twentieth century saw many more great advances in plastic surgery. It also had a positive impact on victim morale after World War II. Many victims of that war had plastic surgery to correct injured or disfigured body parts.

Reconstructive surgery is a form of plastic surgery that involves the rebuilding of normal physical contours and the restoration of function. This type of surgery is often performed on the nose, fingers, jaw, and so on. Due to the increase in automobile accidents in modern society, reconstructive surgery is often required after accidents that have resulted in facial damage. As advances continue in other areas of medicine, such as improvements for curing various diseases, there have also been improvements in the techniques used in reconstructive surgery. Reconstructive surgery requires very complex techniques. Reconstructing the facial area and the hands requires a high level of artistic qualities along with technical skills.

6. What is the main idea of the first paragraph?
   - ❑ A. The primary objective of plastic surgery is to restore loss of function.
   - ❑ B. Malformation can occur for a number of different reasons.
   - ❑ C. Plastic surgery is performed to correct a damaged or deformed body part.
   - ❑ D. A cleft palate is also known as a harelip.

7. In the second paragraph, what is the meaning of the word *habitual*?
   - ❑ A. Unusual
   - ❑ B. Customary
   - ❑ C. Cruel
   - ❑ D. Painful

Most people have heard the name Socrates because he was the greatest philosopher in history. One of the differences between Socrates and other philosophers was that he never accepted payment for any of his teachings. His opinion was that he was only teaching an awareness of the need for more knowledge. Plato, a pupil of Socrates, was responsible for preserving the work of Socrates. Socrates taught that every person has full knowledge of ultimate truth contained within his soul and needs only to be spurred to conscious reflection in order to become aware of it. In Plato's dialogue *Meno*, for example, Socrates guides an untutored slave to the formulation of the Pythagorean theorem, thus demonstrating that such knowledge is innate in the soul, rather than learned from experience. Socrates believed that it was his job and the job of other philosophers to encourage people to think for themselves. He was teaching people a different method of thinking and a way of life. He stressed the needs for analytical examination of the grounds of one's beliefs, for clear definitions of basic concepts, and for a rational and critical approach to ethical problems.

On the other hand, Plato was more of a logical and positive thinker than his teacher. His writings are often seen as a continuation of Socrates' teachings. Both Socrates and Plato regarded ethics as the highest branch of knowledge; he stressed the intellectual basis of virtue, identifying virtue with wisdom. This view led to the so-called

"Socratic paradox" that, as Socrates asserts in *The Protagoras*, "No man does evil voluntarily." Aristotle later noticed that such a conclusion allows no place for moral responsibility. Plato's continued research, ideas, and knowledge eventually became fundamental in Western thought.

The source of Plato's philosophy comes from his Theory of Ideas. This theory basically divides existence into two different realms, an "intelligible realm" of perfect, eternal, and invisible ideas, or forms, and a "sensible realm" of concrete, familiar objects. You can find this theory expressed in several of his dialogues, including *The Republic* and *The Parmenides*.

8. What is the meaning of the word *innate*?
   - ❑ A. Inborn
   - ❑ B. Learned
   - ❑ C. Adopted
   - ❑ D. Unknown

9. According to one philosopher, a philosopher's task is to?
   - ❑ A. Teach people about the unknown
   - ❑ B. Encourage people to think positively
   - ❑ C. Rouse people into thinking for themselves
   - ❑ D. Educate people about basic concepts

10. Which theory divides our being into two different areas?
    - ❑ A. The Socrates theory
    - ❑ B. The Theory of Ideas
    - ❑ C. The Pythagorean theorem
    - ❑ D. The Republic

Grammar, Punctuation, and Usage

Questions 11 through 19 cover grammar, punctuation, and usage. Follow the instructions given for each group of questions.

For questions 11 and 12, identify from the underlined items which part of the sentence, if any, is incorrect.

11. Mom <u>asked,</u> <u>"Did</u> you study for your <u>English</u> <u>test?"</u>
    - ❑ A. asked,
    - ❑ B. "Did
    - ❑ C. English
    - ❑ D. test?"
    - ❑ E. No error

12. <u>Either</u> my sister nor my brother <u>will be</u> going to the party <u>due</u> to prior <u>commitments.</u>

   ❑ A. Either

   ❑ B. will be

   ❑ C. due

   ❑ D. commitments.

   ❑ E. No error

Read questions 13 through 19 and identify which option best corrects the underlined portion of the sentence.

13. If the checks <u>have been received</u> last week, why haven't they been deposited into the bank account?

   ❑ A. were received

   ❑ B. had been received

   ❑ C. was received

   ❑ D. have received

14. If I <u>had the number,</u> I would have called and made a dinner reservation ahead of time.

   ❑ A. have the number,

   ❑ B. had the number;

   ❑ C. have had the number,

   ❑ D. had had the number,

15. According to the weather forecast, the rain <u>will stop</u> by the time we get to the beach.

   ❑ A. will not stop

   ❑ B. will have stopped

   ❑ C. shall have stopped

   ❑ D. will has stopped

16. If Ben <u>would not have missed</u> the final jump, he would have won the gold medal.

   ❑ A. would not have never missed

   ❑ B. would not has missed

   ❑ C. wouldn't have missed

   ❑ D. had not missed

17. After I drove the new car, I decided that mine <u>was the most efficient.</u>

   ❑ A. is the most efficient

   ❑ B. had been more efficient

   ❑ C. was more efficient

   ❑ D. were the most efficient

18. The story explained to the students <u>where</u> the two countries finally ended the war.
   - ❏ A. how
   - ❏ B. were
   - ❏ C. where of
   - ❏ D. what

19. I would wait until after winter to put your house up for sale if I <u>had been</u> you.
   - ❏ A. was
   - ❏ B. have been
   - ❏ C. were
   - ❏ D. where

PRAXIS Mathematics

Questions 20 through 39 present math problems. Choose the mathematically correct answer for each question.

20. Which of the following numbers is divisible by 21?
   - ❏ A. 389
   - ❏ B. 444
   - ❏ C. 312
   - ❏ D. 252

21. What is the greatest common divisor for the following numbers?
24, 30, 42
   - ❏ A. 2
   - ❏ B. 4
   - ❏ C. 6
   - ❏ D. 8

22. What is the least common multiple of the following numbers?
15, 39, 30, 21, 70
   - ❏ A. 2,370
   - ❏ B. 3,270
   - ❏ C. 7,320
   - ❏ D. 2,730

23. Which of the following whole numbers corresponds to the fraction of $\frac{16}{2}$?
   - ❏ A. 2
   - ❏ B. 4
   - ❏ C. 6
   - ❏ D. 8

24. Felicia purchased the following from the market: $\frac{1}{2}$ pound of cheese, $2\frac{1}{4}$ pounds of ham, 2 pounds of butter, and a $16\frac{2}{4}$-pound turkey. What was the total weight of her purchase?

   ❏ A. $20\frac{4}{5}$

   ❏ B. $21\frac{1}{4}$

   ❏ C. $21\frac{1}{2}$

   ❏ D. $20\frac{3}{5}$

25. 35,740 kilometers is equal to how many meters?

   ❏ A. 35,740,000 meters

   ❏ B. 35.740 meters

   ❏ C. 3,574,000 meters

   ❏ D. 357.40 meters

26. How many yards are in 21 meters? Round the answer to the nearest whole number.

   ❏ A. 21,000 yards

   ❏ B. 23 yards

   ❏ C. 19 yards

   ❏ D. 2.1 yards

27. A circle has a radius of 12 cm. What is the area of the circle? Round the answer to the nearest whole number.

   ❏ A. 110

   ❏ B. 38

   ❏ C. 355

   ❏ D. 452

28. How many liters are in 135,000 milliliters?

   ❏ A. 13,500

   ❏ B. 13.5

   ❏ C. 1.35

   ❏ D. 135

29. Don drives his car 200 kilometers and uses 14 liters of gasoline. How many kilometers per liter are used? Round your answer to the nearest whole number.

   ❏ A. 14

   ❏ B. 12

   ❏ C. 15

   ❏ D. 18

30. Which of the following represents the answer to the following equation as a reduced fraction?

    $\frac{3}{4}(\frac{1}{2} \times \frac{2}{3}) = ?$

    ❑ A. $\frac{1}{4}$

    ❑ B. $\frac{3}{4}$

    ❑ C. $\frac{6}{24}$

    ❑ D. $\frac{1}{2}$

31. $17\frac{4}{5} - 6\frac{3}{8}$ equals?

    ❑ A. $11\frac{7}{13}$

    ❑ B. $11\frac{1}{3}$

    ❑ C. $11\frac{17}{40}$

    ❑ D. $11\frac{5}{24}$

32. Which of the following represents the number 23,895.9463 rounded to the nearest hundredth?

    ❑ A. 23,900
    ❑ B. 23,895.9
    ❑ C. 23,000
    ❑ D. 23,895.95

33. What does 35.897 divided by 24.7 equal? Round the answer to the nearest tenth.

    ❑ A. 1.4
    ❑ B. 1.45
    ❑ C. 1.5
    ❑ D. 1.55

34. A salesman makes 12% commission on all his sales. His total sales for one month equal $9,500.00. How much commission will he make?

    ❑ A. $8,360.00
    ❑ B. $2,500.00
    ❑ C. $10,640.00
    ❑ D. $1,140.00

35. An electronic store has a markup of 24%. The cost of a television is $1,400.00. What is the selling price?

    ❑ A. $1,064.00
    ❑ B. $1,736.00
    ❑ C. $1,525.00
    ❑ D. $1,498.00

36. Which of the following represents 15% of 823?
    - ❑ A. 5,486.66
    - ❑ B. 699
    - ❑ C. 123.45
    - ❑ D. 946.45

37. Which of the following represents the decimal value for 5.5%?
    - ❑ A. 5.5
    - ❑ B. 55.0
    - ❑ C. 0.55
    - ❑ D. 0.055

38. Which of the following represents $\frac{23}{24}$ as a decimal rounded to the nearest hundredth?
    - ❑ A. 0.958
    - ❑ B. 0.95
    - ❑ C. 0.96
    - ❑ D. 0.959

39. Which of the following represents $\frac{9}{8}$ as a percent?
    - ❑ A. 112.5%
    - ❑ B. 11.25%
    - ❑ C. 1.125%
    - ❑ D. 1125.0%

PRAXIS Essay

For questions 40 through 45, develop essays based on the given essay topics.

40. Students should not be given morning and afternoon recess breaks in elementary school.

41. Teachers should be required to take college-level courses during summer vacation.

42. Private schools offer better learning and more opportunities for students than public schools.

43. Televisions should be permitted in all classrooms.

44. A teacher without extensive training in a subject area should not be permitted to teach that subject at the secondary level.

45. Any person who is in the spotlight is obligated to act as a role model for teenagers.

Answer Key for Practice Exam #3

1. B   **16.** D   **31.** C

2. A   **17.** C   **32.** D

3. A   **18.** A   **33.** C

4. D   **19.** C   **34.** D

5. B   **20.** D   **35.** B

6. C   **21.** C   **36.** C

7. B   **22.** D   **37.** D

8. A   **23.** D   **38.** C

9. C   **24.** B   **39.** A

10. B   **25.** A   **40.** Answers will vary.

11. E   **26.** B   **41.** Answers will vary.

12. A   **27.** D   **42.** Answers will vary.

13. A   **28.** D   **43.** Answers will vary.

14. D   **29.** A   **44.** Answers will vary.

15. B   **30.** A   **45.** Answers will vary.

Reading Comprehension

Question 1

Answer B is correct. The first paragraph indicates that Charles Theodore's children were illegitimate, which caused problems in having them named princes of the Holy Roman Empire. Therefore, answers A, C, and D are incorrect.

Question 2

Answer A is correct. Frederick the Great did not want to support any moves that would increase Austria's power in the event that it might interfere with his plans of uniting with Prussia. Therefore, answers B, C, and D are incorrect.

Question 3

Answer A is correct. The passage states that Karl Rudolf Koniq, who was a German, designed tuning forks. Therefore, answers B, C, and D are incorrect.

Question 4

Answer D is correct. A cathode-ray oscilloscope can be used to analyze sound after it has been converted into electrical currents. Therefore, answers A, B, and C are incorrect.

Question 5

Answer B is correct. The second paragraph talks about the many advances made in the study of sound during the nineteenth and twentieth centuries. Therefore, answers A, C, and D are incorrect. These are all supporting ideas within the paragraph.

Question 6

Answer C is correct. The main idea of the first paragraph is that plastic surgery is performed to correct a damaged or deformed body part. Therefore, answers A, B, and D are incorrect. The remaining options are all supporting ideas in the first paragraph.

Question 7

Answer B is correct. The word *habitual* also means customary. Therefore, answers A, C, and D are incorrect.

Question 8

Answer A is correct. The word *innate* also means inborn. Therefore, answers B, C, and D are incorrect.

Question 9

Answer C is correct. The passage states that Socrates believed it was a philosopher's task to encourage people to think for themselves. Therefore, answers A, B, and D are incorrect.

Question 10

Answer B is correct. The passage states that the Theory of Ideas divides existence into two realms: an "intelligible realm" and a "sensible realm." Therefore, answers A, C, and D are incorrect.

Grammar, Punctuation, and Usage

Question 11

Answer E is correct. The sentence contains no errors as it is written. Therefore, answers A, B, C, and D are incorrect.

Question 12

Answer A is correct. The correct word that should be used is *neither*. Therefore, answers B, C, D, and E are incorrect.

Question 13

Answer A is correct. The correct phrase is "were received." Therefore, answers B, C, and D are incorrect.

Question 14

Answer D is correct. The underlined part of the sentence should be replaced with "had had the number." Therefore, answers A, B, and C are incorrect.

Question 15

Answer B is correct. The underlined part of the sentence should be changed to "will have stopped." Therefore, answers A, C, and D are incorrect.

Question 16

Answer D is correct. The underlined part of the sentence should be changed to "had not missed." Therefore, answers A, B, and C are incorrect.

Question 17

Answer C is correct. The underlined part of the sentence should be changed to "was more efficient." Therefore, answers A, B, and D are incorrect.

Question 18

Answer A is correct. The underlined part of the sentence should be changed from *where* to *how*. Therefore, answers B, C, and D are incorrect.

Question 19

Answer C is correct. The underlined part of the sentence should be changed from *had been* to *were*. Therefore, answers A, B, and D are incorrect.

PRAXIS Mathematics

Question 20

Answer D is correct. The number 252 is divisible by 21. Therefore, answers A, B, and C are incorrect.

Question 21

Answer C is correct. The greatest common divisor of the given numbers is 6. Therefore, answers A, B, and D are incorrect.

Question 22

Answer D is correct. The least common multiple of the given numbers is 2,730. Therefore, answers A, B, and C are incorrect.

Question 23

Answer D is correct. The number 8 corresponds to the fraction of $\frac{16}{2}$. Therefore, answers A, B, and C are incorrect.

Question 24

Answer B is correct. The answer to the equation is $21\frac{1}{4}$. You can find the answer by adding the whole numbers, changing the fractions so they have a common denominator, and adding the numerators together. Therefore, answers A, C, and D are incorrect.

Question 25

Answer A is correct. There are 1,000 meters in 1 kilometer, so there are 35,740,000 meters in 35,740 kilometers. Therefore, answers B, C, and D are incorrect.

Question 26

Answer B is correct. There are 0.9144 meters in one yard, so there are 22.9658 yards, rounded to 23, in 21 meters. You can find the answer by dividing 21 by 0.9144. Therefore, answers A, C, and D are incorrect.

Question 27

Answer D is correct. The formula to find the area of a circle is $3.14(\text{radius}^2)$, so the area of the circle is 452 ($12^2 = 144$; $144 \times 3.14 = 452$). Therefore, answers A, B, and C are incorrect.

Question 28

Answer D is correct. There are 1,000 milliliters in 1 liter, so there are 135 liters in 135,000 milliliters. Therefore, answers A, B, and C are incorrect.

Question 29

Answer A is correct. Don can drive 14 kilometers per liter. You can find the answer by dividing the number of kilometers driven by the number of liters used. Therefore, answers B, C, and D are incorrect.

Question 30

Answer A is correct. The answer to the equation equals $\frac{1}{4}$. You can find the answer by multiplying the numerators and the denominators. The resulting fraction is $\frac{6}{24}$, which can be reduced to $\frac{1}{4}$. Therefore, answers B, C, and D are incorrect.

Question 31

Answer C is correct. The answer to the equation is $11 \frac{17}{40}$. You can find the answer by subtracting the whole numbers 17–6 to get 11. Then, change the fractions so that they have a common denominator and subtract the numerators to get $\frac{17}{40}$. Therefore, answers A, B, and D are incorrect.

Question 32

Answer D is correct. Because the number 4 is in the hundredths place, it must be rounded up making the answer 23,895.95. Therefore, answers A, B, and C are incorrect.

Question 33

Answer C is correct. 35.897 divided by 24.7 is equal to 1.5 (after being rounded to the nearest tenth). Therefore, answers A, B, and D are incorrect.

Question 34

Answer D is correct. The total amount of commission made for the month is equal to $1,140.00. You can find the answer by multiplying $9,500.00 by .12. Therefore, answers A, B, and C are incorrect.

Question 35

Answer B is correct. The selling price of the television is $1,736.00. You can find the answer by multiplying $1,400.00 by .24 and adding the answer to the cost of the television. Therefore, answers A, C, and D are incorrect.

Question 36

Answer C is correct. 15% of 823 is equal to 123.45. You can find the answer by multiplying 823 by 0.15. Therefore, answers A, B, and D are incorrect.

Question 37

Answer D is correct. The decimal value of 5.5% is equal to 0.055. You can find the answer by dividing the percent by 100. Therefore, answers A, B, and C are incorrect.

Question 38

Answer C is correct. The fraction $\frac{23}{24}$ can also be written in decimal form as 0.96. You can convert the fraction to a decimal by dividing the numerator by the denominator. Then, the answer must be rounded to the nearest hundredth. Therefore, answers A, B, and D are incorrect.

Question 39

Answer A is correct. The fraction $\frac{9}{8}$ can also be written as 112.5%. You can convert the fraction to a percent by dividing the numerator by the denominator and multiplying the answer by 100. Therefore, answers B, C, and D are incorrect.

PRAXIS Essay

Question 40

Answers will vary.

Question 41

Answers will vary.

Question 42

Answers will vary.

Question 43

Answers will vary.

Question 44

Answers will vary.

Question 45

Answers will vary.

PART III
Appendixes

Test Lists

This appendix lists the numbers and names of the specific tests that make up the PRAXIS I and PRAXIS II exams.

PRAXIS I Pre-Professional Skills Test (PPST)

Test Numbers for Praxis I Pre-Professional Skills Test	
Test Number	**Test Name**
10710	PPST: Reading
10730	PPST: Mathematics
20720	PPST: Writing
5710	Computerized PPST: Reading
5730	Computerized PPST: Mathematics
5720	Computerized PPST: Writing

PRAXIS II Subject Assessments

Test Numbers for PRAXIS II Principles of Learning and Teaching (PLT)	
Test Number	**Test Name**
30521	PLT: Early Childhood
30522	PLT: Grades K–6
30523	PLT: Grades 5–9
30524	PLT: Grades 7–12

Test Numbers for PRAXIS II Multiple Subjects Assessment for Teachers (MSAT)	
Test Number	**Test Name**
10140	MSAT: Content Knowledge
20151	MSAT: Content Area Exercises

Test Numbers for PRAXIS II Subject Assessments	
Test Number	**Test Name**
10700	Agriculture
10900	Agriculture (CA)
10780	Agriculture (PA)
10133	Art: Content Knowledge
20131	Art Making
20132	Art: Content, Traditions, Criticism, and Aesthetics
10340	Audiology
20030	Biology and General Science
30233	Biology: Content Essays
20231	Biology: Content Knowledge, Part 1
20232	Biology: Content Knowledge, Part 2
20235	Biology: Content Knowledge
10100	Business Education
30242	Chemistry: Content Essays
20241	Chemistry: Content Knowledge
20245	Chemistry: Content Knowledge
10070	Chemistry, Physics, and General Science
10087	Citizenship Education: Content Knowledge

(continued)

Test Numbers for PRAXIS II Subject Assessments *(continued)*	
Test Number	**Test Name**
20800	Communication (PA)
10810	Cooperative Education
10867	Driver Education
10020	Early Childhood Education
20571	Earth and Space Sciences: Content Knowledge
10910	Economics
10271	Education of Deaf and Hard-of-Hearing Students
20353	Education of Exceptional Students: Core Content Knowledge
10382	Education of Exceptional Students: Learning Disabilities
10542	Education of Exceptional Students: Mild to Moderate Disabilities
10544	Education of Exceptional Students: Severe to Profound Disabilities
20021	Education of Young Children
10410	Educational Leadership: Administration and Supervision
20012	Elementary Education: Content Area Exercises
10014	Elementary Education: Content Knowledge
10011	Elementary Education: Curriculum, Instruction, and Assessment
10016	Elementary Education: Curriculum, Instruction, and Assessment K–5
10041	English Language, Literature, and Composition: Content Knowledge
20042	English Language, Literature, and Composition: Essays
30043	English Language, Literature, and Composition: Pedagogy
20360	English to Speakers of Other Languages
10830	Environmental Education
10120	Family and Consumer Sciences
10840	Foreign Language Pedagogy
20173	French: Content Knowledge
10171	French: Productive Language Skills
30511	Fundamental Subjects: Content Knowledge
30067	General Mathematics (WV)
30433	General Science: Content Essays
10431	General Science: Content Knowledge, Part 1
10432	General Science: Content Knowledge, Part 2
10435	General Science: Content Knowledge
30920	Geography
20181	German: Content Knowledge

(continued)

Test Number	Test Name
Test Numbers for PRAXIS II Subject Assessments *(continued)*	
Test Number	**Test Name**
30182	German: Productive Language Skills
10357	Gifted Education
10930	Government/Political Science
20856	Health and Physical Education: Content Knowledge
20550	Health Education
10200	Introduction to the Teaching of Reading
10600	Latin
10310	Library Media Specialist
30234	Life Science: Pedagogy
10560	Marketing Education
10061	Mathematics: Content Knowledge
30065	Mathematics: Pedagogy
20063	Mathematics: Proofs, Models, and Problems, Part 1
20146	Middle School: Content Knowledge
10049	Middle School English Language Arts
20069	Middle School Mathematics
10439	Middle School Science
20089	Middle School Social Studies
20112	Music: Analysis
30111	Music: Concepts and Processes
10113	Music: Content Knowledge
10110	Music Education
10091	Physical Education: Content Knowledge
30092	Physical Education: Movement Forms—Analysis and Design
20093	Physical Education: Movement Forms—Video Evaluation
20481	Physical Science: Content Knowledge
30483	Physical Science: Pedagogy
30260	Physics
30262	Physics: Content Essays
10261	Physics: Content Knowledge
10265	Physics: Content Knowledge
20530	Pre-Kindergarten Education
20390	Psychology

(continued)

Test Number	Test Name
Test Numbers for PRAXIS II Subject Assessments *(continued)*	
20201	Reading Across the Curriculum: Elementary
20202	Reading Across the Curriculum: Secondary
20300	Reading Specialist
10860	Safety/Driver Education
20420	School Guidance and Counseling
10400	School Psychologist
20211	School Social Worker: Content Knowledge
10951	Social Sciences: Content Knowledge
20082	Social Studies: Analytical Essays
10081	Social Studies: Content Knowledge
20085	Social Studies: Interpretation and Analysis
20083	Social Studies: Interpretation of Materials
30084	Social Studies: Pedagogy
20950	Sociology
10191	Spanish: Content Knowledge
30194	Spanish: Pedagogy
20192	Spanish: Productive Language Skills
10352	Special Education: Application of Core Principles Across Categories of Disability
20351	Special Education: Knowledge-Based Core Principles
10690	Special Education: Preschool/Early Childhood
20371	Special Education: Teaching Students with Behavioral Disorders/Emotional Disturbances
20381	Special Education: Teaching Students with Learning Disabilities
20321	Special Education: Teaching Students with Mental Retardation
10220	Speech Communication
20330	Speech-Language Pathology
10088	Teaching Foundations: History-Social Science
10068	Teaching Foundations: Mathematics
10048	Teaching Foundations: Reading/Language Arts
10438	Teaching Foundations: Science
10528	Teaching Foundations: Multiple Subjects
10880	Teaching Speech to Students with Language Impairments

(continued)

Test Numbers for PRAXIS II Subject Assessments *(continued)*	
Test Number	**Test Name**
10290	Teaching Students with Orthopedic Impairments
10280	Teaching Students with Visual Impairments
10050	Technology Education
10640	Theater
10890	Vocational General Knowledge
10940	World and U.S. History
10941	World and U.S. History: Content Knowledge

What's on the CD

The CD that accompanies this book features a state-of-the-art exam preparation engine from ExamForce called CramMaster. This uniquely powerful program identifies gaps in your knowledge and helps you turn them into strengths.

The CramMaster Engine

This innovative exam engine systematically prepares you for a successful test. Working your way through CramMaster is the fastest, surest route to a successful exam. The presentation of questions is weighted according to your unique requirements. Your answer history determines which questions you'll see next. The exam engine determines what you don't know and forces you to overcome those shortcomings. You won't waste time answering easy questions about things you already know.

Multiple Test Modes

The CramMaster test engine from ExamForce has three unique testing modes to systematically prepare you for a successful exam.

Pretest Mode

Pretest mode is used to establish your baseline skill set. You train CramMaster by taking two or three pretests. There is neither review nor feedback on answers in this mode. You view your topic-by-topic skill levels from the History menu on the main screen. Effective exam preparation begins when you attack your weakest topics first in Adaptive Drill mode.

Adaptive Drill Mode

Adaptive Drill mode allows you to focus on specific exam objectives. CramMaster learns which questions you find difficult and drills you until you master them. As you gain proficiency in one area, it seeks out the next with which to challenge you. Even the most complex concepts of the exam are mastered in this mode.

Simulated Exam Mode

Simulated Exam mode approximates the real exam. By the time you reach this level, you've already mastered the exam material. This is your opportunity to exercise those skills while building your mental and physical stamina.

Installing CramMaster for the PRAXIS I Exam

The minimum system requirements for installation are as follows:

➤ Windows 95, 98, ME, NT4, 2000, or XP

➤ 64MB RAM

➤ 18MB disk space

NOTE | If you need technical support, please contact ExamForce at 800-845-8569 or email support@examforce.com. Additional product support can be found at www.examforce.com.

To install the CramMaster CD-ROM, follow these instructions:

1. Close all applications before beginning this installation.

2. Insert the CD into your CD-ROM drive. If the setup starts automatically, go to step 6. If the setup does not start automatically, continue with step 3.

3. From the Start menu, select Run.

4. Click Browse to locate the CramMaster CD. In the Browse dialog box, from the Look In drop-down list, select the CD-ROM drive.

5. In the Browse dialog box, double-click on `Setup.exe`. In the Run dialog box, click OK to begin the installation.

6. On the Welcome screen, click Next.

7. To agree to the End User License Agreement (EULA), click Next.

8. On the Choose Destination Location screen, click Next to install the software to `C:\Program Files\CramMaster`.

9. On the Select Program Manager Group screen, verify that the Program Manager group is set to CramMaster, and click Next.

10. On the Start Installation screen, click Next.

11. On the Installation Complete screen, verify that the Launch CramMaster Now box is checked, and click Finish.

12. For your convenience, a shortcut to CramMaster will be automatically created on your desktop.

Using CramMaster for the PRAXIS I Exam

An Introduction slide show starts when CramMaster first launches. It teaches you how to get the most out of this uniquely powerful program. Uncheck the Show on Startup box to suppress the Introduction from showing each time the application is launched. You may review it at any time from the Help menu on the main screen. Tips on using other CramMaster features can be found there as well.

Customer Support

If you encounter problems installing or using CramMaster for the PRAXIS I exam, please contact ExamForce at 800-845-8569 or email support@ examforce.com. Support hours are from 8:30 a.m. to 5:30 p.m. EST Monday through Friday. Additional product support can be found at www. examforce.com.

If you would like to purchase additional ExamForce products, telephone 800-845-8569, or visit www.examforce.com.

Index

adverbs, 90-91
answer keys (practice exams), 237-238, 255-263
nouns, 84
    common nouns, 85
    plural nouns, 85
    possessive nouns, 85
    pronouns, 85-87
    proper nouns, 85
questions, 226-227, 249-254
verbs
    auxiliary verbs, 89
    finite verbs, 89
    infinitive verbs, 90
    non-finite verbs, 89
    tenses, 88
graphs
    bar graphs, 41
    circle graphs, 41
    legends, 42
    line graphs, 42
    XY plots, 42
greatest common factors (fractions), 12

H - I

hyphenated form compound words, 94-95
hypotenuse (triangles), 36

ideas, organizing (essay writing), 118-121
identifying
    main ideas (reading), 63-64
    purposes (reading), 64-65
idioms, 100-102
improper fractions, 13
independent clauses, 91
    commas, 95
    complex sentences, 92
    compound sentences, 92
    simple sentences, 92
inequalities
    solutions, 27-29
    symbols of, 26
inferential comprehension, PPST (Pre-Professional Skills Test), 62
infinitive verbs, 90
information, locating (reading), 69
installing CramMaster exam preparation engine, 274-275
Instruction and Assessment category (PLT exams), 149-150
interference (reading), 67-68
intersecting lines (geometry), 32

introductory paragraphs (essays)
    reader attention, 122
    topic sentence, 122-123
inverse operations (equations), 21
issues (essays), 114

J - K - L

K-6 sample questions, PLT (Principles of Learning and Teaching, 152-154
keys (charts/graphs), 42
Kohlberg, 148

launching CramMaster exam preparation engine, 275
legends (charts/graphs), 42
legs (triangles), 36
line graphs, 42
lines (geometry)
    intersecting lines, 32
    parallel lines, 32
    perpendicular lines, 32
literal comprehension, PPST (Pre-Professional Skills Test), 62
locating information (reading), 69
lowest terms (fractions), 12

M

main ideas, identifying (reading), 63-64
mapping (brainstorming), 116
Maslow, 149
mathematics
    addition, 4
        decimals, 17
        division, 17
        fractions, 13-15
        mixed numbers, 13
        negative numbers, 6
        positive numbers, 6
    averages, 8-9
    charts
        legends, 42
        pie charts, 41
    cubes, 25
        surface area calculation formula, 40
        volume calculation formula, 39
    decimals
        adding, 17
        converting fractions to, 21
        converting to fractions, 21
        dividing, 17
        multiplying, 17

How can we make this index more useful? Email us at indexes@quepublishing.com

O - P

If you would like more answer sheets than are available here, visit this book's website at www.examcram.com. You can download and print as many answer sheets as you want.

Answer Sheet for Practice Exam

Directions: Read each question carefully and choose the best answer. Fill in the oval completely with a soft lead pencil.

1. Ⓐ Ⓑ Ⓒ Ⓓ Ⓔ
2. Ⓐ Ⓑ Ⓒ Ⓓ Ⓔ
3. Ⓐ Ⓑ Ⓒ Ⓓ Ⓔ
4. Ⓐ Ⓑ Ⓒ Ⓓ Ⓔ
5. Ⓐ Ⓑ Ⓒ Ⓓ Ⓔ
6. Ⓐ Ⓑ Ⓒ Ⓓ Ⓔ
7. Ⓐ Ⓑ Ⓒ Ⓓ Ⓔ
8. Ⓐ Ⓑ Ⓒ Ⓓ Ⓔ
9. Ⓐ Ⓑ Ⓒ Ⓓ Ⓔ
10. Ⓐ Ⓑ Ⓒ Ⓓ Ⓔ
11. Ⓐ Ⓑ Ⓒ Ⓓ Ⓔ
12. Ⓐ Ⓑ Ⓒ Ⓓ Ⓔ
13. Ⓐ Ⓑ Ⓒ Ⓓ Ⓔ
14. Ⓐ Ⓑ Ⓒ Ⓓ Ⓔ
15. Ⓐ Ⓑ Ⓒ Ⓓ Ⓔ
16. Ⓐ Ⓑ Ⓒ Ⓓ Ⓔ
17. Ⓐ Ⓑ Ⓒ Ⓓ Ⓔ
18. Ⓐ Ⓑ Ⓒ Ⓓ Ⓔ

19. Ⓐ Ⓑ Ⓒ Ⓓ Ⓔ
20. Ⓐ Ⓑ Ⓒ Ⓓ Ⓔ
21. Ⓐ Ⓑ Ⓒ Ⓓ Ⓔ
22. Ⓐ Ⓑ Ⓒ Ⓓ Ⓔ
23. Ⓐ Ⓑ Ⓒ Ⓓ Ⓔ
24. Ⓐ Ⓑ Ⓒ Ⓓ Ⓔ
25. Ⓐ Ⓑ Ⓒ Ⓓ Ⓔ
26. Ⓐ Ⓑ Ⓒ Ⓓ Ⓔ
27. Ⓐ Ⓑ Ⓒ Ⓓ Ⓔ
28. Ⓐ Ⓑ Ⓒ Ⓓ Ⓔ
29. Ⓐ Ⓑ Ⓒ Ⓓ Ⓔ
30. Ⓐ Ⓑ Ⓒ Ⓓ Ⓔ
31. Ⓐ Ⓑ Ⓒ Ⓓ Ⓔ
32. Ⓐ Ⓑ Ⓒ Ⓓ Ⓔ
33. Ⓐ Ⓑ Ⓒ Ⓓ Ⓔ
34. Ⓐ Ⓑ Ⓒ Ⓓ Ⓔ
35. Ⓐ Ⓑ Ⓒ Ⓓ Ⓔ
36. Ⓐ Ⓑ Ⓒ Ⓓ Ⓔ

37. Ⓐ Ⓑ Ⓒ Ⓓ Ⓔ
38. Ⓐ Ⓑ Ⓒ Ⓓ Ⓔ
39. Ⓐ Ⓑ Ⓒ Ⓓ Ⓔ
40. Ⓐ Ⓑ Ⓒ Ⓓ Ⓔ
41. Ⓐ Ⓑ Ⓒ Ⓓ Ⓔ
42. Ⓐ Ⓑ Ⓒ Ⓓ Ⓔ
43. Ⓐ Ⓑ Ⓒ Ⓓ Ⓔ
44. Ⓐ Ⓑ Ⓒ Ⓓ Ⓔ
45. Ⓐ Ⓑ Ⓒ Ⓓ Ⓔ
46. Ⓐ Ⓑ Ⓒ Ⓓ Ⓔ
47. Ⓐ Ⓑ Ⓒ Ⓓ Ⓔ
48. Ⓐ Ⓑ Ⓒ Ⓓ Ⓔ
49. Ⓐ Ⓑ Ⓒ Ⓓ Ⓔ
50. Ⓐ Ⓑ Ⓒ Ⓓ Ⓔ
51. Ⓐ Ⓑ Ⓒ Ⓓ Ⓔ
52. Ⓐ Ⓑ Ⓒ Ⓓ Ⓔ
53. Ⓐ Ⓑ Ⓒ Ⓓ Ⓔ
54. Ⓐ Ⓑ Ⓒ Ⓓ Ⓔ

55. Ⓐ Ⓑ Ⓒ Ⓓ Ⓔ   58. Ⓐ Ⓑ Ⓒ Ⓓ Ⓔ   61. Ⓐ Ⓑ Ⓒ Ⓓ Ⓔ

56. Ⓐ Ⓑ Ⓒ Ⓓ Ⓔ   59. Ⓐ Ⓑ Ⓒ Ⓓ Ⓔ   62. Ⓐ Ⓑ Ⓒ Ⓓ Ⓔ

57. Ⓐ Ⓑ Ⓒ Ⓓ Ⓔ   60. Ⓐ Ⓑ Ⓒ Ⓓ Ⓔ   63. Ⓐ Ⓑ Ⓒ Ⓓ Ⓔ

Answer Sheet for Practice Exam

Directions: Read each question carefully and choose the best answer. Fill in the oval completely with a soft lead pencil.

1. Ⓐ Ⓑ Ⓒ Ⓓ Ⓔ   20. Ⓐ Ⓑ Ⓒ Ⓓ Ⓔ   39. Ⓐ Ⓑ Ⓒ Ⓓ Ⓔ

2. Ⓐ Ⓑ Ⓒ Ⓓ Ⓔ   21. Ⓐ Ⓑ Ⓒ Ⓓ Ⓔ   40. Ⓐ Ⓑ Ⓒ Ⓓ Ⓔ

3. Ⓐ Ⓑ Ⓒ Ⓓ Ⓔ   22. Ⓐ Ⓑ Ⓒ Ⓓ Ⓔ   41. Ⓐ Ⓑ Ⓒ Ⓓ Ⓔ

4. Ⓐ Ⓑ Ⓒ Ⓓ Ⓔ   23. Ⓐ Ⓑ Ⓒ Ⓓ Ⓔ   42. Ⓐ Ⓑ Ⓒ Ⓓ Ⓔ

5. Ⓐ Ⓑ Ⓒ Ⓓ Ⓔ   24. Ⓐ Ⓑ Ⓒ Ⓓ Ⓔ   43. Ⓐ Ⓑ Ⓒ Ⓓ Ⓔ

6. Ⓐ Ⓑ Ⓒ Ⓓ Ⓔ   25. Ⓐ Ⓑ Ⓒ Ⓓ Ⓔ   44. Ⓐ Ⓑ Ⓒ Ⓓ Ⓔ

7. Ⓐ Ⓑ Ⓒ Ⓓ Ⓔ   26. Ⓐ Ⓑ Ⓒ Ⓓ Ⓔ   45. Ⓐ Ⓑ Ⓒ Ⓓ Ⓔ

8. Ⓐ Ⓑ Ⓒ Ⓓ Ⓔ   27. Ⓐ Ⓑ Ⓒ Ⓓ Ⓔ   46. Ⓐ Ⓑ Ⓒ Ⓓ Ⓔ

9. Ⓐ Ⓑ Ⓒ Ⓓ Ⓔ   28. Ⓐ Ⓑ Ⓒ Ⓓ Ⓔ   47. Ⓐ Ⓑ Ⓒ Ⓓ Ⓔ

10. Ⓐ Ⓑ Ⓒ Ⓓ Ⓔ   29. Ⓐ Ⓑ Ⓒ Ⓓ Ⓔ   48. Ⓐ Ⓑ Ⓒ Ⓓ Ⓔ

11. Ⓐ Ⓑ Ⓒ Ⓓ Ⓔ   30. Ⓐ Ⓑ Ⓒ Ⓓ Ⓔ   49. Ⓐ Ⓑ Ⓒ Ⓓ Ⓔ

12. Ⓐ Ⓑ Ⓒ Ⓓ Ⓔ   31. Ⓐ Ⓑ Ⓒ Ⓓ Ⓔ   50. Ⓐ Ⓑ Ⓒ Ⓓ Ⓔ

13. Ⓐ Ⓑ Ⓒ Ⓓ Ⓔ   32. Ⓐ Ⓑ Ⓒ Ⓓ Ⓔ   51. Ⓐ Ⓑ Ⓒ Ⓓ Ⓔ

14. Ⓐ Ⓑ Ⓒ Ⓓ Ⓔ   33. Ⓐ Ⓑ Ⓒ Ⓓ Ⓔ   52. Ⓐ Ⓑ Ⓒ Ⓓ Ⓔ

15. Ⓐ Ⓑ Ⓒ Ⓓ Ⓔ   34. Ⓐ Ⓑ Ⓒ Ⓓ Ⓔ   53. Ⓐ Ⓑ Ⓒ Ⓓ Ⓔ

16. Ⓐ Ⓑ Ⓒ Ⓓ Ⓔ   35. Ⓐ Ⓑ Ⓒ Ⓓ Ⓔ   54. Ⓐ Ⓑ Ⓒ Ⓓ Ⓔ

17. Ⓐ Ⓑ Ⓒ Ⓓ Ⓔ   36. Ⓐ Ⓑ Ⓒ Ⓓ Ⓔ   55. Ⓐ Ⓑ Ⓒ Ⓓ Ⓔ

18. Ⓐ Ⓑ Ⓒ Ⓓ Ⓔ   37. Ⓐ Ⓑ Ⓒ Ⓓ Ⓔ   56. Ⓐ Ⓑ Ⓒ Ⓓ Ⓔ

19. Ⓐ Ⓑ Ⓒ Ⓓ Ⓔ   38. Ⓐ Ⓑ Ⓒ Ⓓ Ⓔ   57. Ⓐ Ⓑ Ⓒ Ⓓ Ⓔ

58. Ⓐ Ⓑ Ⓒ Ⓓ Ⓔ   60. Ⓐ Ⓑ Ⓒ Ⓓ Ⓔ   62. Ⓐ Ⓑ Ⓒ Ⓓ Ⓔ

59. Ⓐ Ⓑ Ⓒ Ⓓ Ⓔ   61. Ⓐ Ⓑ Ⓒ Ⓓ Ⓔ   63. Ⓐ Ⓑ Ⓒ Ⓓ Ⓔ

Answer Sheet for Practice Exam

Directions: Read each question carefully and choose the best answer. Fill in the oval completely with a soft lead pencil.

1. Ⓐ Ⓑ Ⓒ Ⓓ Ⓔ   20. Ⓐ Ⓑ Ⓒ Ⓓ Ⓔ   39. Ⓐ Ⓑ Ⓒ Ⓓ Ⓔ

2. Ⓐ Ⓑ Ⓒ Ⓓ Ⓔ   21. Ⓐ Ⓑ Ⓒ Ⓓ Ⓔ   40. Ⓐ Ⓑ Ⓒ Ⓓ Ⓔ

3. Ⓐ Ⓑ Ⓒ Ⓓ Ⓔ   22. Ⓐ Ⓑ Ⓒ Ⓓ Ⓔ   41. Ⓐ Ⓑ Ⓒ Ⓓ Ⓔ

4. Ⓐ Ⓑ Ⓒ Ⓓ Ⓔ   23. Ⓐ Ⓑ Ⓒ Ⓓ Ⓔ   42. Ⓐ Ⓑ Ⓒ Ⓓ Ⓔ

5. Ⓐ Ⓑ Ⓒ Ⓓ Ⓔ   24. Ⓐ Ⓑ Ⓒ Ⓓ Ⓔ   43. Ⓐ Ⓑ Ⓒ Ⓓ Ⓔ

6. Ⓐ Ⓑ Ⓒ Ⓓ Ⓔ   25. Ⓐ Ⓑ Ⓒ Ⓓ Ⓔ   44. Ⓐ Ⓑ Ⓒ Ⓓ Ⓔ

7. Ⓐ Ⓑ Ⓒ Ⓓ Ⓔ   26. Ⓐ Ⓑ Ⓒ Ⓓ Ⓔ   45. Ⓐ Ⓑ Ⓒ Ⓓ Ⓔ

8. Ⓐ Ⓑ Ⓒ Ⓓ Ⓔ   27. Ⓐ Ⓑ Ⓒ Ⓓ Ⓔ   46. Ⓐ Ⓑ Ⓒ Ⓓ Ⓔ

9. Ⓐ Ⓑ Ⓒ Ⓓ Ⓔ   28. Ⓐ Ⓑ Ⓒ Ⓓ Ⓔ   47. Ⓐ Ⓑ Ⓒ Ⓓ Ⓔ

10. Ⓐ Ⓑ Ⓒ Ⓓ Ⓔ   29. Ⓐ Ⓑ Ⓒ Ⓓ Ⓔ   48. Ⓐ Ⓑ Ⓒ Ⓓ Ⓔ

11. Ⓐ Ⓑ Ⓒ Ⓓ Ⓔ   30. Ⓐ Ⓑ Ⓒ Ⓓ Ⓔ   49. Ⓐ Ⓑ Ⓒ Ⓓ Ⓔ

12. Ⓐ Ⓑ Ⓒ Ⓓ Ⓔ   31. Ⓐ Ⓑ Ⓒ Ⓓ Ⓔ   50. Ⓐ Ⓑ Ⓒ Ⓓ Ⓔ

13. Ⓐ Ⓑ Ⓒ Ⓓ Ⓔ   32. Ⓐ Ⓑ Ⓒ Ⓓ Ⓔ   51. Ⓐ Ⓑ Ⓒ Ⓓ Ⓔ

14. Ⓐ Ⓑ Ⓒ Ⓓ Ⓔ   33. Ⓐ Ⓑ Ⓒ Ⓓ Ⓔ   52. Ⓐ Ⓑ Ⓒ Ⓓ Ⓔ

15. Ⓐ Ⓑ Ⓒ Ⓓ Ⓔ   34. Ⓐ Ⓑ Ⓒ Ⓓ Ⓔ   53. Ⓐ Ⓑ Ⓒ Ⓓ Ⓔ

16. Ⓐ Ⓑ Ⓒ Ⓓ Ⓔ   35. Ⓐ Ⓑ Ⓒ Ⓓ Ⓔ   54. Ⓐ Ⓑ Ⓒ Ⓓ Ⓔ

17. Ⓐ Ⓑ Ⓒ Ⓓ Ⓔ   36. Ⓐ Ⓑ Ⓒ Ⓓ Ⓔ   55. Ⓐ Ⓑ Ⓒ Ⓓ Ⓔ

18. Ⓐ Ⓑ Ⓒ Ⓓ Ⓔ   37. Ⓐ Ⓑ Ⓒ Ⓓ Ⓔ   56. Ⓐ Ⓑ Ⓒ Ⓓ Ⓔ

19. Ⓐ Ⓑ Ⓒ Ⓓ Ⓔ   38. Ⓐ Ⓑ Ⓒ Ⓓ Ⓔ   57. Ⓐ Ⓑ Ⓒ Ⓓ Ⓔ

Answer Sheet

58. Ⓐ Ⓑ Ⓒ Ⓓ Ⓔ   60. Ⓐ Ⓑ Ⓒ Ⓓ Ⓔ   62. Ⓐ Ⓑ Ⓒ Ⓓ Ⓔ

59. Ⓐ Ⓑ Ⓒ Ⓓ Ⓔ   61. Ⓐ Ⓑ Ⓒ Ⓓ Ⓔ   63. Ⓐ Ⓑ Ⓒ Ⓓ Ⓔ

Answer Sheet for Practice Exam

Directions: Read each question carefully and choose the best answer. Fill in the oval completely with a soft lead pencil.

1. Ⓐ Ⓑ Ⓒ Ⓓ Ⓔ
2. Ⓐ Ⓑ Ⓒ Ⓓ Ⓔ
3. Ⓐ Ⓑ Ⓒ Ⓓ Ⓔ
4. Ⓐ Ⓑ Ⓒ Ⓓ Ⓔ
5. Ⓐ Ⓑ Ⓒ Ⓓ Ⓔ
6. Ⓐ Ⓑ Ⓒ Ⓓ Ⓔ
7. Ⓐ Ⓑ Ⓒ Ⓓ Ⓔ
8. Ⓐ Ⓑ Ⓒ Ⓓ Ⓔ
9. Ⓐ Ⓑ Ⓒ Ⓓ Ⓔ
10. Ⓐ Ⓑ Ⓒ Ⓓ Ⓔ
11. Ⓐ Ⓑ Ⓒ Ⓓ Ⓔ
12. Ⓐ Ⓑ Ⓒ Ⓓ Ⓔ
13. Ⓐ Ⓑ Ⓒ Ⓓ Ⓔ
14. Ⓐ Ⓑ Ⓒ Ⓓ Ⓔ
15. Ⓐ Ⓑ Ⓒ Ⓓ Ⓔ
16. Ⓐ Ⓑ Ⓒ Ⓓ Ⓔ
17. Ⓐ Ⓑ Ⓒ Ⓓ Ⓔ
18. Ⓐ Ⓑ Ⓒ Ⓓ Ⓔ
19. Ⓐ Ⓑ Ⓒ Ⓓ Ⓔ

20. Ⓐ Ⓑ Ⓒ Ⓓ Ⓔ
21. Ⓐ Ⓑ Ⓒ Ⓓ Ⓔ
22. Ⓐ Ⓑ Ⓒ Ⓓ Ⓔ
23. Ⓐ Ⓑ Ⓒ Ⓓ Ⓔ
24. Ⓐ Ⓑ Ⓒ Ⓓ Ⓔ
25. Ⓐ Ⓑ Ⓒ Ⓓ Ⓔ
26. Ⓐ Ⓑ Ⓒ Ⓓ Ⓔ
27. Ⓐ Ⓑ Ⓒ Ⓓ Ⓔ
28. Ⓐ Ⓑ Ⓒ Ⓓ Ⓔ
29. Ⓐ Ⓑ Ⓒ Ⓓ Ⓔ
30. Ⓐ Ⓑ Ⓒ Ⓓ Ⓔ
31. Ⓐ Ⓑ Ⓒ Ⓓ Ⓔ
32. Ⓐ Ⓑ Ⓒ Ⓓ Ⓔ
33. Ⓐ Ⓑ Ⓒ Ⓓ Ⓔ
34. Ⓐ Ⓑ Ⓒ Ⓓ Ⓔ
35. Ⓐ Ⓑ Ⓒ Ⓓ Ⓔ
36. Ⓐ Ⓑ Ⓒ Ⓓ Ⓔ
37. Ⓐ Ⓑ Ⓒ Ⓓ Ⓔ
38. Ⓐ Ⓑ Ⓒ Ⓓ Ⓔ

39. Ⓐ Ⓑ Ⓒ Ⓓ Ⓔ
40. Ⓐ Ⓑ Ⓒ Ⓓ Ⓔ
41. Ⓐ Ⓑ Ⓒ Ⓓ Ⓔ
42. Ⓐ Ⓑ Ⓒ Ⓓ Ⓔ
43. Ⓐ Ⓑ Ⓒ Ⓓ Ⓔ
44. Ⓐ Ⓑ Ⓒ Ⓓ Ⓔ
45. Ⓐ Ⓑ Ⓒ Ⓓ Ⓔ
46. Ⓐ Ⓑ Ⓒ Ⓓ Ⓔ
47. Ⓐ Ⓑ Ⓒ Ⓓ Ⓔ
48. Ⓐ Ⓑ Ⓒ Ⓓ Ⓔ
49. Ⓐ Ⓑ Ⓒ Ⓓ Ⓔ
50. Ⓐ Ⓑ Ⓒ Ⓓ Ⓔ
51. Ⓐ Ⓑ Ⓒ Ⓓ Ⓔ
52. Ⓐ Ⓑ Ⓒ Ⓓ Ⓔ
53. Ⓐ Ⓑ Ⓒ Ⓓ Ⓔ
54. Ⓐ Ⓑ Ⓒ Ⓓ Ⓔ
55. Ⓐ Ⓑ Ⓒ Ⓓ Ⓔ
56. Ⓐ Ⓑ Ⓒ Ⓓ Ⓔ
57. Ⓐ Ⓑ Ⓒ Ⓓ Ⓔ

Answer Sheet for Practice Exam

Directions: Read each question carefully and choose the best answer. Fill in the oval completely with a soft lead pencil.

1. Ⓐ Ⓑ Ⓒ Ⓓ Ⓔ   20. Ⓐ Ⓑ Ⓒ Ⓓ Ⓔ   39. Ⓐ Ⓑ Ⓒ Ⓓ Ⓔ

2. Ⓐ Ⓑ Ⓒ Ⓓ Ⓔ   21. Ⓐ Ⓑ Ⓒ Ⓓ Ⓔ   40. Ⓐ Ⓑ Ⓒ Ⓓ Ⓔ

3. Ⓐ Ⓑ Ⓒ Ⓓ Ⓔ   22. Ⓐ Ⓑ Ⓒ Ⓓ Ⓔ   41. Ⓐ Ⓑ Ⓒ Ⓓ Ⓔ

4. Ⓐ Ⓑ Ⓒ Ⓓ Ⓔ   23. Ⓐ Ⓑ Ⓒ Ⓓ Ⓔ   42. Ⓐ Ⓑ Ⓒ Ⓓ Ⓔ

5. Ⓐ Ⓑ Ⓒ Ⓓ Ⓔ   24. Ⓐ Ⓑ Ⓒ Ⓓ Ⓔ   43. Ⓐ Ⓑ Ⓒ Ⓓ Ⓔ

6. Ⓐ Ⓑ Ⓒ Ⓓ Ⓔ   25. Ⓐ Ⓑ Ⓒ Ⓓ Ⓔ   44. Ⓐ Ⓑ Ⓒ Ⓓ Ⓔ

7. Ⓐ Ⓑ Ⓒ Ⓓ Ⓔ   26. Ⓐ Ⓑ Ⓒ Ⓓ Ⓔ   45. Ⓐ Ⓑ Ⓒ Ⓓ Ⓔ

8. Ⓐ Ⓑ Ⓒ Ⓓ Ⓔ   27. Ⓐ Ⓑ Ⓒ Ⓓ Ⓔ   46. Ⓐ Ⓑ Ⓒ Ⓓ Ⓔ

9. Ⓐ Ⓑ Ⓒ Ⓓ Ⓔ   28. Ⓐ Ⓑ Ⓒ Ⓓ Ⓔ   47. Ⓐ Ⓑ Ⓒ Ⓓ Ⓔ

10. Ⓐ Ⓑ Ⓒ Ⓓ Ⓔ   29. Ⓐ Ⓑ Ⓒ Ⓓ Ⓔ   48. Ⓐ Ⓑ Ⓒ Ⓓ Ⓔ

11. Ⓐ Ⓑ Ⓒ Ⓓ Ⓔ   30. Ⓐ Ⓑ Ⓒ Ⓓ Ⓔ   49. Ⓐ Ⓑ Ⓒ Ⓓ Ⓔ

12. Ⓐ Ⓑ Ⓒ Ⓓ Ⓔ   31. Ⓐ Ⓑ Ⓒ Ⓓ Ⓔ   50. Ⓐ Ⓑ Ⓒ Ⓓ Ⓔ

13. Ⓐ Ⓑ Ⓒ Ⓓ Ⓔ   32. Ⓐ Ⓑ Ⓒ Ⓓ Ⓔ   51. Ⓐ Ⓑ Ⓒ Ⓓ Ⓔ

14. Ⓐ Ⓑ Ⓒ Ⓓ Ⓔ   33. Ⓐ Ⓑ Ⓒ Ⓓ Ⓔ   52. Ⓐ Ⓑ Ⓒ Ⓓ Ⓔ

15. Ⓐ Ⓑ Ⓒ Ⓓ Ⓔ   34. Ⓐ Ⓑ Ⓒ Ⓓ Ⓔ   53. Ⓐ Ⓑ Ⓒ Ⓓ Ⓔ

16. Ⓐ Ⓑ Ⓒ Ⓓ Ⓔ   35. Ⓐ Ⓑ Ⓒ Ⓓ Ⓔ   54. Ⓐ Ⓑ Ⓒ Ⓓ Ⓔ

17. Ⓐ Ⓑ Ⓒ Ⓓ Ⓔ   36. Ⓐ Ⓑ Ⓒ Ⓓ Ⓔ   55. Ⓐ Ⓑ Ⓒ Ⓓ Ⓔ

18. Ⓐ Ⓑ Ⓒ Ⓓ Ⓔ   37. Ⓐ Ⓑ Ⓒ Ⓓ Ⓔ   56. Ⓐ Ⓑ Ⓒ Ⓓ Ⓔ

19. Ⓐ Ⓑ Ⓒ Ⓓ Ⓔ   38. Ⓐ Ⓑ Ⓒ Ⓓ Ⓔ   57. Ⓐ Ⓑ Ⓒ Ⓓ Ⓔ

58. Ⓐ Ⓑ Ⓒ Ⓓ Ⓔ   60. Ⓐ Ⓑ Ⓒ Ⓓ Ⓔ   62. Ⓐ Ⓑ Ⓒ Ⓓ Ⓔ

59. Ⓐ Ⓑ Ⓒ Ⓓ Ⓔ   61. Ⓐ Ⓑ Ⓒ Ⓓ Ⓔ   63. Ⓐ Ⓑ Ⓒ Ⓓ Ⓔ

Answer Sheet for Practice Exam

Directions: Read each question carefully and choose the best answer. Fill in the oval completely with a soft lead pencil.

1. Ⓐ Ⓑ Ⓒ Ⓓ Ⓔ   20. Ⓐ Ⓑ Ⓒ Ⓓ Ⓔ   39. Ⓐ Ⓑ Ⓒ Ⓓ Ⓔ

2. Ⓐ Ⓑ Ⓒ Ⓓ Ⓔ   21. Ⓐ Ⓑ Ⓒ Ⓓ Ⓔ   40. Ⓐ Ⓑ Ⓒ Ⓓ Ⓔ

3. Ⓐ Ⓑ Ⓒ Ⓓ Ⓔ   22. Ⓐ Ⓑ Ⓒ Ⓓ Ⓔ   41. Ⓐ Ⓑ Ⓒ Ⓓ Ⓔ

4. Ⓐ Ⓑ Ⓒ Ⓓ Ⓔ   23. Ⓐ Ⓑ Ⓒ Ⓓ Ⓔ   42. Ⓐ Ⓑ Ⓒ Ⓓ Ⓔ

5. Ⓐ Ⓑ Ⓒ Ⓓ Ⓔ   24. Ⓐ Ⓑ Ⓒ Ⓓ Ⓔ   43. Ⓐ Ⓑ Ⓒ Ⓓ Ⓔ

6. Ⓐ Ⓑ Ⓒ Ⓓ Ⓔ   25. Ⓐ Ⓑ Ⓒ Ⓓ Ⓔ   44. Ⓐ Ⓑ Ⓒ Ⓓ Ⓔ

7. Ⓐ Ⓑ Ⓒ Ⓓ Ⓔ   26. Ⓐ Ⓑ Ⓒ Ⓓ Ⓔ   45. Ⓐ Ⓑ Ⓒ Ⓓ Ⓔ

8. Ⓐ Ⓑ Ⓒ Ⓓ Ⓔ   27. Ⓐ Ⓑ Ⓒ Ⓓ Ⓔ   46. Ⓐ Ⓑ Ⓒ Ⓓ Ⓔ

9. Ⓐ Ⓑ Ⓒ Ⓓ Ⓔ   28. Ⓐ Ⓑ Ⓒ Ⓓ Ⓔ   47. Ⓐ Ⓑ Ⓒ Ⓓ Ⓔ

10. Ⓐ Ⓑ Ⓒ Ⓓ Ⓔ   29. Ⓐ Ⓑ Ⓒ Ⓓ Ⓔ   48. Ⓐ Ⓑ Ⓒ Ⓓ Ⓔ

11. Ⓐ Ⓑ Ⓒ Ⓓ Ⓔ   30. Ⓐ Ⓑ Ⓒ Ⓓ Ⓔ   49. Ⓐ Ⓑ Ⓒ Ⓓ Ⓔ

12. Ⓐ Ⓑ Ⓒ Ⓓ Ⓔ   31. Ⓐ Ⓑ Ⓒ Ⓓ Ⓔ   50. Ⓐ Ⓑ Ⓒ Ⓓ Ⓔ

13. Ⓐ Ⓑ Ⓒ Ⓓ Ⓔ   32. Ⓐ Ⓑ Ⓒ Ⓓ Ⓔ   51. Ⓐ Ⓑ Ⓒ Ⓓ Ⓔ

14. Ⓐ Ⓑ Ⓒ Ⓓ Ⓔ   33. Ⓐ Ⓑ Ⓒ Ⓓ Ⓔ   52. Ⓐ Ⓑ Ⓒ Ⓓ Ⓔ

15. Ⓐ Ⓑ Ⓒ Ⓓ Ⓔ   34. Ⓐ Ⓑ Ⓒ Ⓓ Ⓔ   53. Ⓐ Ⓑ Ⓒ Ⓓ Ⓔ

16. Ⓐ Ⓑ Ⓒ Ⓓ Ⓔ   35. Ⓐ Ⓑ Ⓒ Ⓓ Ⓔ   54. Ⓐ Ⓑ Ⓒ Ⓓ Ⓔ

17. Ⓐ Ⓑ Ⓒ Ⓓ Ⓔ   36. Ⓐ Ⓑ Ⓒ Ⓓ Ⓔ   55. Ⓐ Ⓑ Ⓒ Ⓓ Ⓔ

18. Ⓐ Ⓑ Ⓒ Ⓓ Ⓔ   37. Ⓐ Ⓑ Ⓒ Ⓓ Ⓔ   56. Ⓐ Ⓑ Ⓒ Ⓓ Ⓔ

19. Ⓐ Ⓑ Ⓒ Ⓓ Ⓔ   38. Ⓐ Ⓑ Ⓒ Ⓓ Ⓔ   57. Ⓐ Ⓑ Ⓒ Ⓓ Ⓔ

Answer Sheet

58. Ⓐ Ⓑ Ⓒ Ⓓ Ⓔ   60. Ⓐ Ⓑ Ⓒ Ⓓ Ⓔ   62. Ⓐ Ⓑ Ⓒ Ⓓ Ⓔ

59. Ⓐ Ⓑ Ⓒ Ⓓ Ⓔ   61. Ⓐ Ⓑ Ⓒ Ⓓ Ⓔ   63. Ⓐ Ⓑ Ⓒ Ⓓ Ⓔ

Answer Sheet for Practice Exam

Directions: Read each question carefully and choose the best answer. Fill in the oval completely with a soft lead pencil.

1. Ⓐ Ⓑ Ⓒ Ⓓ Ⓔ
2. Ⓐ Ⓑ Ⓒ Ⓓ Ⓔ
3. Ⓐ Ⓑ Ⓒ Ⓓ Ⓔ
4. Ⓐ Ⓑ Ⓒ Ⓓ Ⓔ
5. Ⓐ Ⓑ Ⓒ Ⓓ Ⓔ
6. Ⓐ Ⓑ Ⓒ Ⓓ Ⓔ
7. Ⓐ Ⓑ Ⓒ Ⓓ Ⓔ
8. Ⓐ Ⓑ Ⓒ Ⓓ Ⓔ
9. Ⓐ Ⓑ Ⓒ Ⓓ Ⓔ
10. Ⓐ Ⓑ Ⓒ Ⓓ Ⓔ
11. Ⓐ Ⓑ Ⓒ Ⓓ Ⓔ
12. Ⓐ Ⓑ Ⓒ Ⓓ Ⓔ
13. Ⓐ Ⓑ Ⓒ Ⓓ Ⓔ
14. Ⓐ Ⓑ Ⓒ Ⓓ Ⓔ
15. Ⓐ Ⓑ Ⓒ Ⓓ Ⓔ
16. Ⓐ Ⓑ Ⓒ Ⓓ Ⓔ
17. Ⓐ Ⓑ Ⓒ Ⓓ Ⓔ
18. Ⓐ Ⓑ Ⓒ Ⓓ Ⓔ
19. Ⓐ Ⓑ Ⓒ Ⓓ Ⓔ

20. Ⓐ Ⓑ Ⓒ Ⓓ Ⓔ
21. Ⓐ Ⓑ Ⓒ Ⓓ Ⓔ
22. Ⓐ Ⓑ Ⓒ Ⓓ Ⓔ
23. Ⓐ Ⓑ Ⓒ Ⓓ Ⓔ
24. Ⓐ Ⓑ Ⓒ Ⓓ Ⓔ
25. Ⓐ Ⓑ Ⓒ Ⓓ Ⓔ
26. Ⓐ Ⓑ Ⓒ Ⓓ Ⓔ
27. Ⓐ Ⓑ Ⓒ Ⓓ Ⓔ
28. Ⓐ Ⓑ Ⓒ Ⓓ Ⓔ
29. Ⓐ Ⓑ Ⓒ Ⓓ Ⓔ
30. Ⓐ Ⓑ Ⓒ Ⓓ Ⓔ
31. Ⓐ Ⓑ Ⓒ Ⓓ Ⓔ
32. Ⓐ Ⓑ Ⓒ Ⓓ Ⓔ
33. Ⓐ Ⓑ Ⓒ Ⓓ Ⓔ
34. Ⓐ Ⓑ Ⓒ Ⓓ Ⓔ
35. Ⓐ Ⓑ Ⓒ Ⓓ Ⓔ
36. Ⓐ Ⓑ Ⓒ Ⓓ Ⓔ
37. Ⓐ Ⓑ Ⓒ Ⓓ Ⓔ
38. Ⓐ Ⓑ Ⓒ Ⓓ Ⓔ

39. Ⓐ Ⓑ Ⓒ Ⓓ Ⓔ
40. Ⓐ Ⓑ Ⓒ Ⓓ Ⓔ
41. Ⓐ Ⓑ Ⓒ Ⓓ Ⓔ
42. Ⓐ Ⓑ Ⓒ Ⓓ Ⓔ
43. Ⓐ Ⓑ Ⓒ Ⓓ Ⓔ
44. Ⓐ Ⓑ Ⓒ Ⓓ Ⓔ
45. Ⓐ Ⓑ Ⓒ Ⓓ Ⓔ
46. Ⓐ Ⓑ Ⓒ Ⓓ Ⓔ
47. Ⓐ Ⓑ Ⓒ Ⓓ Ⓔ
48. Ⓐ Ⓑ Ⓒ Ⓓ Ⓔ
49. Ⓐ Ⓑ Ⓒ Ⓓ Ⓔ
50. Ⓐ Ⓑ Ⓒ Ⓓ Ⓔ
51. Ⓐ Ⓑ Ⓒ Ⓓ Ⓔ
52. Ⓐ Ⓑ Ⓒ Ⓓ Ⓔ
53. Ⓐ Ⓑ Ⓒ Ⓓ Ⓔ
54. Ⓐ Ⓑ Ⓒ Ⓓ Ⓔ
55. Ⓐ Ⓑ Ⓒ Ⓓ Ⓔ
56. Ⓐ Ⓑ Ⓒ Ⓓ Ⓔ
57. Ⓐ Ⓑ Ⓒ Ⓓ Ⓔ

58. Ⓐ Ⓑ Ⓒ Ⓓ Ⓔ   60. Ⓐ Ⓑ Ⓒ Ⓓ Ⓔ   62. Ⓐ Ⓑ Ⓒ Ⓓ Ⓔ

59. Ⓐ Ⓑ Ⓒ Ⓓ Ⓔ   61. Ⓐ Ⓑ Ⓒ Ⓓ Ⓔ   63. Ⓐ Ⓑ Ⓒ Ⓓ Ⓔ

Answer Sheet for Practice Exam

Directions: Read each question carefully and choose the best answer. Fill in the oval completely with a soft lead pencil.

1. Ⓐ Ⓑ Ⓒ Ⓓ Ⓔ   20. Ⓐ Ⓑ Ⓒ Ⓓ Ⓔ   39. Ⓐ Ⓑ Ⓒ Ⓓ Ⓔ

2. Ⓐ Ⓑ Ⓒ Ⓓ Ⓔ   21. Ⓐ Ⓑ Ⓒ Ⓓ Ⓔ   40. Ⓐ Ⓑ Ⓒ Ⓓ Ⓔ

3. Ⓐ Ⓑ Ⓒ Ⓓ Ⓔ   22. Ⓐ Ⓑ Ⓒ Ⓓ Ⓔ   41. Ⓐ Ⓑ Ⓒ Ⓓ Ⓔ

4. Ⓐ Ⓑ Ⓒ Ⓓ Ⓔ   23. Ⓐ Ⓑ Ⓒ Ⓓ Ⓔ   42. Ⓐ Ⓑ Ⓒ Ⓓ Ⓔ

5. Ⓐ Ⓑ Ⓒ Ⓓ Ⓔ   24. Ⓐ Ⓑ Ⓒ Ⓓ Ⓔ   43. Ⓐ Ⓑ Ⓒ Ⓓ Ⓔ

6. Ⓐ Ⓑ Ⓒ Ⓓ Ⓔ   25. Ⓐ Ⓑ Ⓒ Ⓓ Ⓔ   44. Ⓐ Ⓑ Ⓒ Ⓓ Ⓔ

7. Ⓐ Ⓑ Ⓒ Ⓓ Ⓔ   26. Ⓐ Ⓑ Ⓒ Ⓓ Ⓔ   45. Ⓐ Ⓑ Ⓒ Ⓓ Ⓔ

8. Ⓐ Ⓑ Ⓒ Ⓓ Ⓔ   27. Ⓐ Ⓑ Ⓒ Ⓓ Ⓔ   46. Ⓐ Ⓑ Ⓒ Ⓓ Ⓔ

9. Ⓐ Ⓑ Ⓒ Ⓓ Ⓔ   28. Ⓐ Ⓑ Ⓒ Ⓓ Ⓔ   47. Ⓐ Ⓑ Ⓒ Ⓓ Ⓔ

10. Ⓐ Ⓑ Ⓒ Ⓓ Ⓔ   29. Ⓐ Ⓑ Ⓒ Ⓓ Ⓔ   48. Ⓐ Ⓑ Ⓒ Ⓓ Ⓔ

11. Ⓐ Ⓑ Ⓒ Ⓓ Ⓔ   30. Ⓐ Ⓑ Ⓒ Ⓓ Ⓔ   49. Ⓐ Ⓑ Ⓒ Ⓓ Ⓔ

12. Ⓐ Ⓑ Ⓒ Ⓓ Ⓔ   31. Ⓐ Ⓑ Ⓒ Ⓓ Ⓔ   50. Ⓐ Ⓑ Ⓒ Ⓓ Ⓔ

13. Ⓐ Ⓑ Ⓒ Ⓓ Ⓔ   32. Ⓐ Ⓑ Ⓒ Ⓓ Ⓔ   51. Ⓐ Ⓑ Ⓒ Ⓓ Ⓔ

14. Ⓐ Ⓑ Ⓒ Ⓓ Ⓔ   33. Ⓐ Ⓑ Ⓒ Ⓓ Ⓔ   52. Ⓐ Ⓑ Ⓒ Ⓓ Ⓔ

15. Ⓐ Ⓑ Ⓒ Ⓓ Ⓔ   34. Ⓐ Ⓑ Ⓒ Ⓓ Ⓔ   53. Ⓐ Ⓑ Ⓒ Ⓓ Ⓔ

16. Ⓐ Ⓑ Ⓒ Ⓓ Ⓔ   35. Ⓐ Ⓑ Ⓒ Ⓓ Ⓔ   54. Ⓐ Ⓑ Ⓒ Ⓓ Ⓔ

17. Ⓐ Ⓑ Ⓒ Ⓓ Ⓔ   36. Ⓐ Ⓑ Ⓒ Ⓓ Ⓔ   55. Ⓐ Ⓑ Ⓒ Ⓓ Ⓔ

18. Ⓐ Ⓑ Ⓒ Ⓓ Ⓔ   37. Ⓐ Ⓑ Ⓒ Ⓓ Ⓔ   56. Ⓐ Ⓑ Ⓒ Ⓓ Ⓔ

19. Ⓐ Ⓑ Ⓒ Ⓓ Ⓔ   38. Ⓐ Ⓑ Ⓒ Ⓓ Ⓔ   57. Ⓐ Ⓑ Ⓒ Ⓓ Ⓔ

58. Ⓐ Ⓑ Ⓒ Ⓓ Ⓔ   60. Ⓐ Ⓑ Ⓒ Ⓓ Ⓔ   62. Ⓐ Ⓑ Ⓒ Ⓓ Ⓔ

59. Ⓐ Ⓑ Ⓒ Ⓓ Ⓔ   61. Ⓐ Ⓑ Ⓒ Ⓓ Ⓔ   63. Ⓐ Ⓑ Ⓒ Ⓓ Ⓔ